Chapter 24

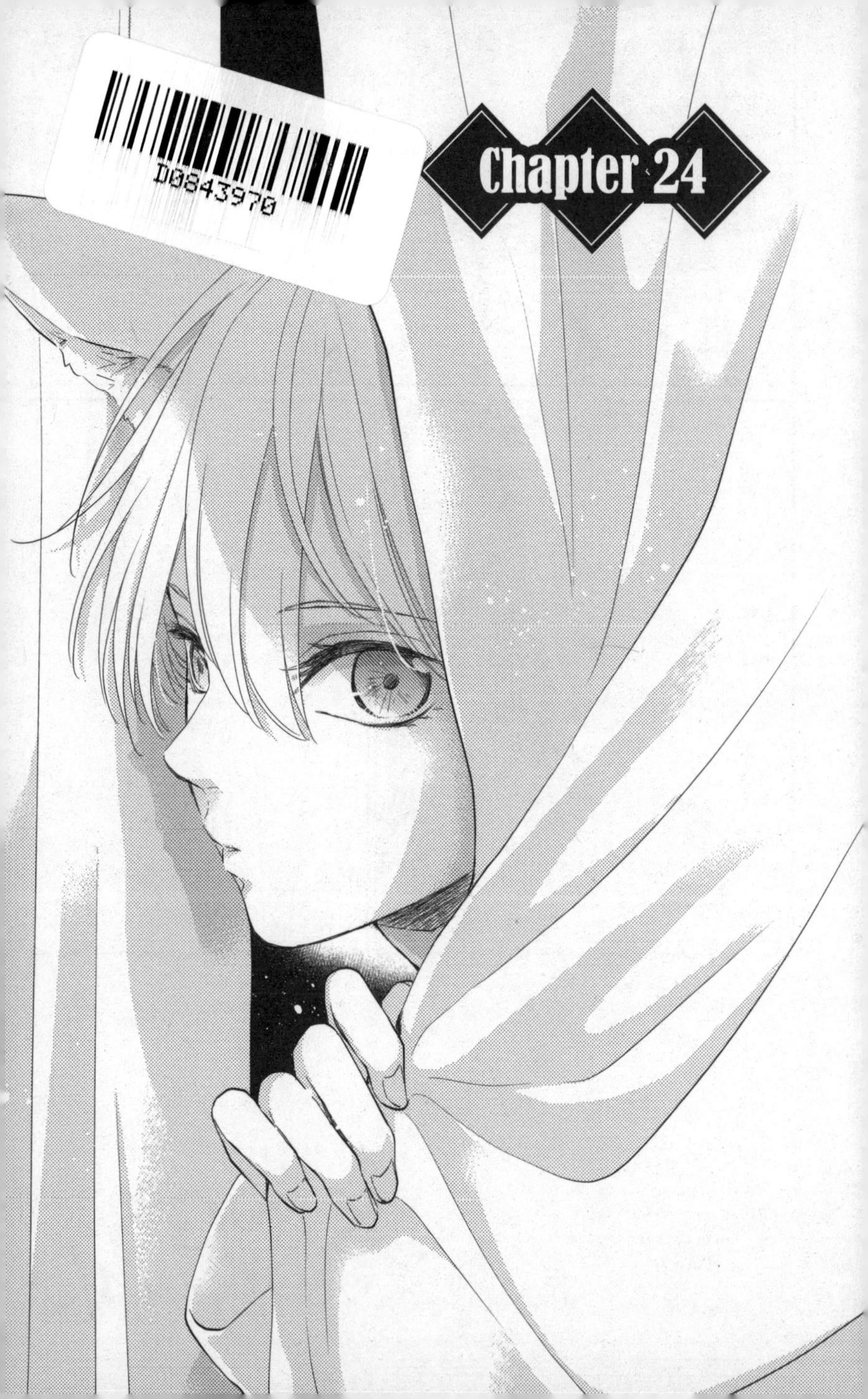

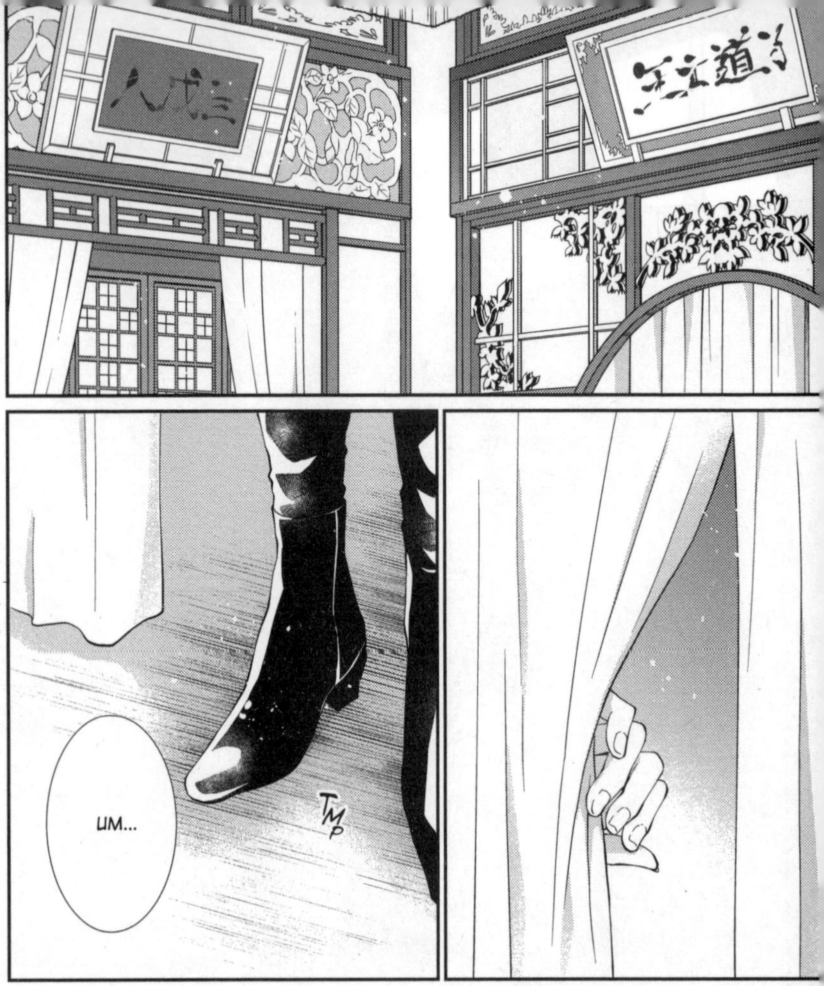
TMP
UM...

THE KING'S Beast

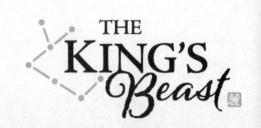

THE KING'S Beast 麗

7

STORY & ART BY

Rei Toma

THE KING'S Beast 麗

CHARACTERS

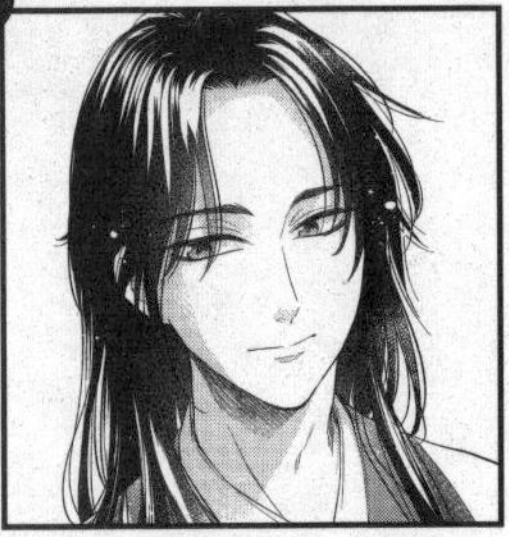

Tenyou

The fourth prince. Kindhearted, he is trying to clean up the intrigues in the imperial palace.

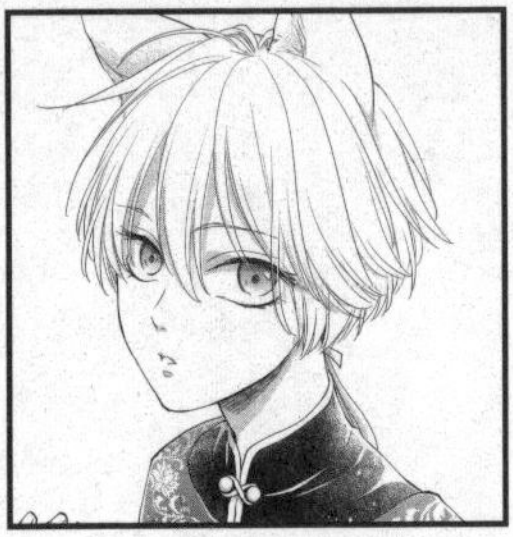

Rangetsu

To avenge her younger brother's death, she hides her true identity as a woman and becomes Prince Tenyou's beast-servant.

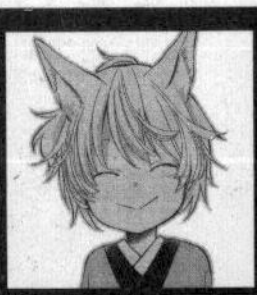

The Assassination of Sogetsu

Rangetsu's twin was brought to the imperial palace to serve Prince Tenyou as his beast-servant, but he was brutally killed soon after.

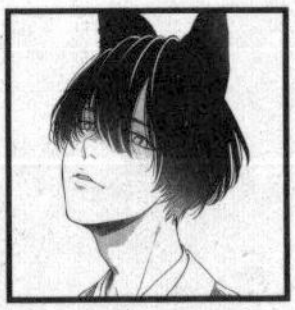

Boku

Prince Kougai's beast-servant.

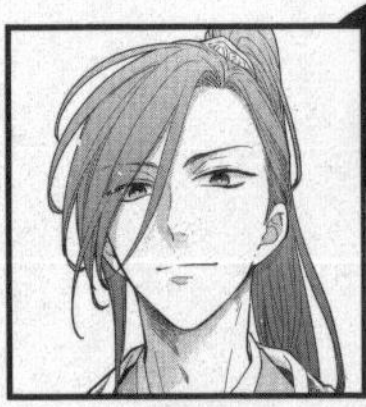

Kougai

The third prince. Two-faced and ambitious.

CONTENTS

◆◆◆

In a world where humans rule the half-beast Ajin, Rangetsu disguises herself as a man to become Fourth Prince Tenyou's beast-servant. When Third Prince Kougai becomes obsessed with Rangetsu, it sparks an unfathomable rage in Prince Tenyou even as his feelings for Rangetsu grow stronger.

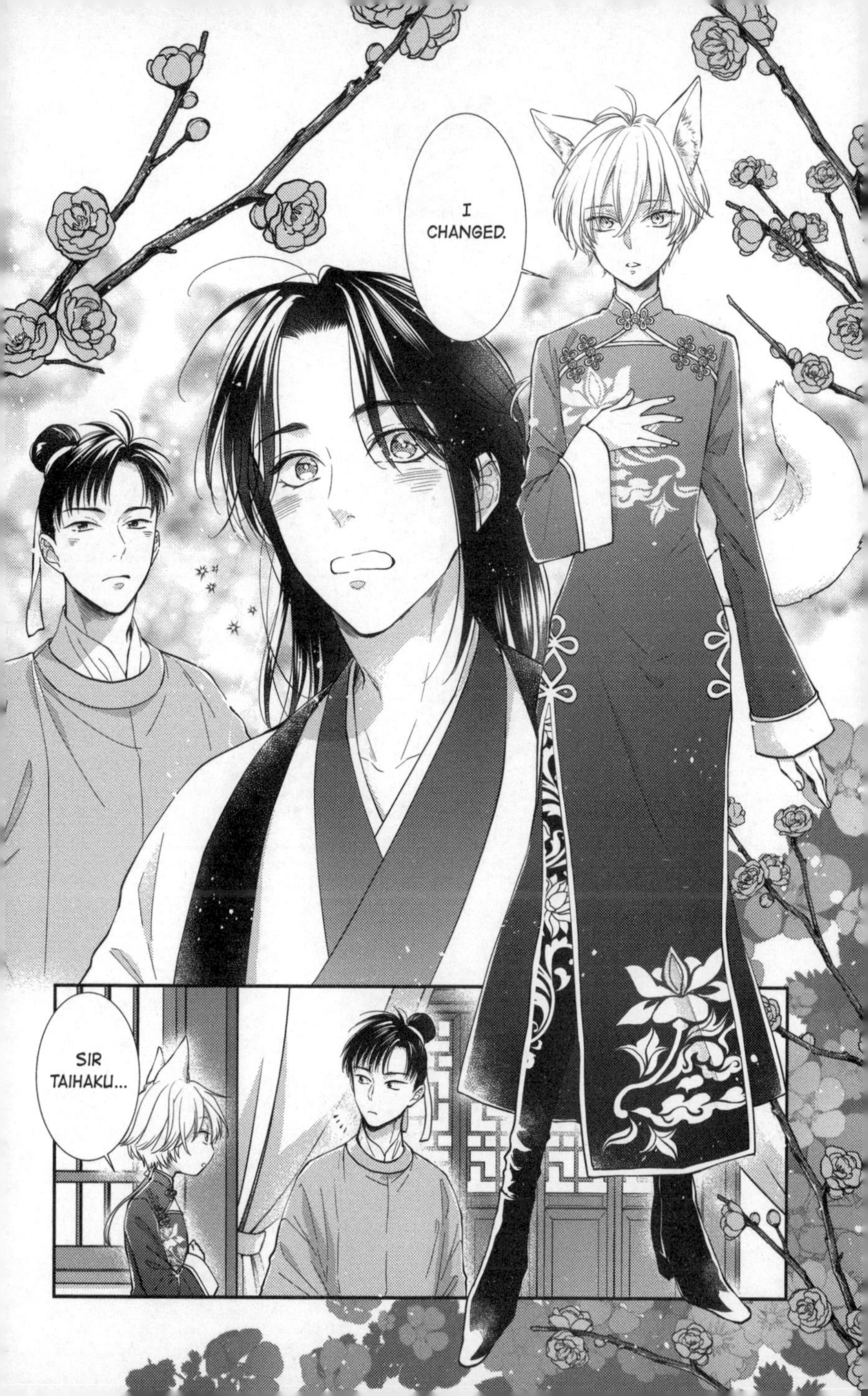
I CHANGED.
SIR TAIHAKU...

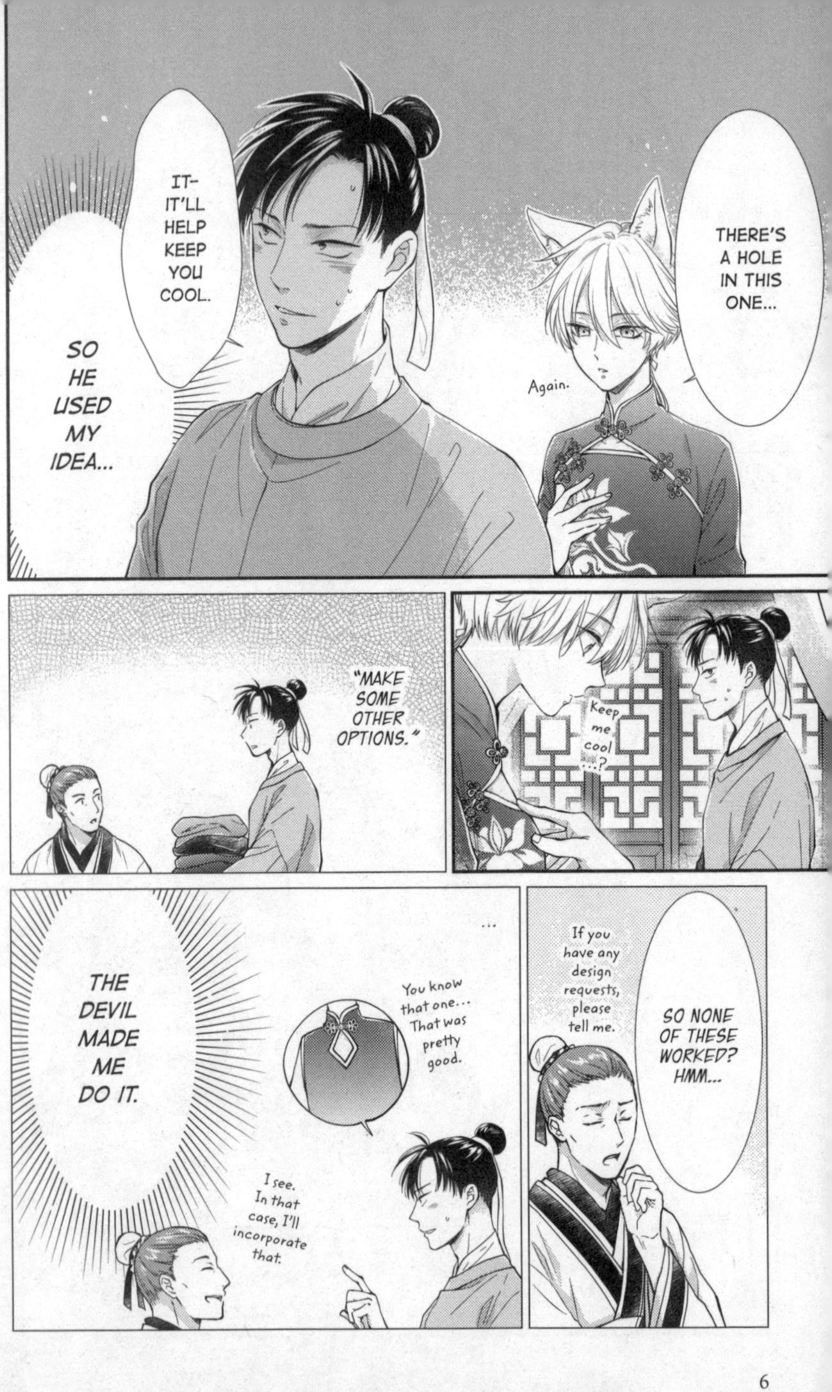
THERE'S A HOLE IN THIS ONE...
Again.
IT-IT'LL HELP KEEP YOU COOL.
SO HE USED MY IDEA...
Keep me cool...?
"MAKE SOME OTHER OPTIONS."
SO NONE OF THESE WORKED? HMM...
If you have any design requests, please tell me.
...
You know that one... That was pretty good.
I see. In that case, I'll incorporate that.
THE DEVIL MADE ME DO IT.

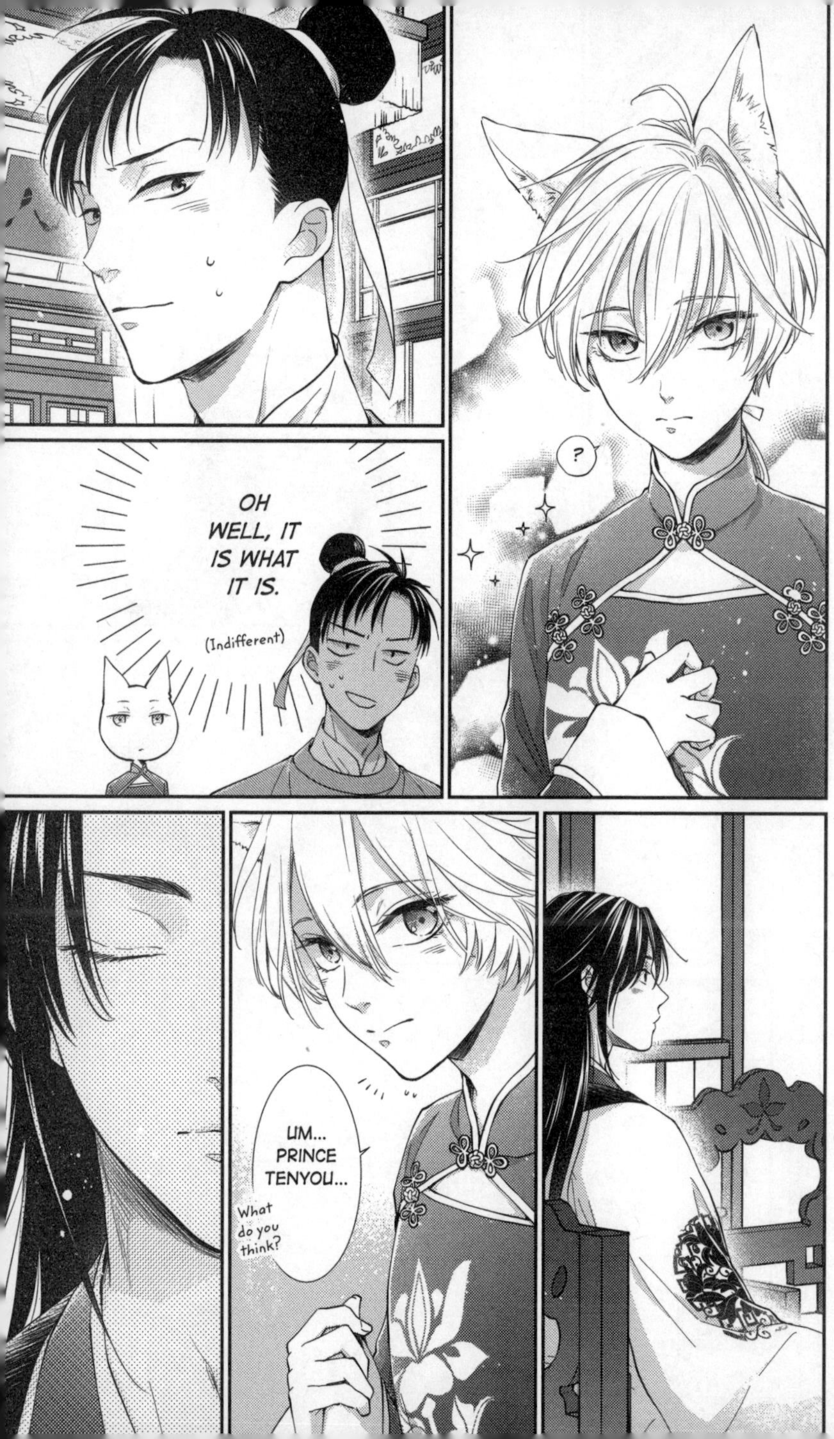
?
OH WELL, IT IS WHAT IT IS.
(Indifferent)
UM... PRINCE TENYOU...
What do you think?

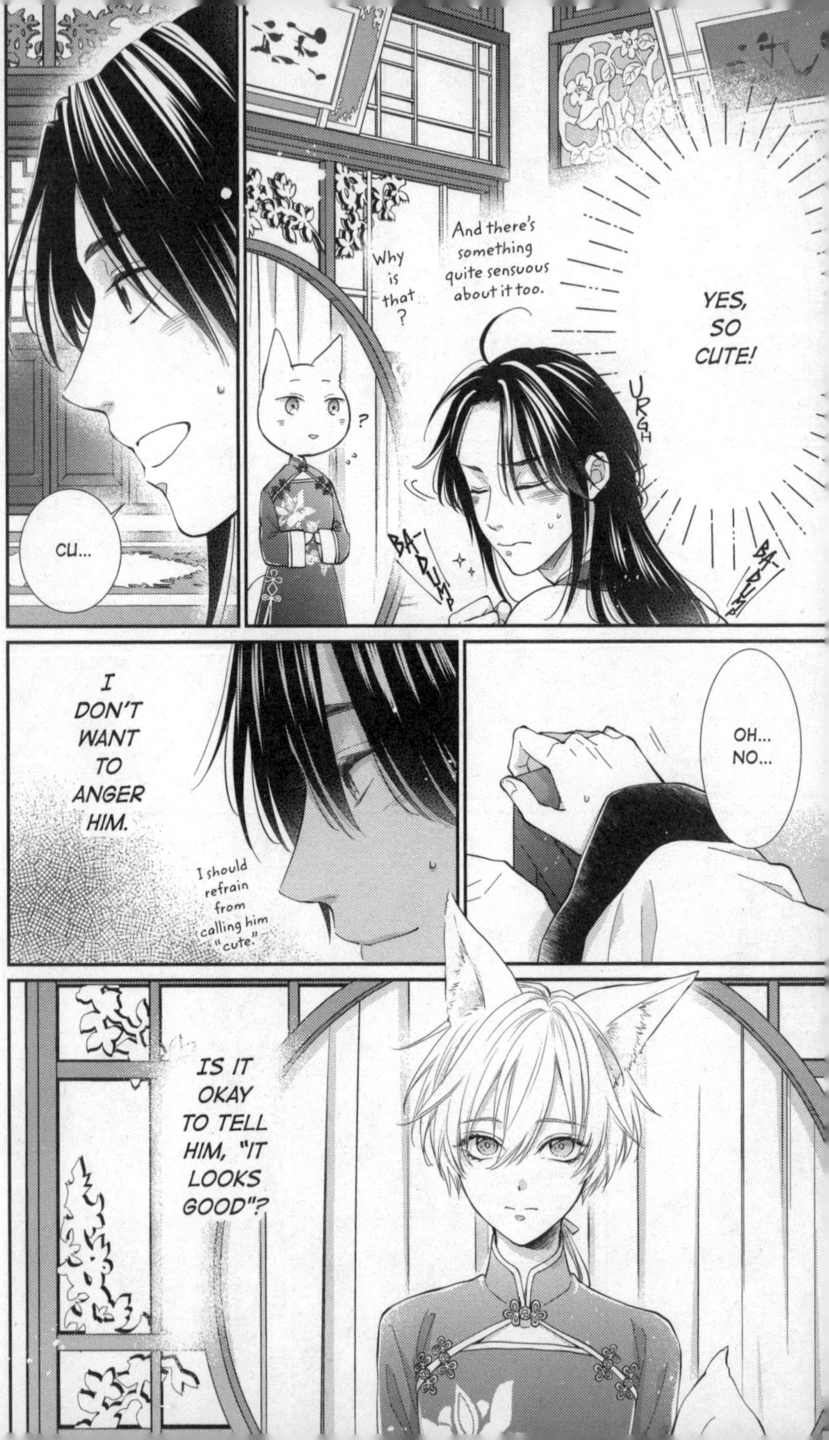
YES, SO CUTE!
And there's something quite sensuous about it too.
Why is that?
?
URGH
BA-DUMP
BA-DUMP
CU...
OH... NO...
I DON'T WANT TO ANGER HIM.
I should refrain from calling him "cute."
IS IT OKAY TO TELL HIM, "IT LOOKS GOOD"?

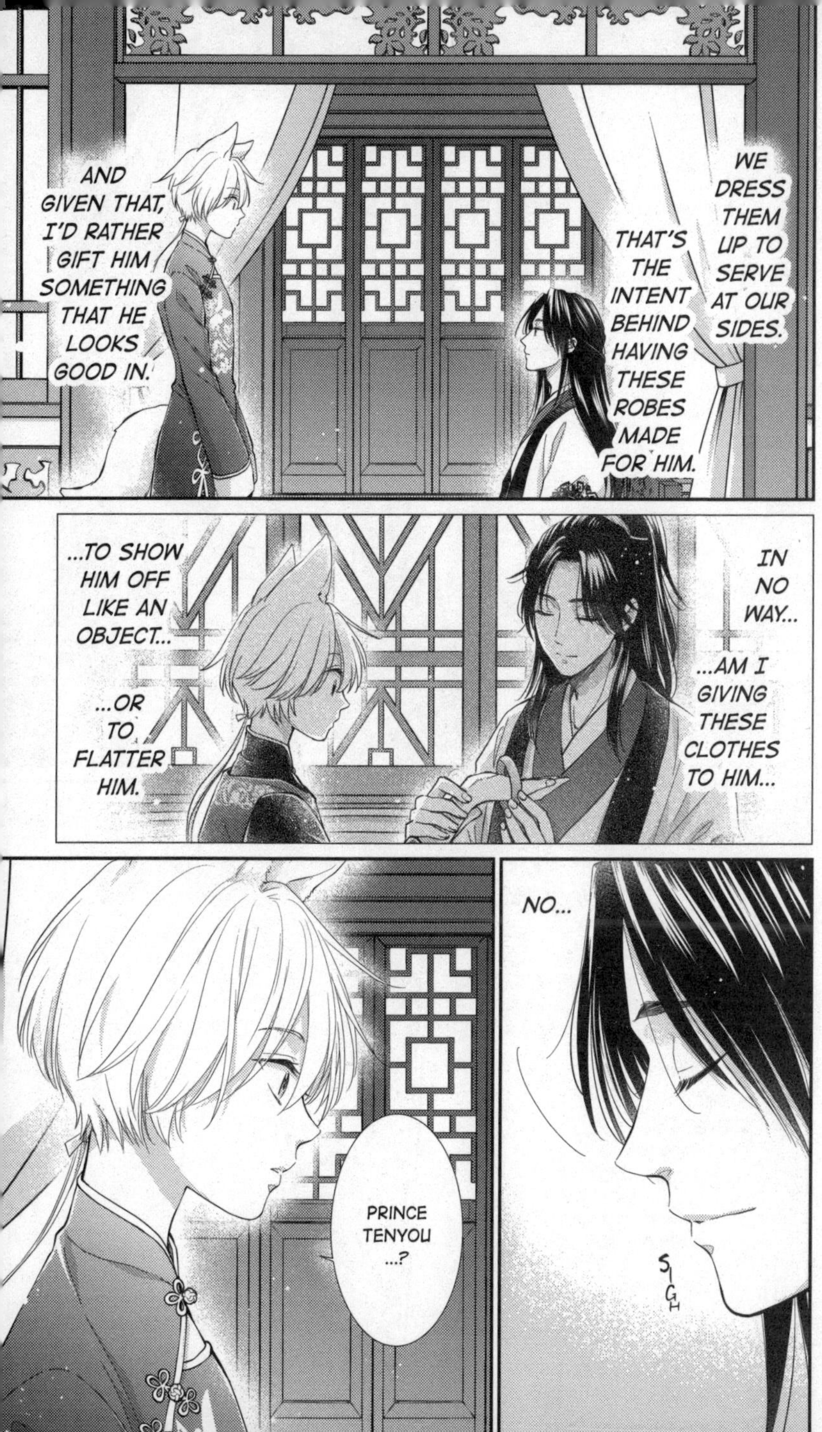
WE DRESS THEM UP TO SERVE AT OUR SIDES.
THAT'S THE INTENT BEHIND HAVING THESE ROBES MADE FOR HIM.
AND GIVEN THAT, I'D RATHER GIFT HIM SOMETHING THAT HE LOOKS GOOD IN.
IN NO WAY...
...AM I GIVING THESE CLOTHES TO HIM...
...TO SHOW HIM OFF LIKE AN OBJECT...
...OR TO FLATTER HIM.
NO...
SIGH
PRINCE TENYOU ...?

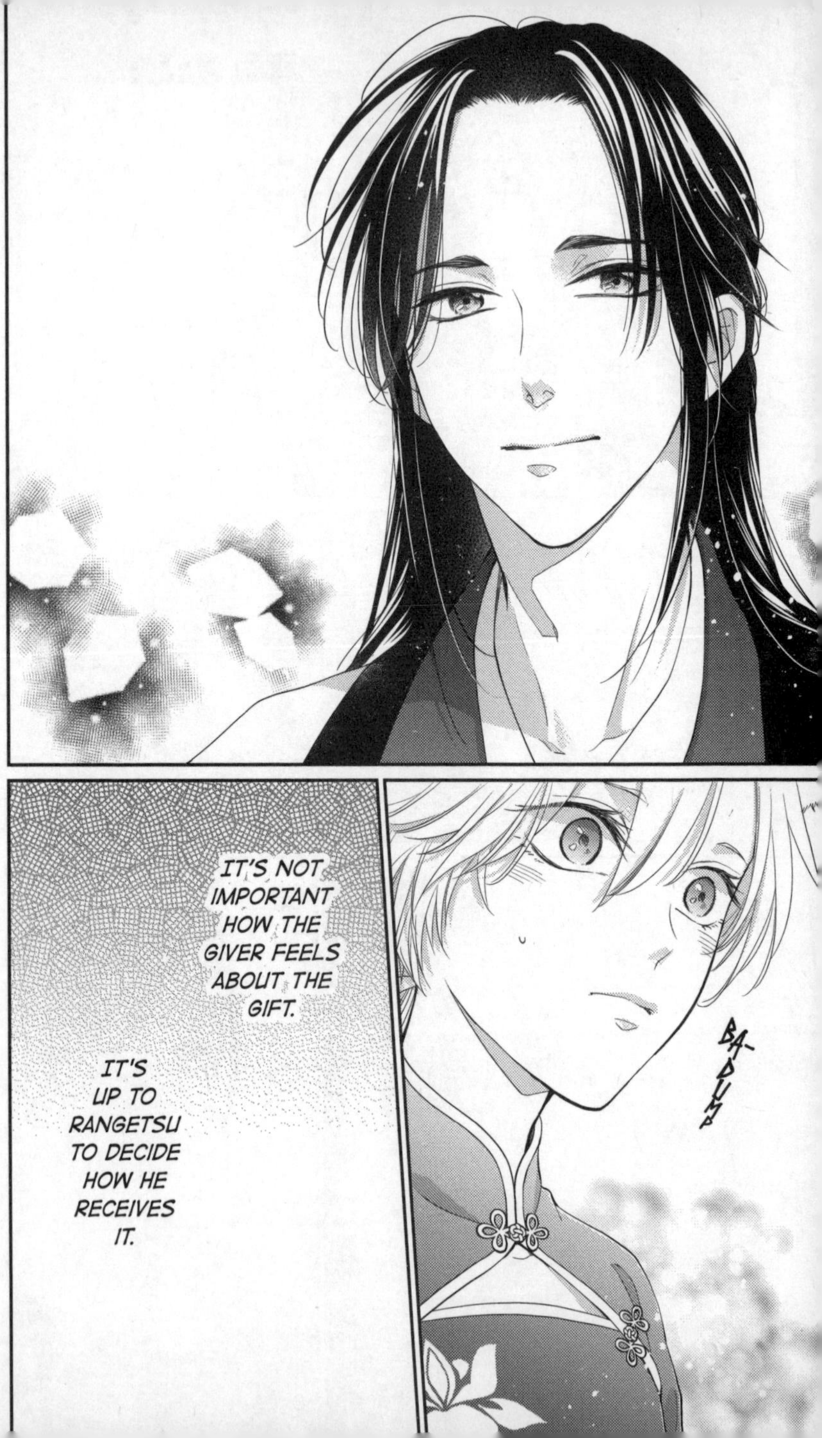
BA-DUMP
IT'S NOT IMPORTANT HOW THE GIVER FEELS ABOUT THE GIFT.
IT'S UP TO RANGETSU TO DECIDE HOW HE RECEIVES IT.

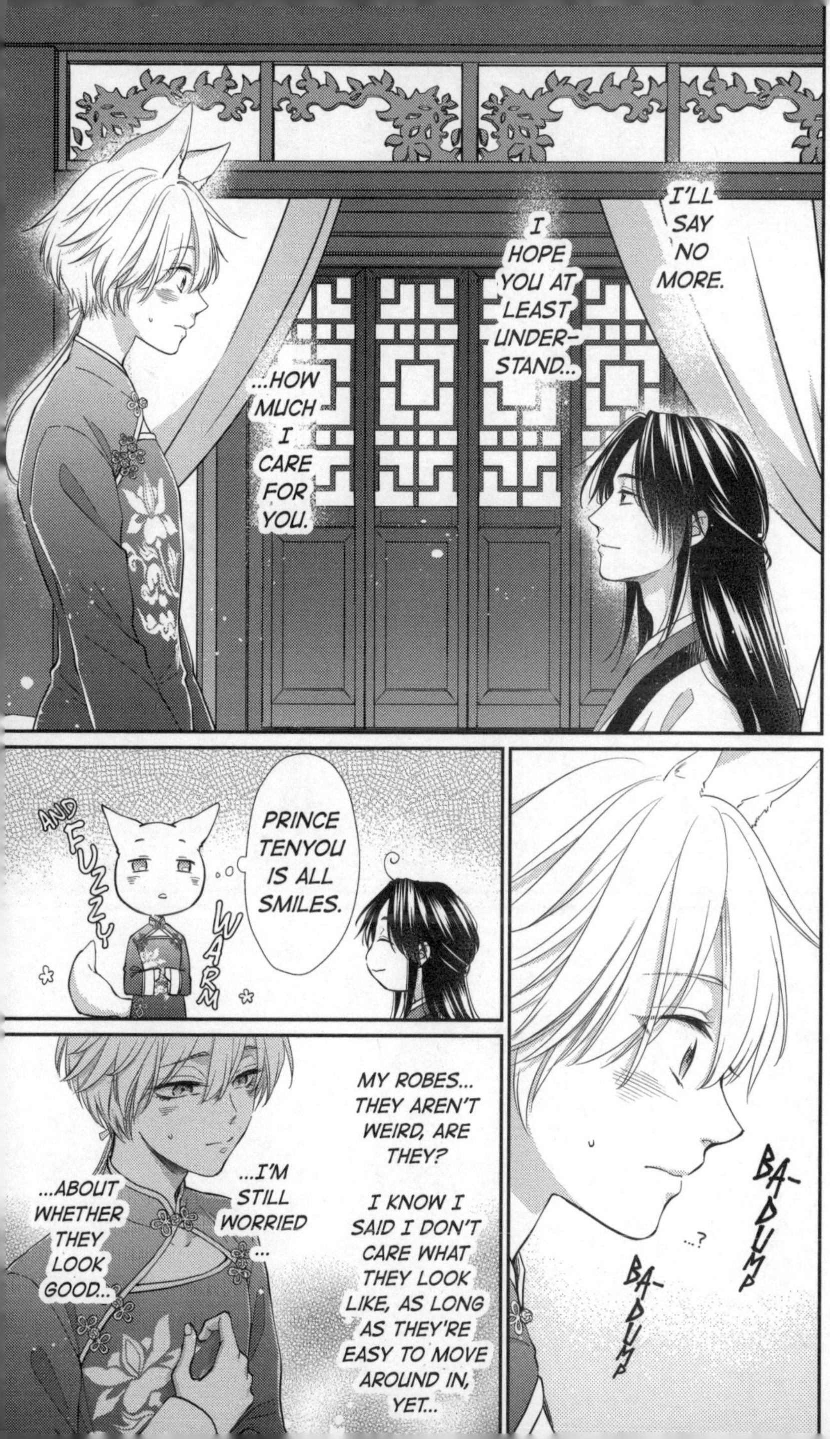
I'LL SAY NO MORE.
I HOPE YOU AT LEAST UNDER-STAND...
...HOW MUCH I CARE FOR YOU.
BA-DUMP
BA-DUMP
...?
PRINCE TENYOU IS ALL SMILES.
AND FUZZY
WARM
MY ROBES... THEY AREN'T WEIRD, ARE THEY?
I KNOW I SAID I DON'T CARE WHAT THEY LOOK LIKE, AS LONG AS THEY'RE EASY TO MOVE AROUND IN, YET...
...I'M STILL WORRIED...
...ABOUT WHETHER THEY LOOK GOOD...

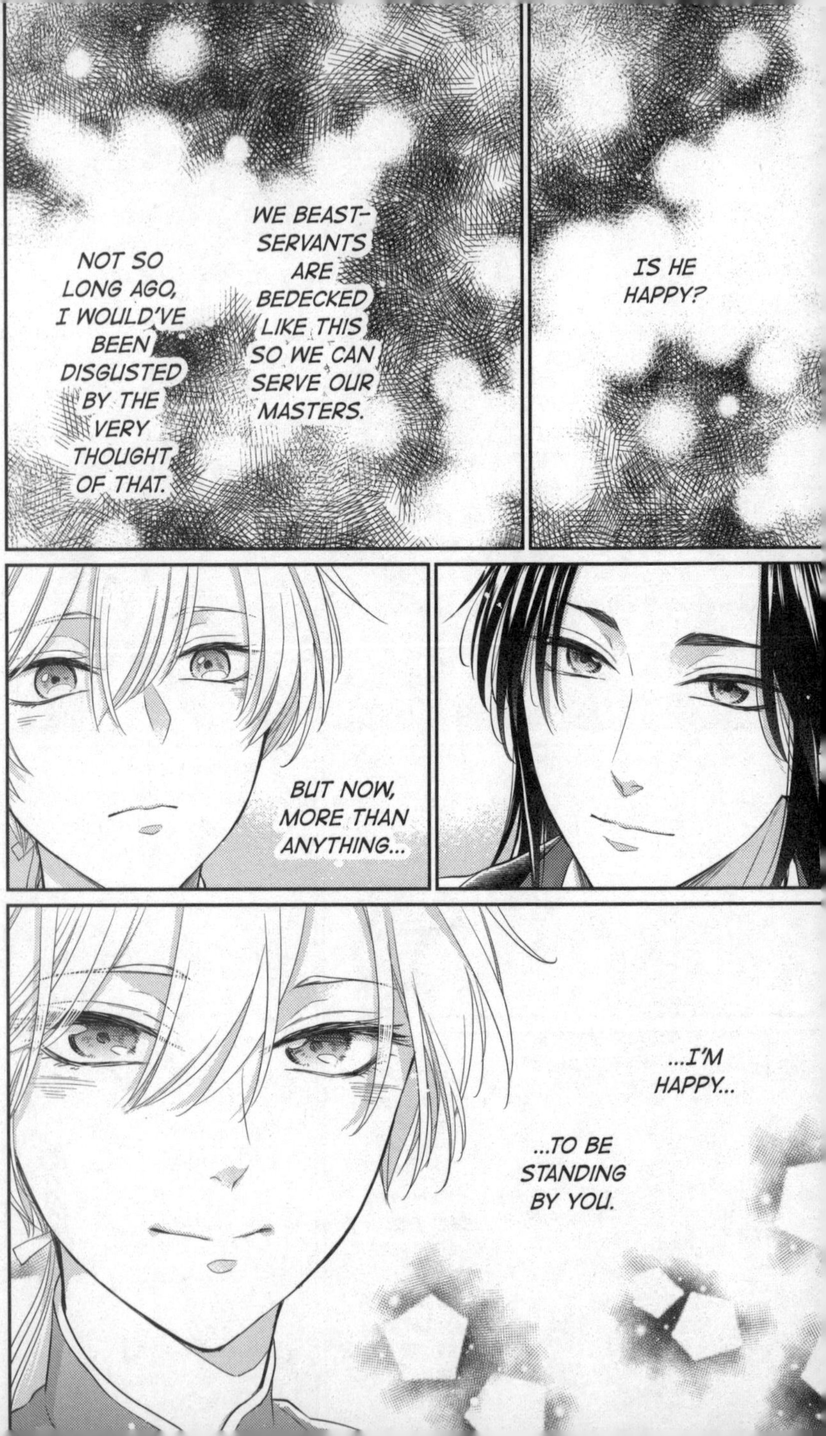
IS HE HAPPY?
WE BEAST-SERVANTS ARE BEDECKED LIKE THIS SO WE CAN SERVE OUR MASTERS.
NOT SO LONG AGO, I WOULD'VE BEEN DISGUSTED BY THE VERY THOUGHT OF THAT.
BUT NOW, MORE THAN ANYTHING...
...I'M HAPPY...
...TO BE STANDING BY YOU.

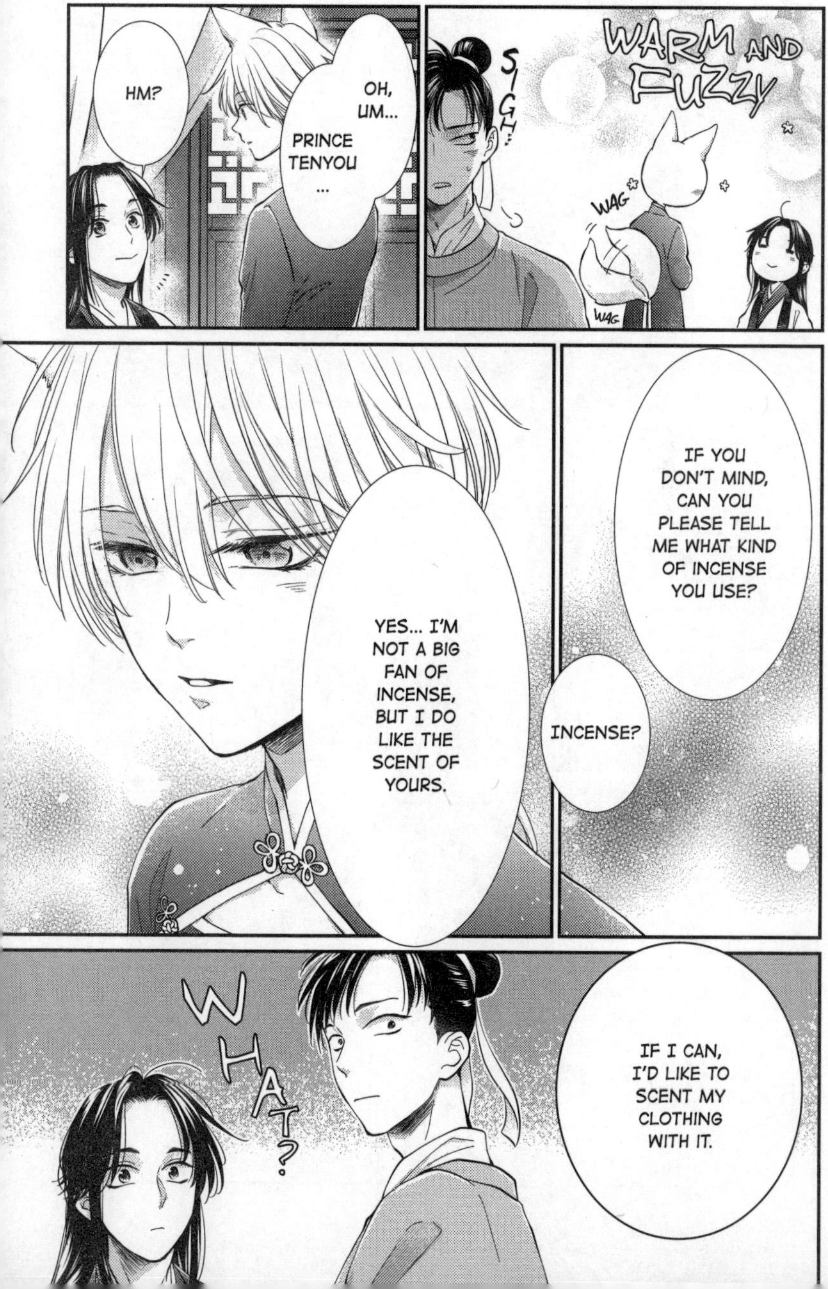
WARM AND FUZZY
SIGH...
WAG
WAG
OH, UM... PRINCE TENYOU ...
HM?
IF YOU DON'T MIND, CAN YOU PLEASE TELL ME WHAT KIND OF INCENSE YOU USE?
INCENSE?
YES... I'M NOT A BIG FAN OF INCENSE, BUT I DO LIKE THE SCENT OF YOURS.
IF I CAN, I'D LIKE TO SCENT MY CLOTHING WITH IT.
WHAT?

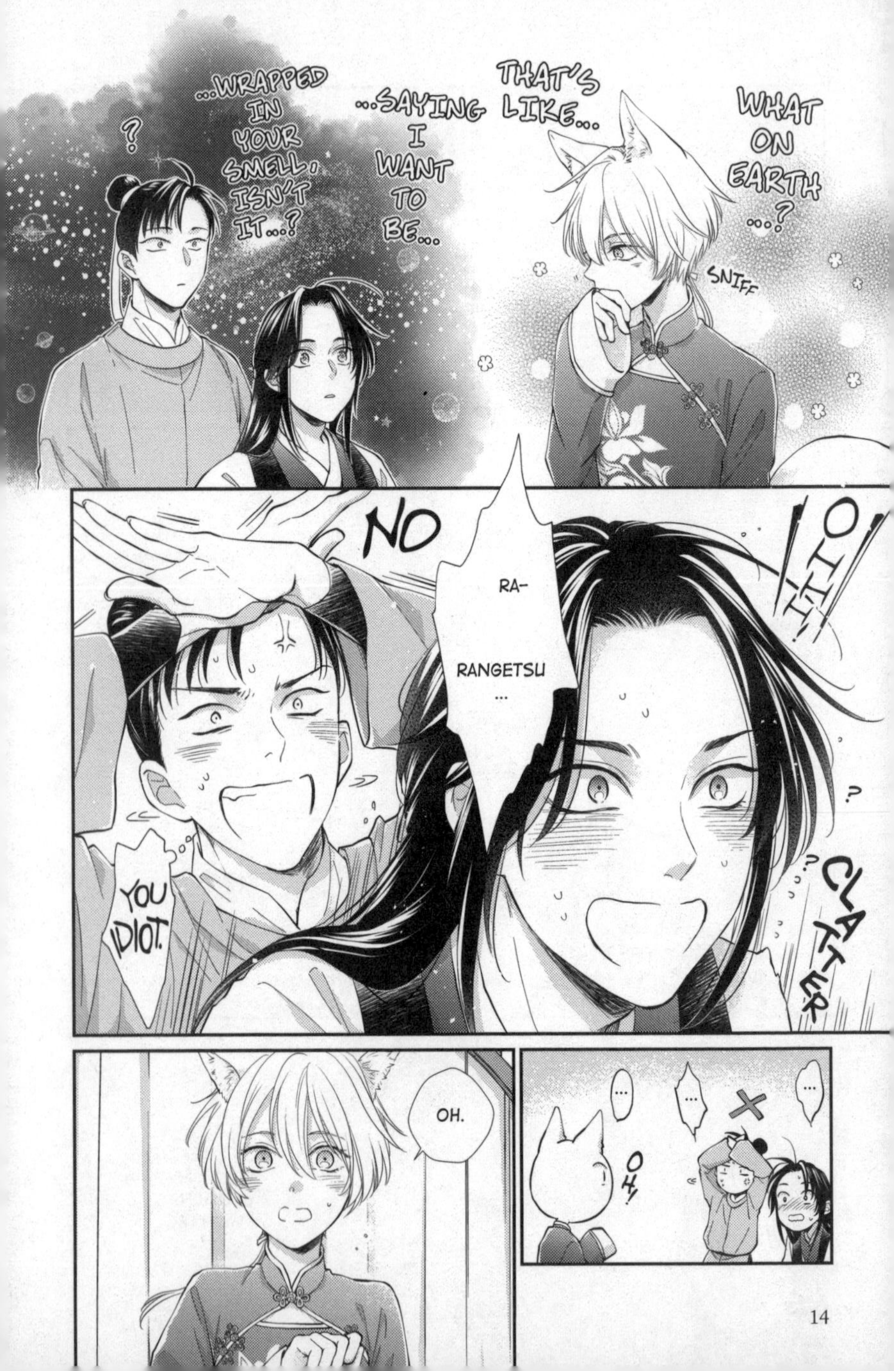
WHAT ON EARTH ...?
SNIFF
THAT'S LIKE...
...SAYING I WANT TO BE...
...WRAPPED IN YOUR SMELL, ISN'T IT...?
?
OHHH!
?
?
CLATTER
RA- RANGETSU ...
NO
YOU IDIOT.
...
...
...
OH!
OH.

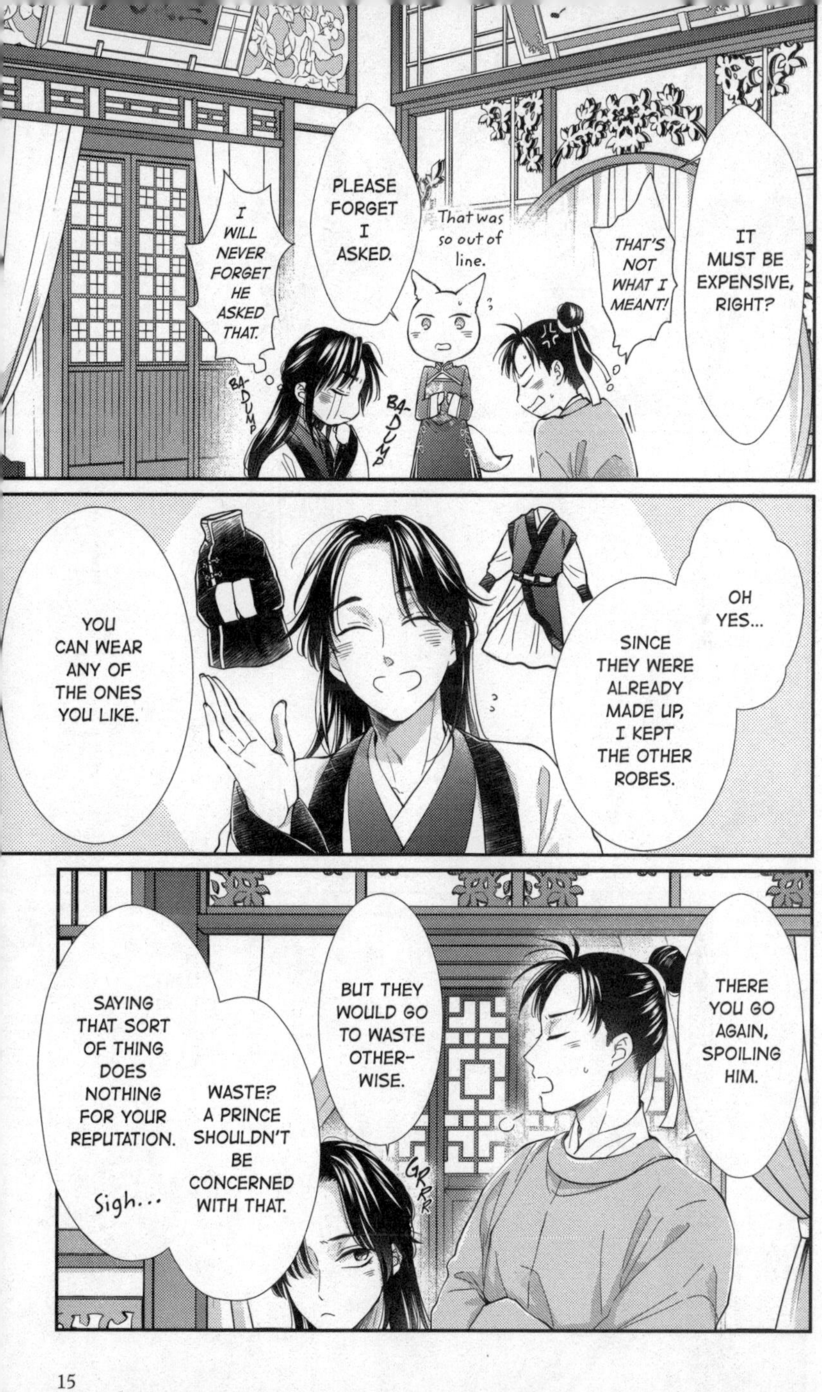
IT MUST BE EXPENSIVE, RIGHT?
THAT'S NOT WHAT I MEANT!
That was so out of line.
PLEASE FORGET I ASKED.
I WILL NEVER FORGET HE ASKED THAT.
BA-DUMP
BA-DUMP
OH YES...
SINCE THEY WERE ALREADY MADE UP, I KEPT THE OTHER ROBES.
YOU CAN WEAR ANY OF THE ONES YOU LIKE.
THERE YOU GO AGAIN, SPOILING HIM.
BUT THEY WOULD GO TO WASTE OTHER-WISE.
GRRR
WASTE? A PRINCE SHOULDN'T BE CONCERNED WITH THAT.
SAYING THAT SORT OF THING DOES NOTHING FOR YOUR REPUTATION.
Sigh...

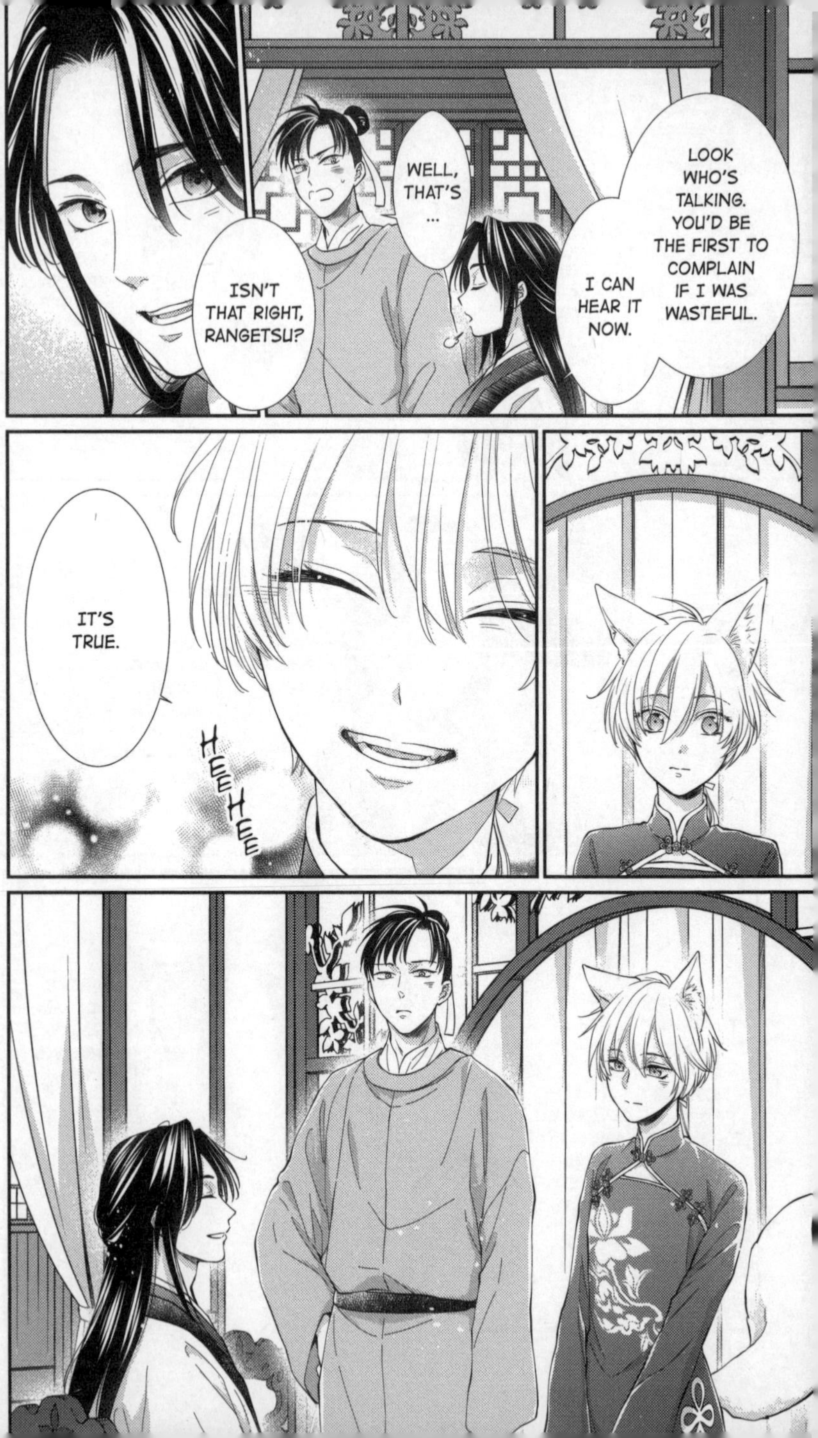
LOOK WHO'S TALKING. YOU'D BE THE FIRST TO COMPLAIN IF I WAS WASTEFUL.
I CAN HEAR IT NOW.
WELL, THAT'S ...
ISN'T THAT RIGHT, RANGETSU?
IT'S TRUE.
HEE HEE

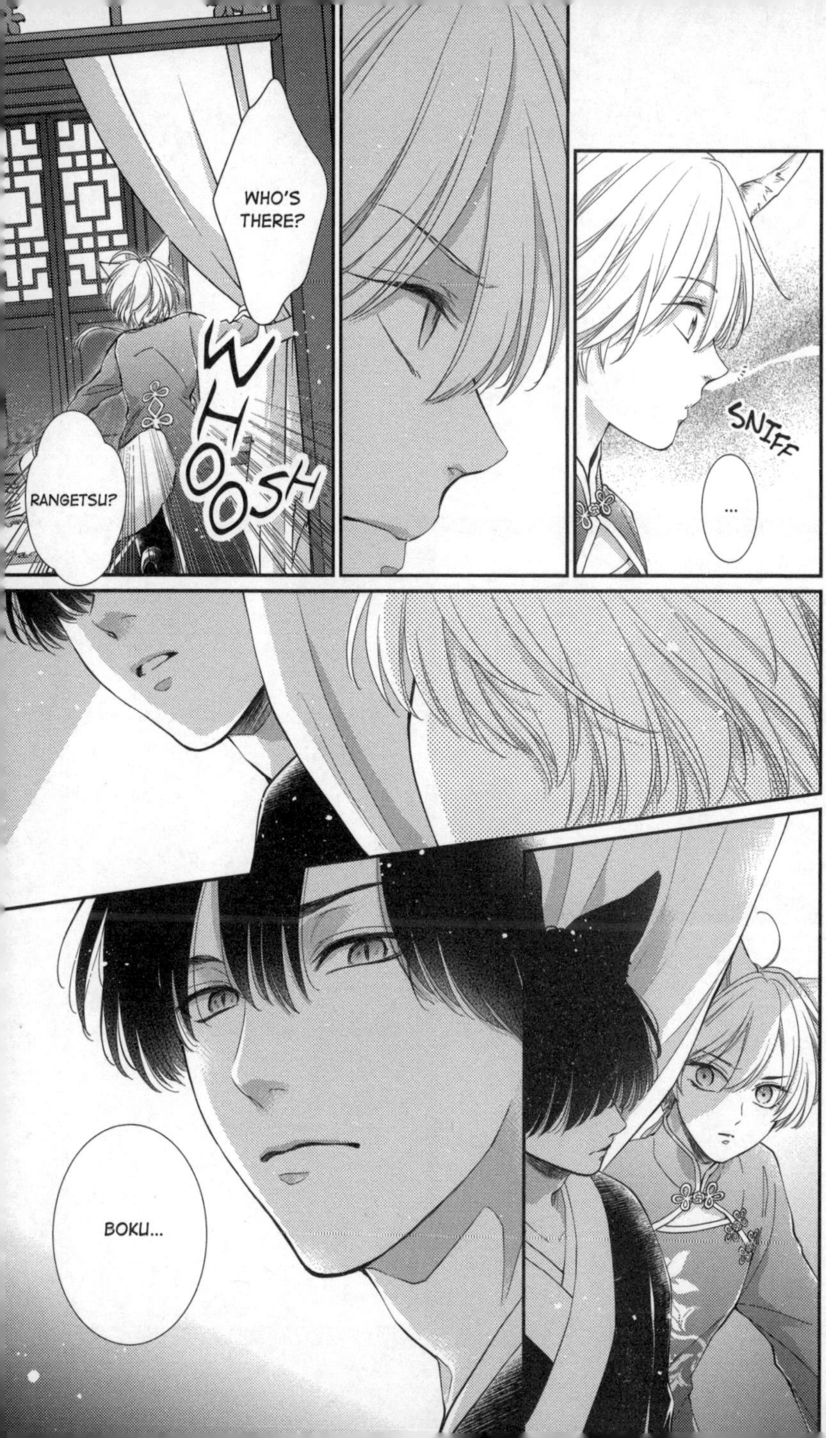
SNIFF
...
WHO'S THERE?
WHOOSH
RANGETSU?
BOKU...

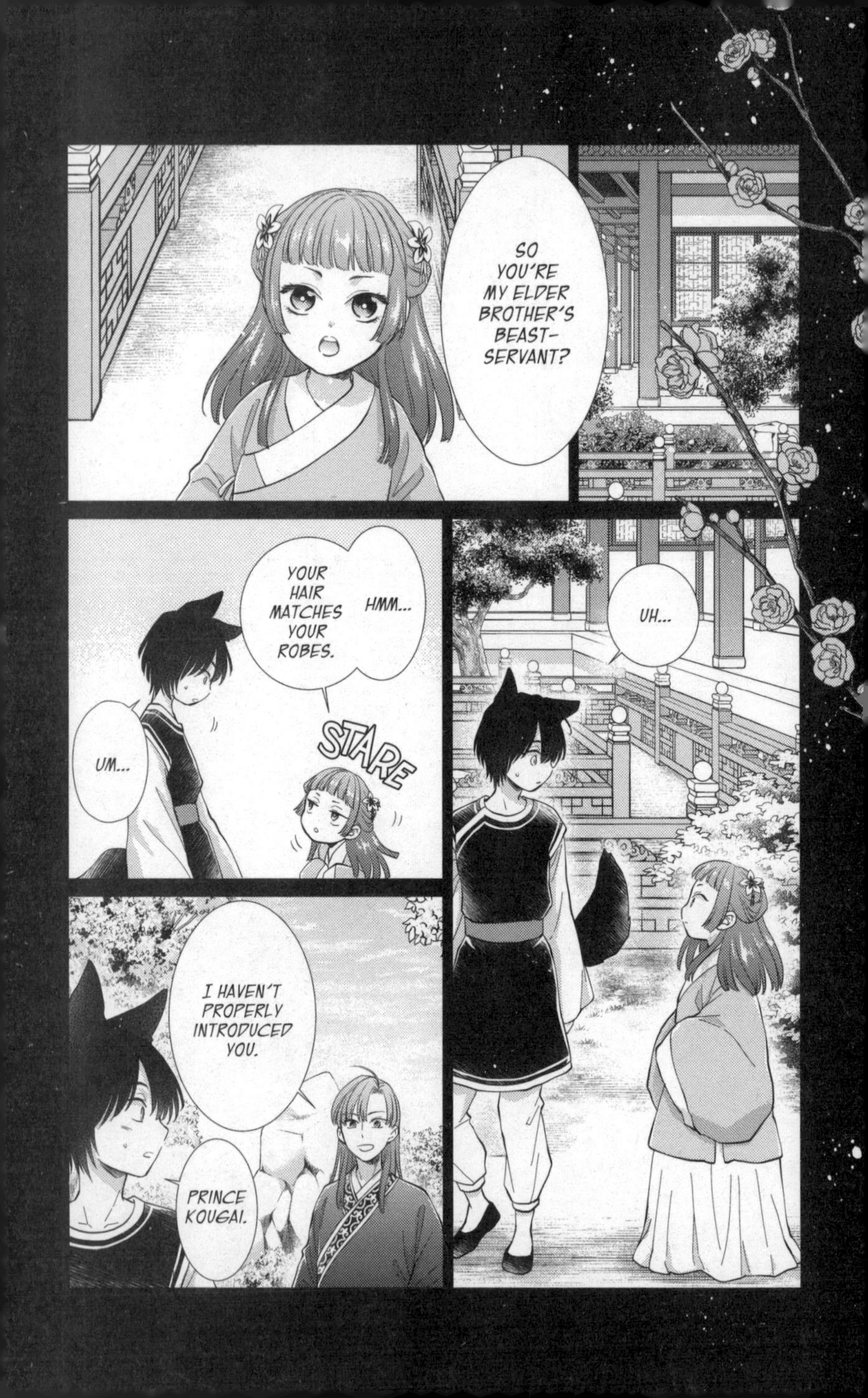
SO YOU'RE MY ELDER BROTHER'S BEAST-SERVANT?
UH...
HMM...
YOUR HAIR MATCHES YOUR ROBES.
STARE
UM...
I HAVEN'T PROPERLY INTRODUCED YOU.
PRINCE KOUGAI.

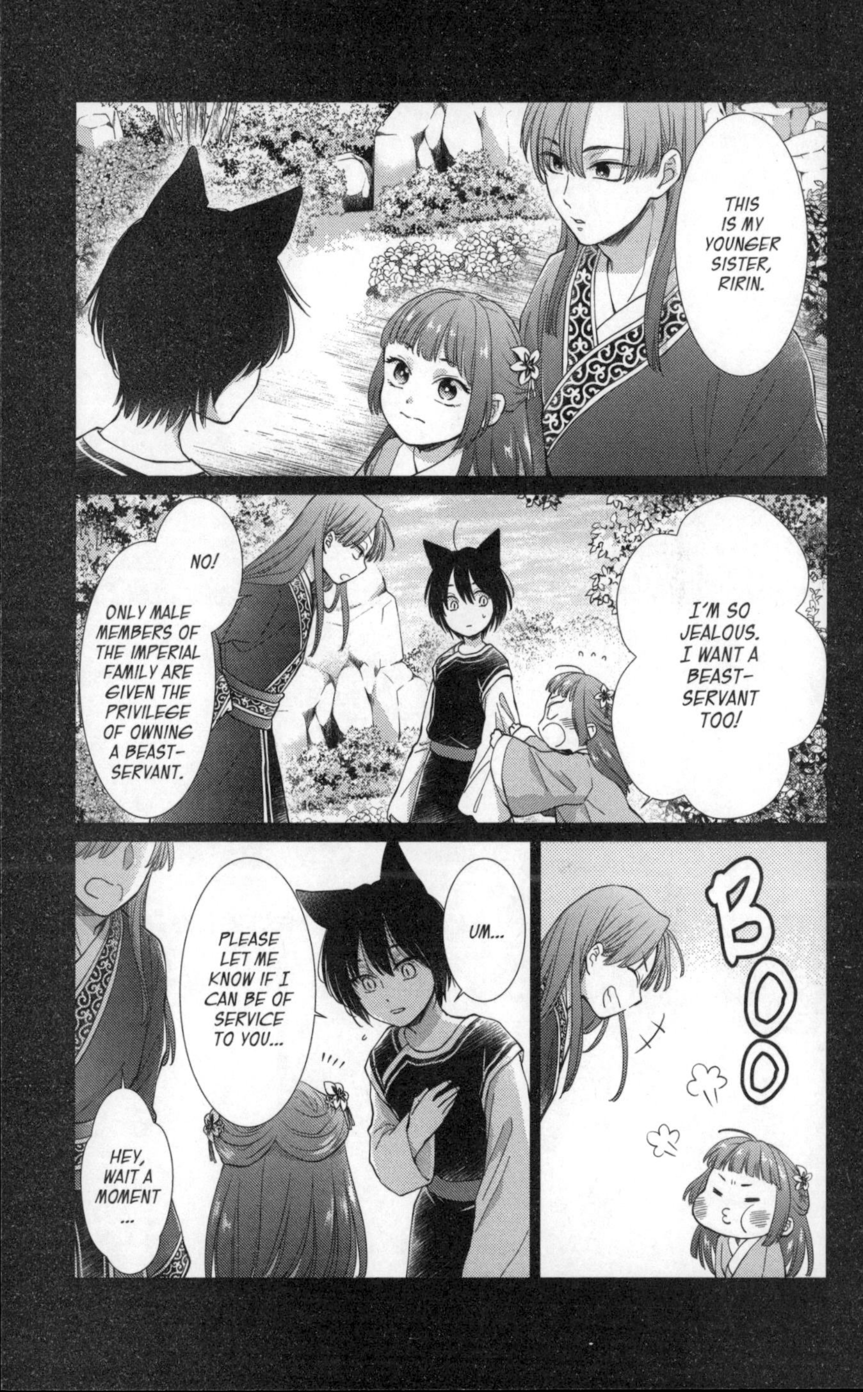
THIS IS MY YOUNGER SISTER, RIRIN.
I'M SO JEALOUS. I WANT A BEAST-SERVANT TOO!
NO!
ONLY MALE MEMBERS OF THE IMPERIAL FAMILY ARE GIVEN THE PRIVILEGE OF OWNING A BEAST-SERVANT.
BOO
UM...
PLEASE LET ME KNOW IF I CAN BE OF SERVICE TO YOU...
HEY, WAIT A MOMENT ...

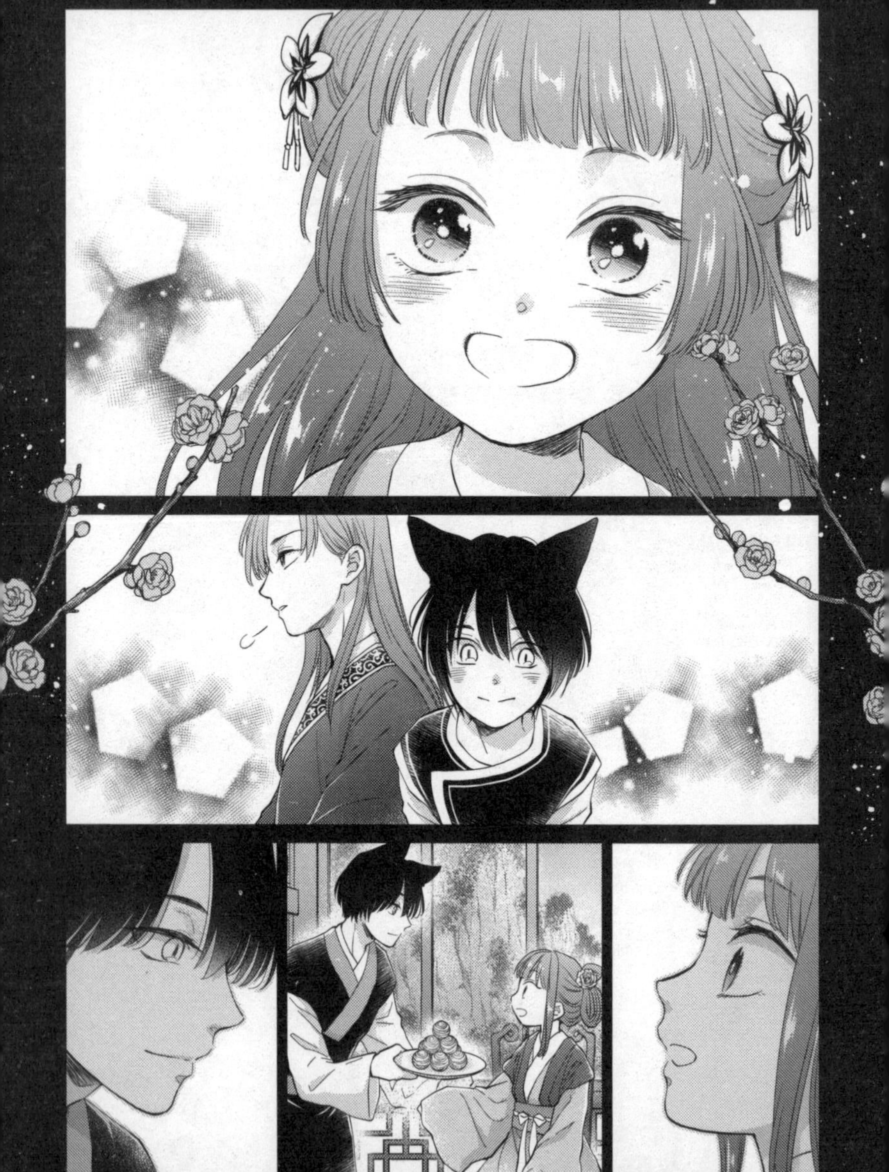

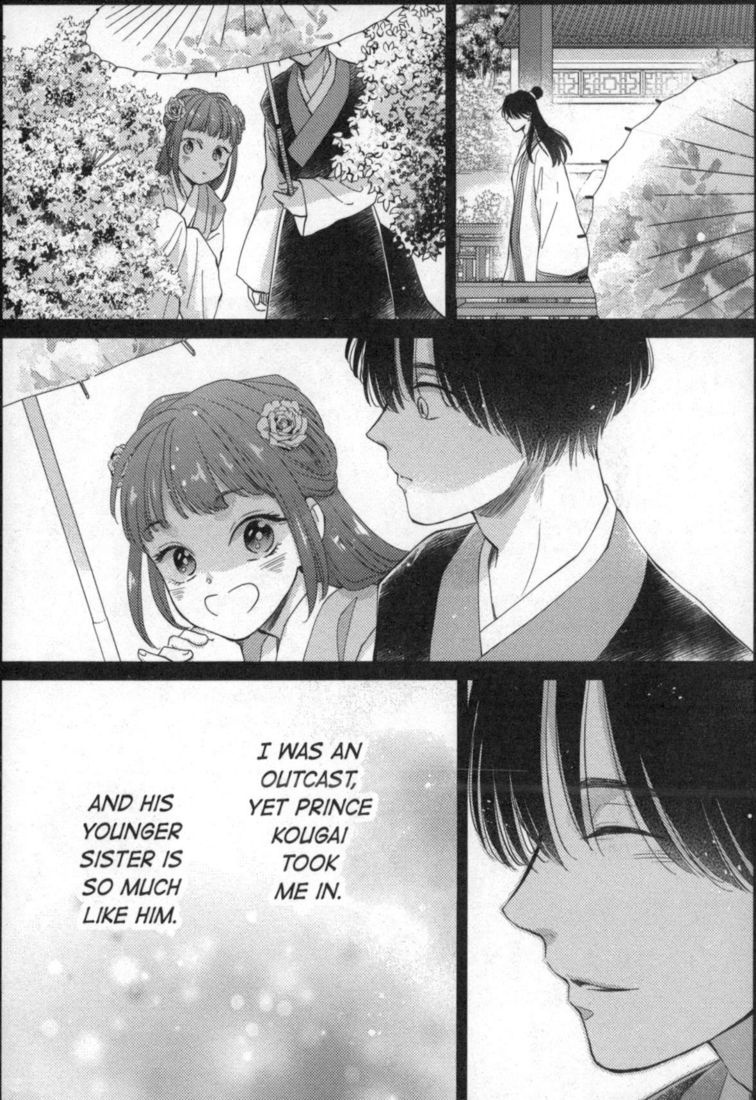
I WAS AN OUTCAST, YET PRINCE KOUGAI TOOK ME IN.
AND HIS YOUNGER SISTER IS SO MUCH LIKE HIM.

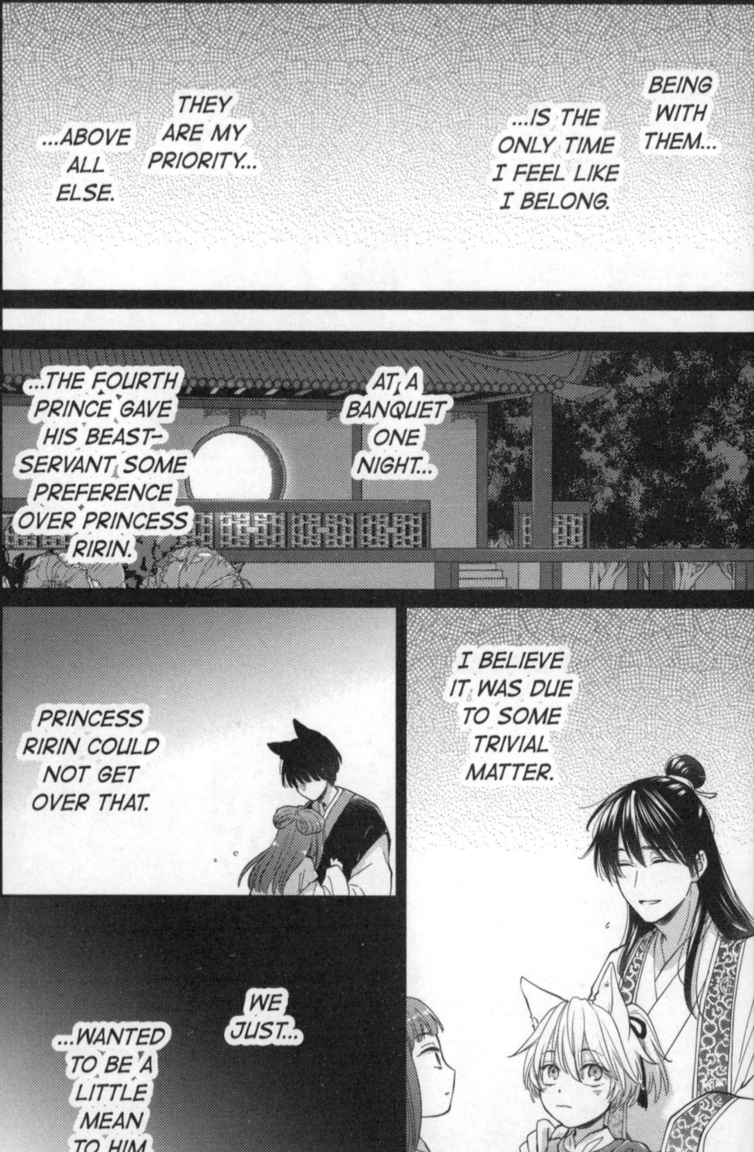
BEING WITH THEM...
...IS THE ONLY TIME I FEEL LIKE I BELONG.
THEY ARE MY PRIORITY...
...ABOVE ALL ELSE.
AT A BANQUET ONE NIGHT...
...THE FOURTH PRINCE GAVE HIS BEAST-SERVANT SOME PREFERENCE OVER PRINCESS RIRIN.
I BELIEVE IT WAS DUE TO SOME TRIVIAL MATTER.
PRINCESS RIRIN COULD NOT GET OVER THAT.
WE JUST...
...WANTED TO BE A LITTLE MEAN TO HIM.

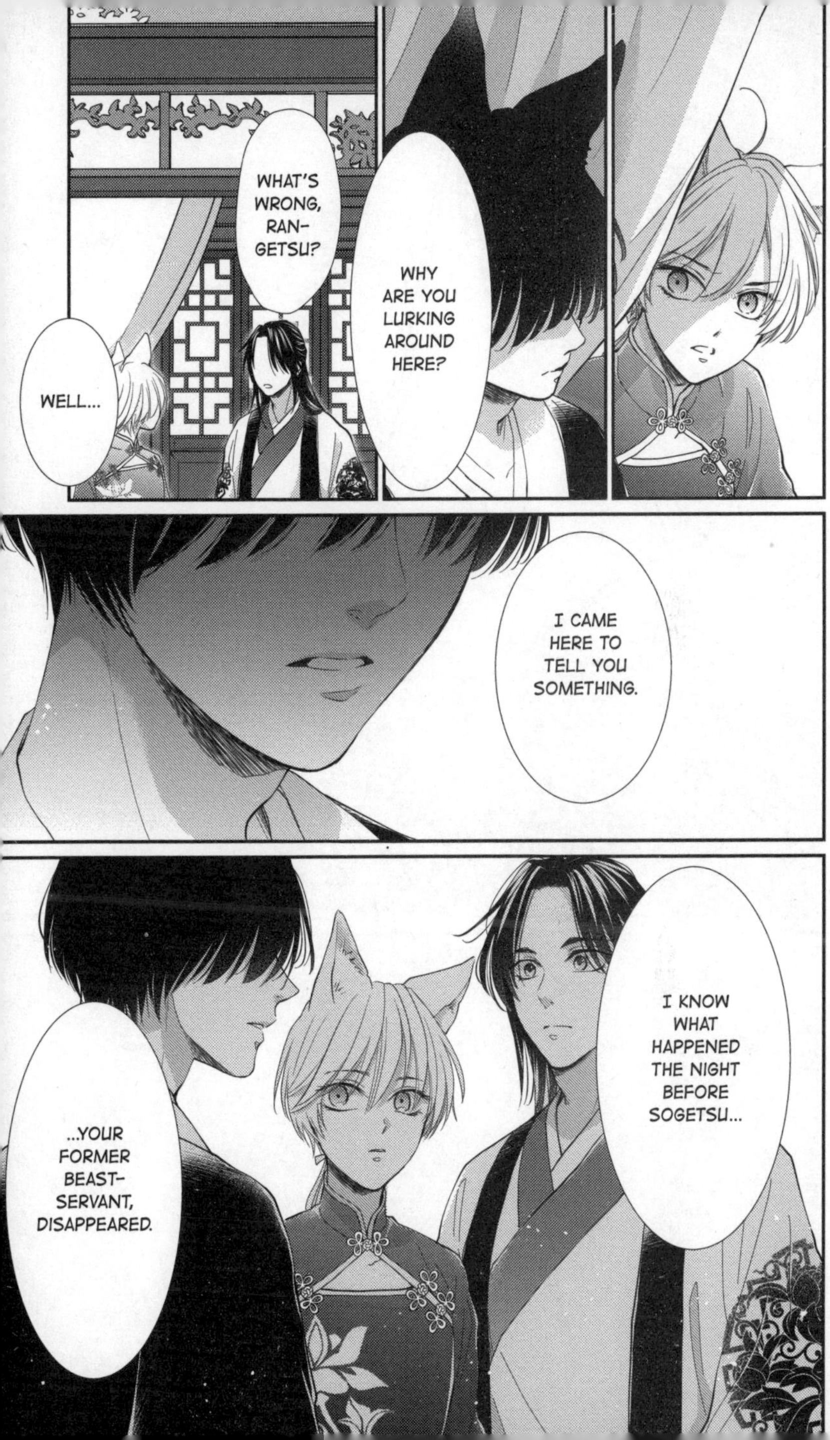
WHY ARE YOU LURKING AROUND HERE?
WHAT'S WRONG, RAN-GETSU?
WELL...
I CAME HERE TO TELL YOU SOMETHING.
I KNOW WHAT HAPPENED THE NIGHT BEFORE SOGETSU...
...YOUR FORMER BEAST-SERVANT, DISAPPEARED.

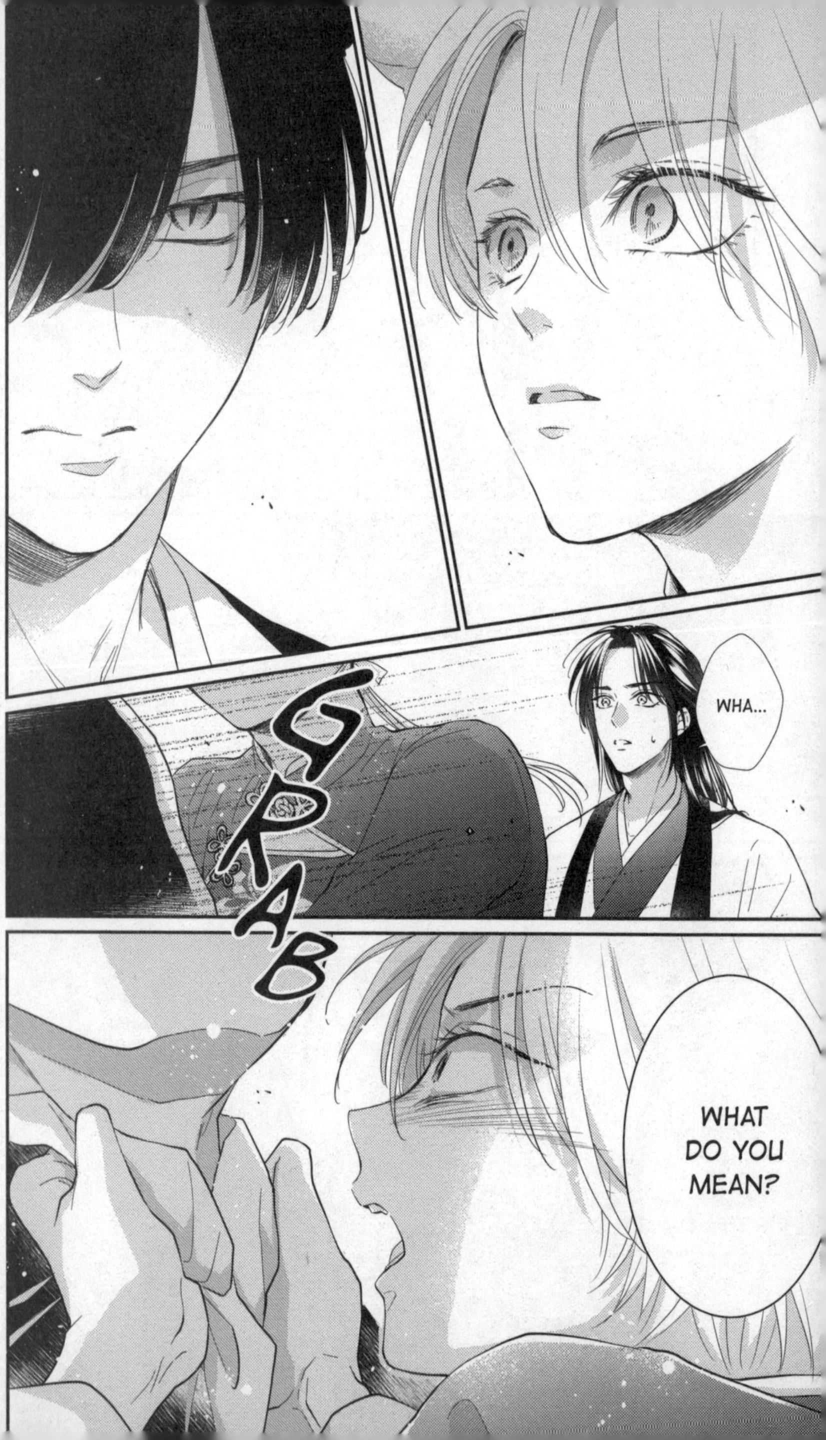
WHA...
GRAB
WHAT DO YOU MEAN?

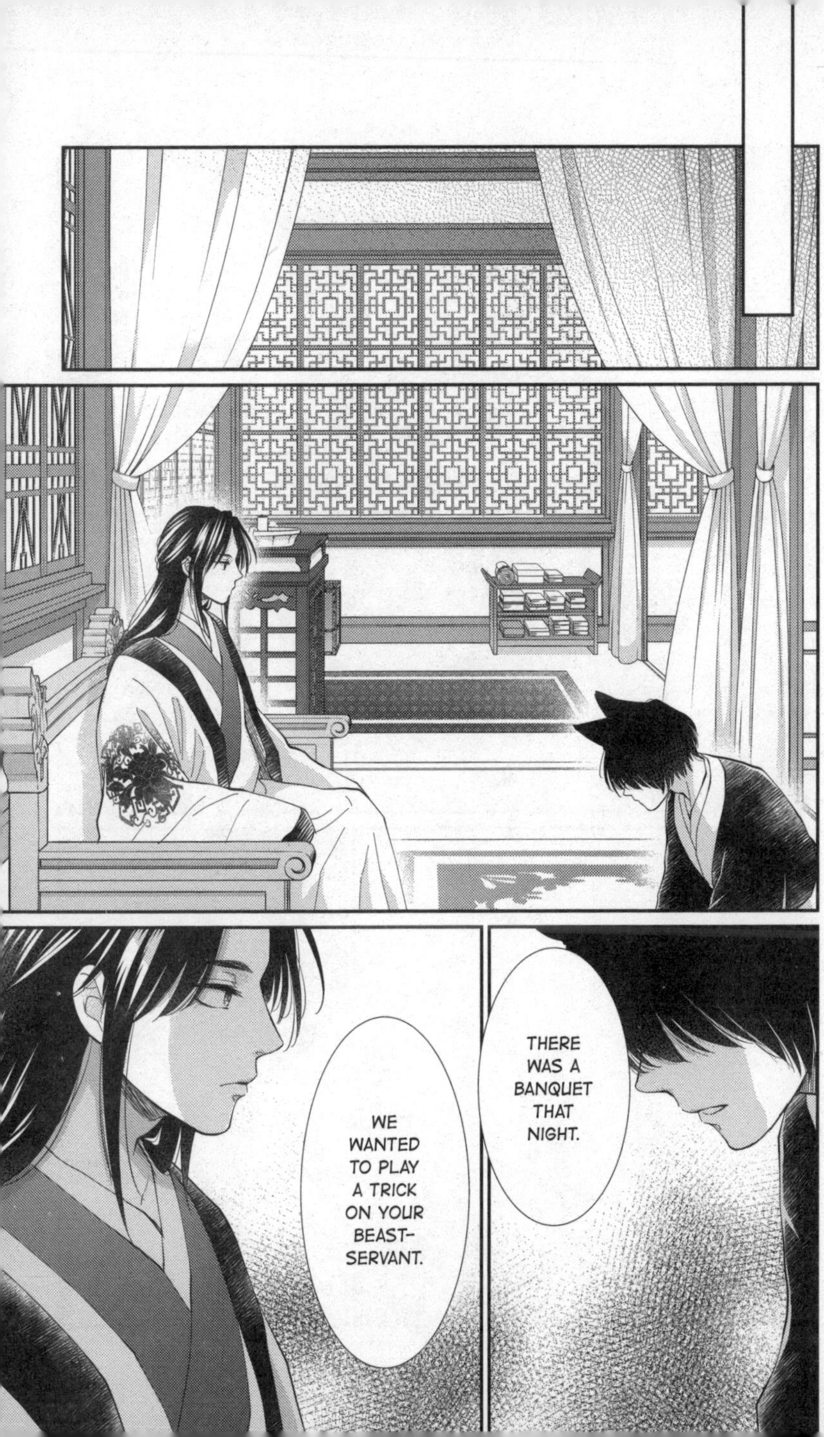
THERE WAS A BANQUET THAT NIGHT.
WE WANTED TO PLAY A TRICK ON YOUR BEAST-SERVANT.

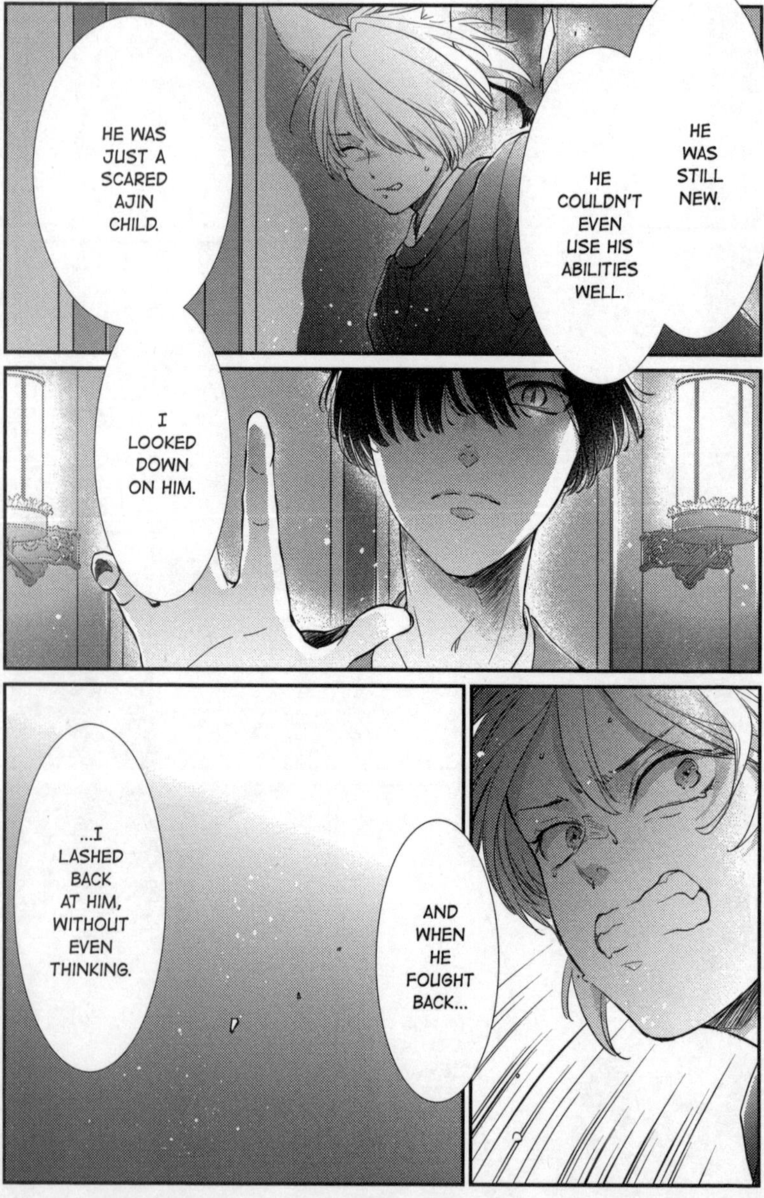
HE WAS STILL NEW.
HE COULDN'T EVEN USE HIS ABILITIES WELL.
HE WAS JUST A SCARED AJIN CHILD.
I LOOKED DOWN ON HIM.
AND WHEN HE FOUGHT BACK...
...I LASHED BACK AT HIM, WITHOUT EVEN THINKING.

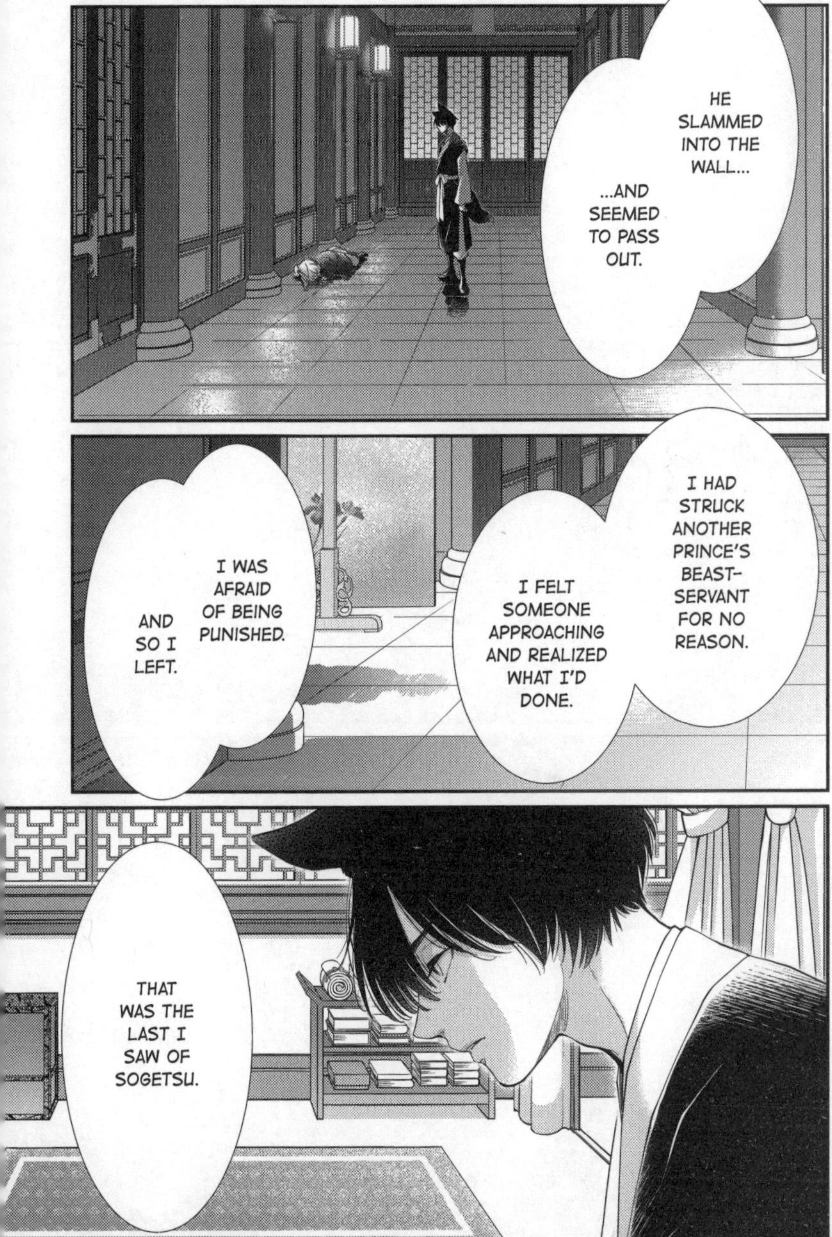
HE SLAMMED INTO THE WALL...
...AND SEEMED TO PASS OUT.
I HAD STRUCK ANOTHER PRINCE'S BEAST-SERVANT FOR NO REASON.
I FELT SOMEONE APPROACHING AND REALIZED WHAT I'D DONE.
I WAS AFRAID OF BEING PUNISHED.
AND SO I LEFT.
THAT WAS THE LAST I SAW OF SOGETSU.

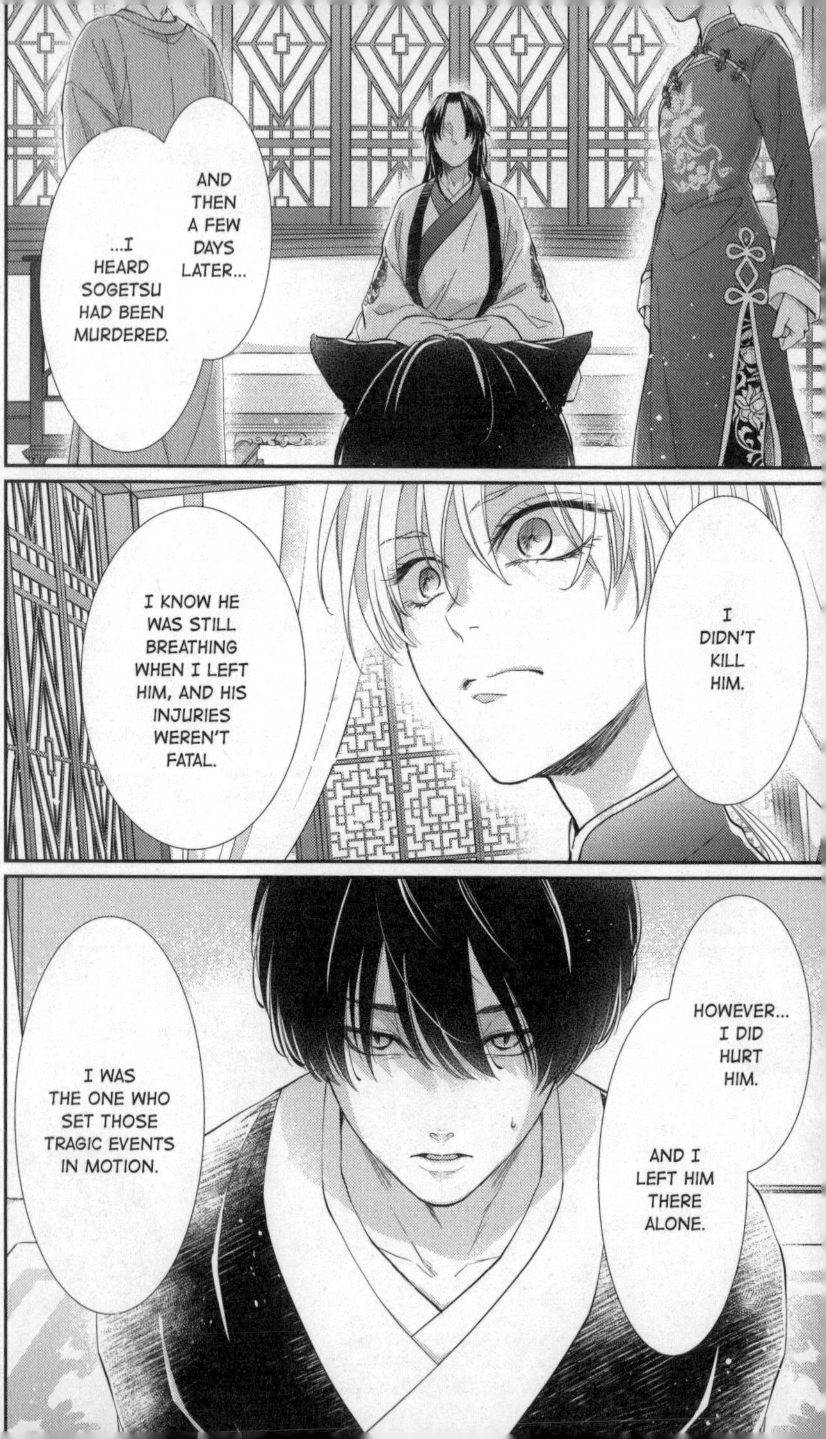
AND THEN A FEW DAYS LATER...
...I HEARD SOGETSU HAD BEEN MURDERED.
I DIDN'T KILL HIM.
I KNOW HE WAS STILL BREATHING WHEN I LEFT HIM, AND HIS INJURIES WEREN'T FATAL.
HOWEVER... I DID HURT HIM.
AND I LEFT HIM THERE ALONE.
I WAS THE ONE WHO SET THOSE TRAGIC EVENTS IN MOTION.

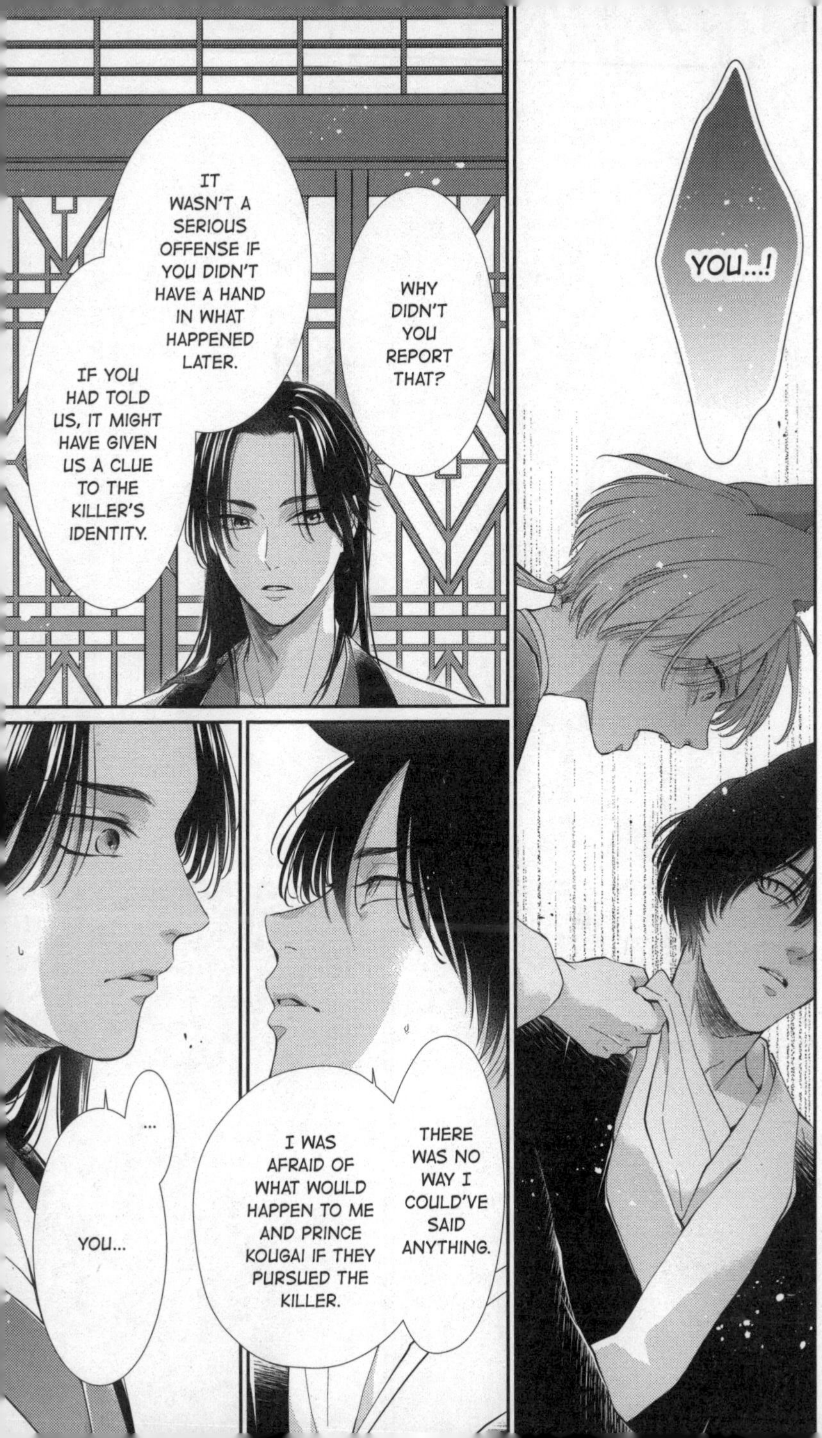
YOU...!
WHY DIDN'T YOU REPORT THAT?
IT WASN'T A SERIOUS OFFENSE IF YOU DIDN'T HAVE A HAND IN WHAT HAPPENED LATER.
IF YOU HAD TOLD US, IT MIGHT HAVE GIVEN US A CLUE TO THE KILLER'S IDENTITY.
THERE WAS NO WAY I COULD'VE SAID ANYTHING.
I WAS AFRAID OF WHAT WOULD HAPPEN TO ME AND PRINCE KOUGAI IF THEY PURSUED THE KILLER.
...
YOU...

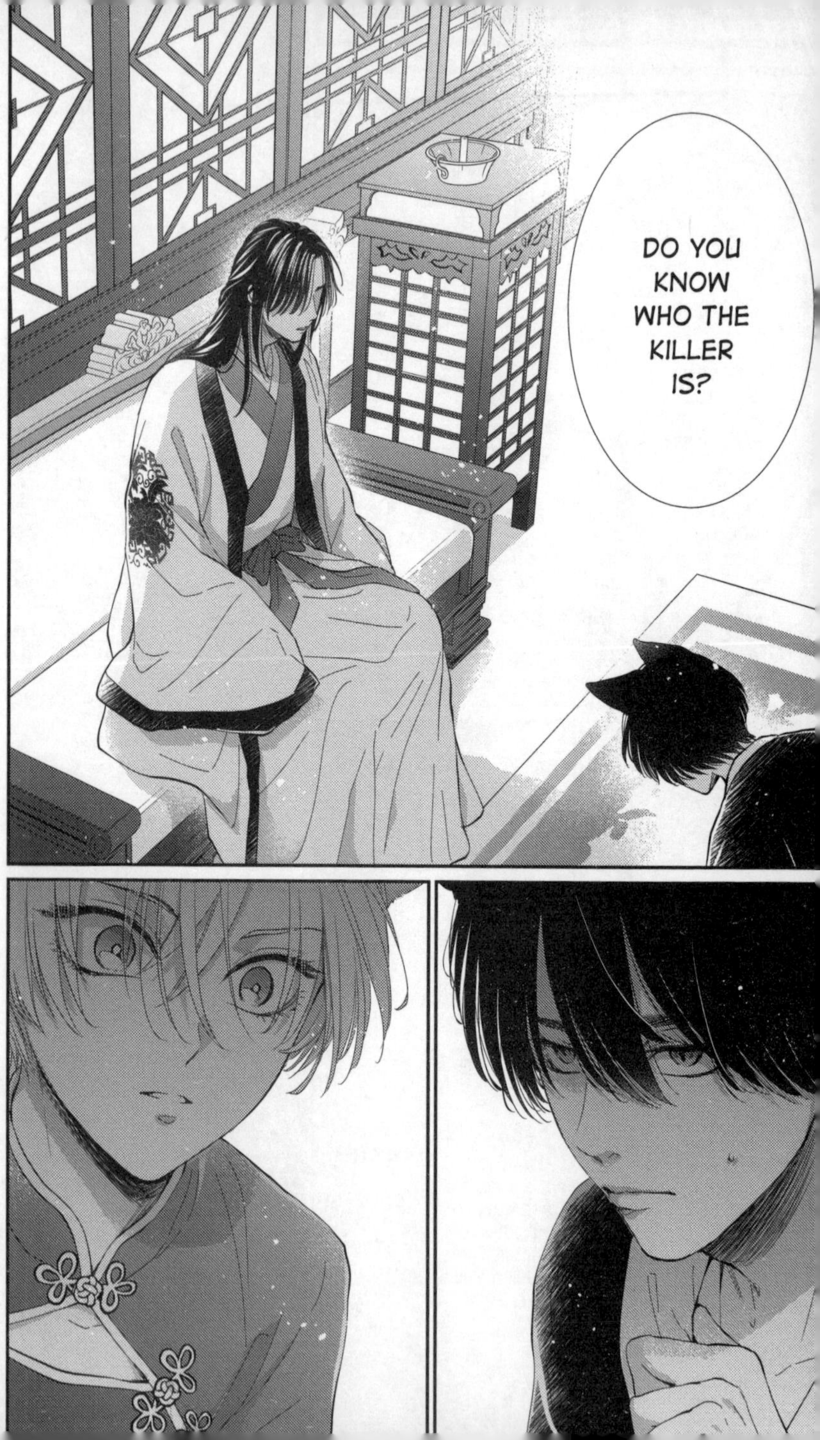
DO YOU KNOW WHO THE KILLER IS?

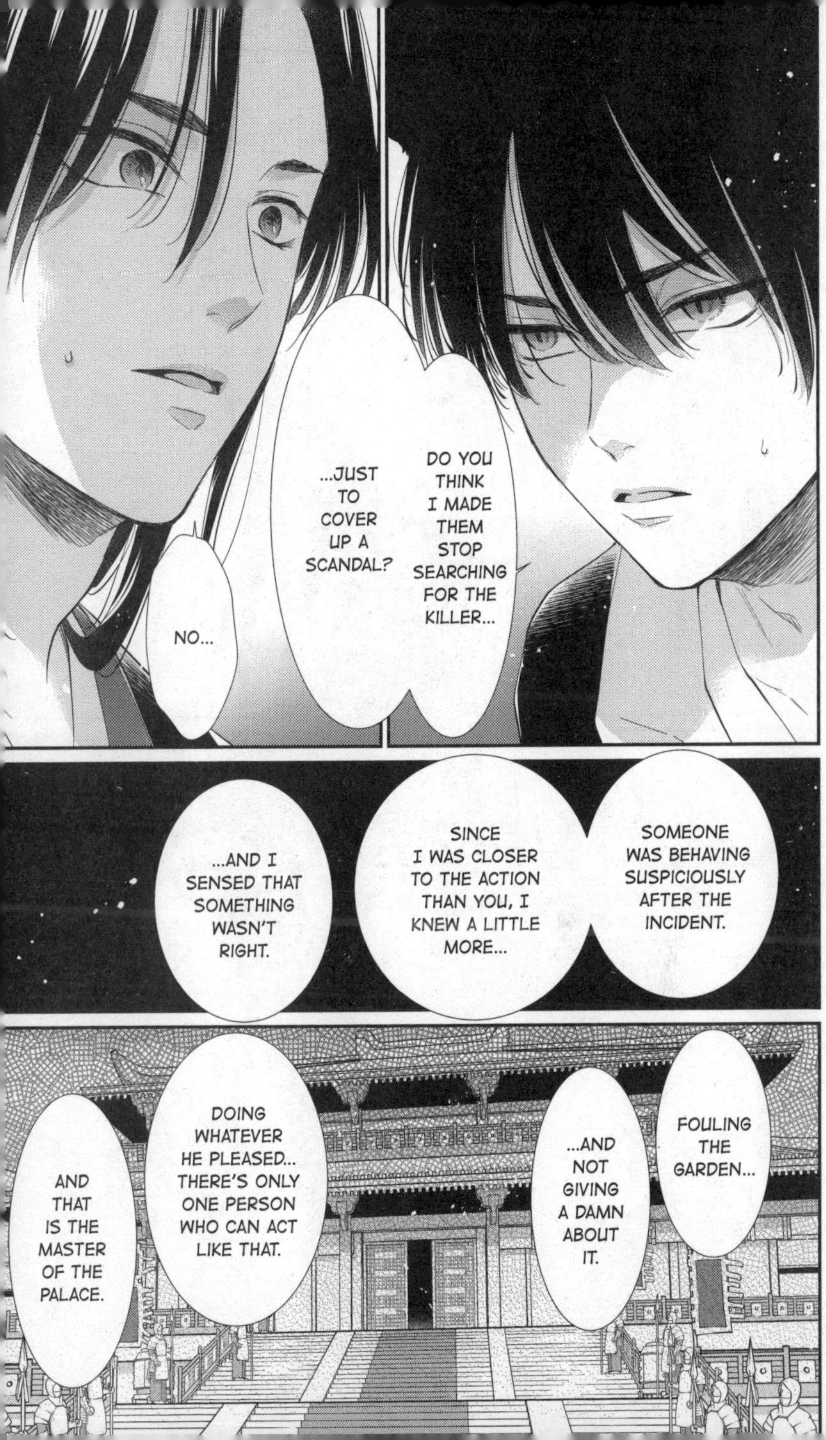
DO YOU THINK I MADE THEM STOP SEARCHING FOR THE KILLER...
...JUST TO COVER UP A SCANDAL?
NO...
SOMEONE WAS BEHAVING SUSPICIOUSLY AFTER THE INCIDENT.
SINCE I WAS CLOSER TO THE ACTION THAN YOU, I KNEW A LITTLE MORE...
...AND I SENSED THAT SOMETHING WASN'T RIGHT.
FOULING THE GARDEN...
...AND NOT GIVING A DAMN ABOUT IT.
DOING WHATEVER HE PLEASED... THERE'S ONLY ONE PERSON WHO CAN ACT LIKE THAT.
AND THAT IS THE MASTER OF THE PALACE.

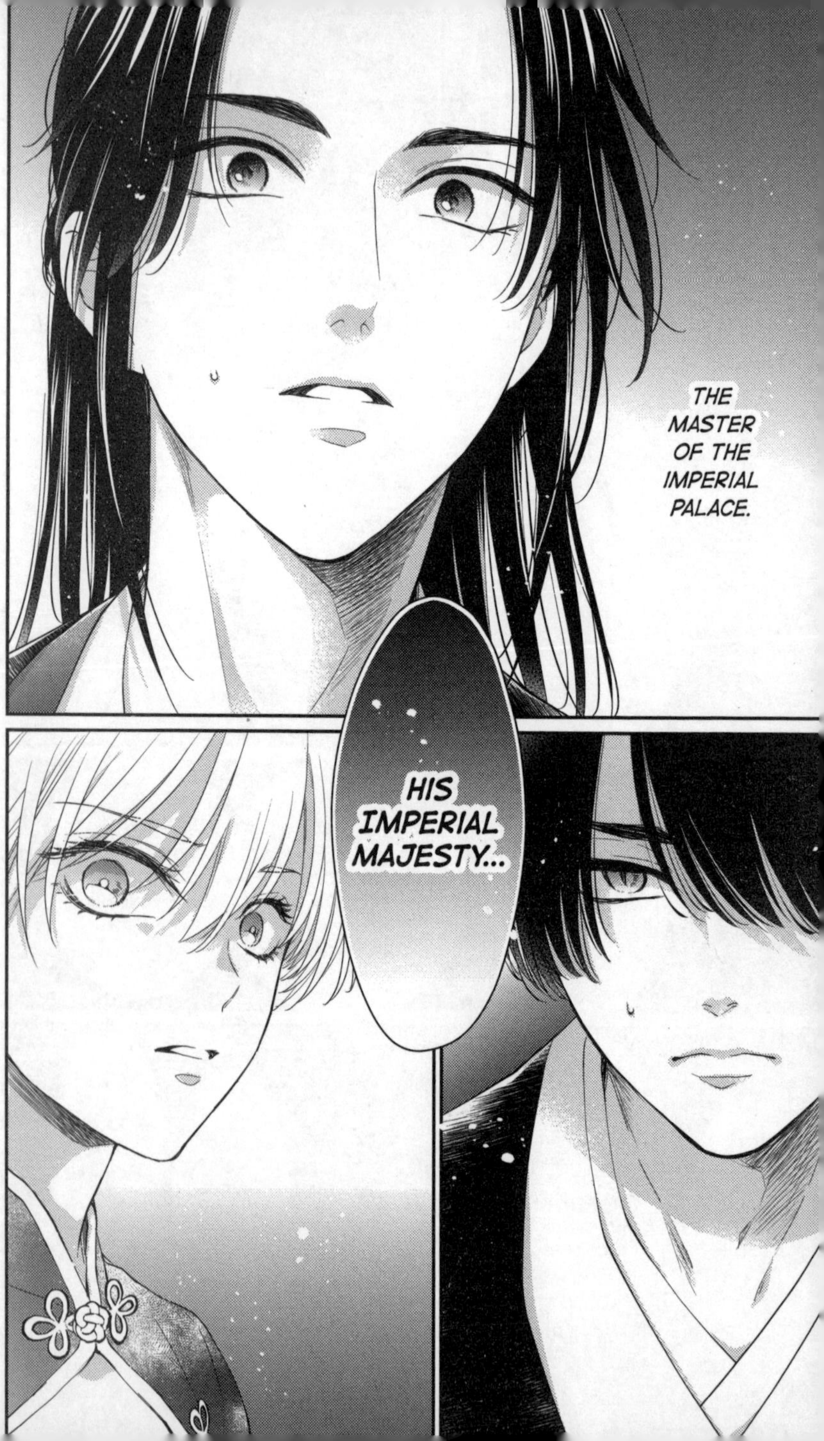
THE MASTER OF THE IMPERIAL PALACE.
HIS IMPERIAL MAJESTY...

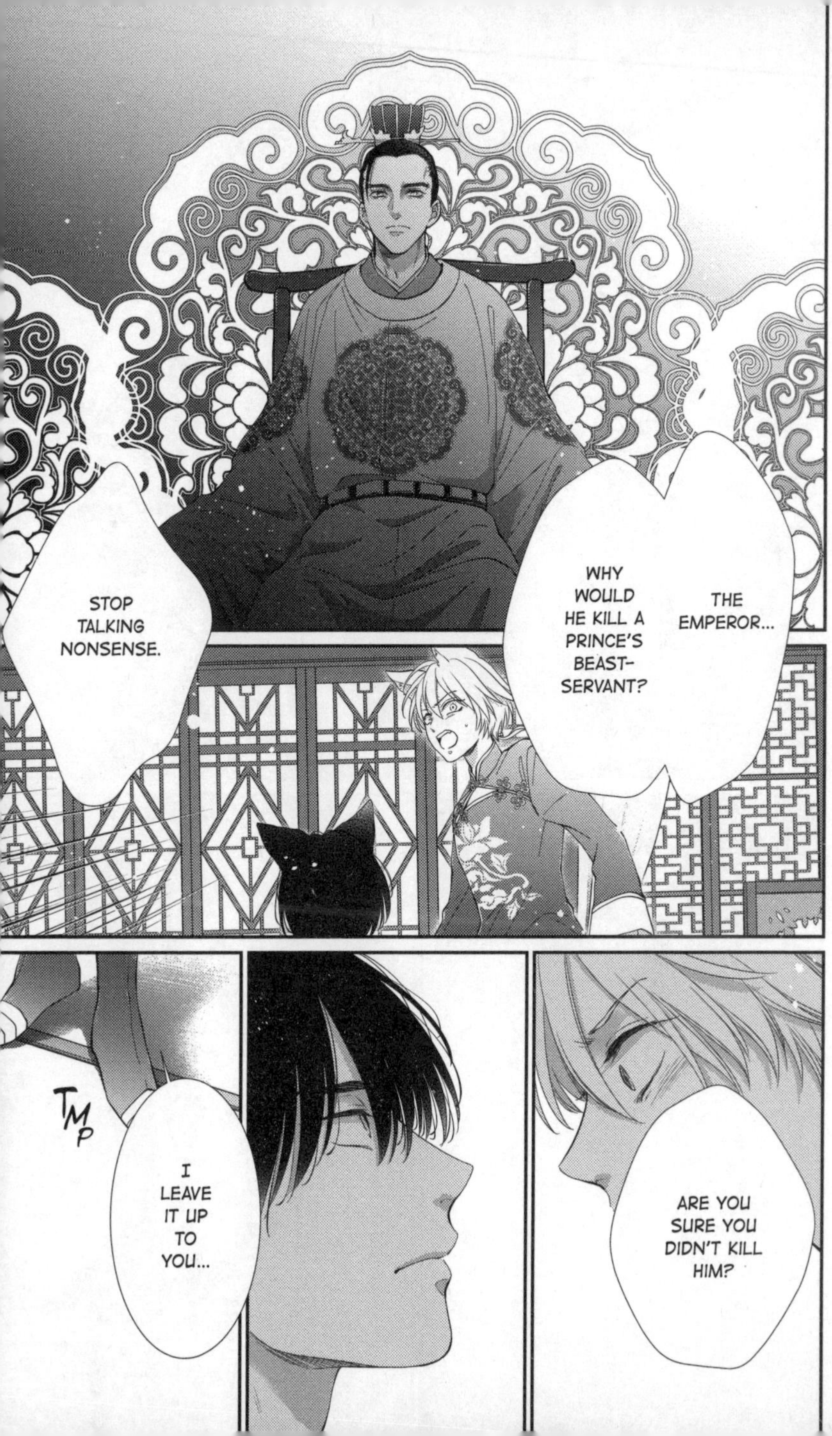
THE EMPEROR...
WHY WOULD HE KILL A PRINCE'S BEAST-SERVANT?
STOP TALKING NONSENSE.
ARE YOU SURE YOU DIDN'T KILL HIM?
I LEAVE IT UP TO YOU...
TMP

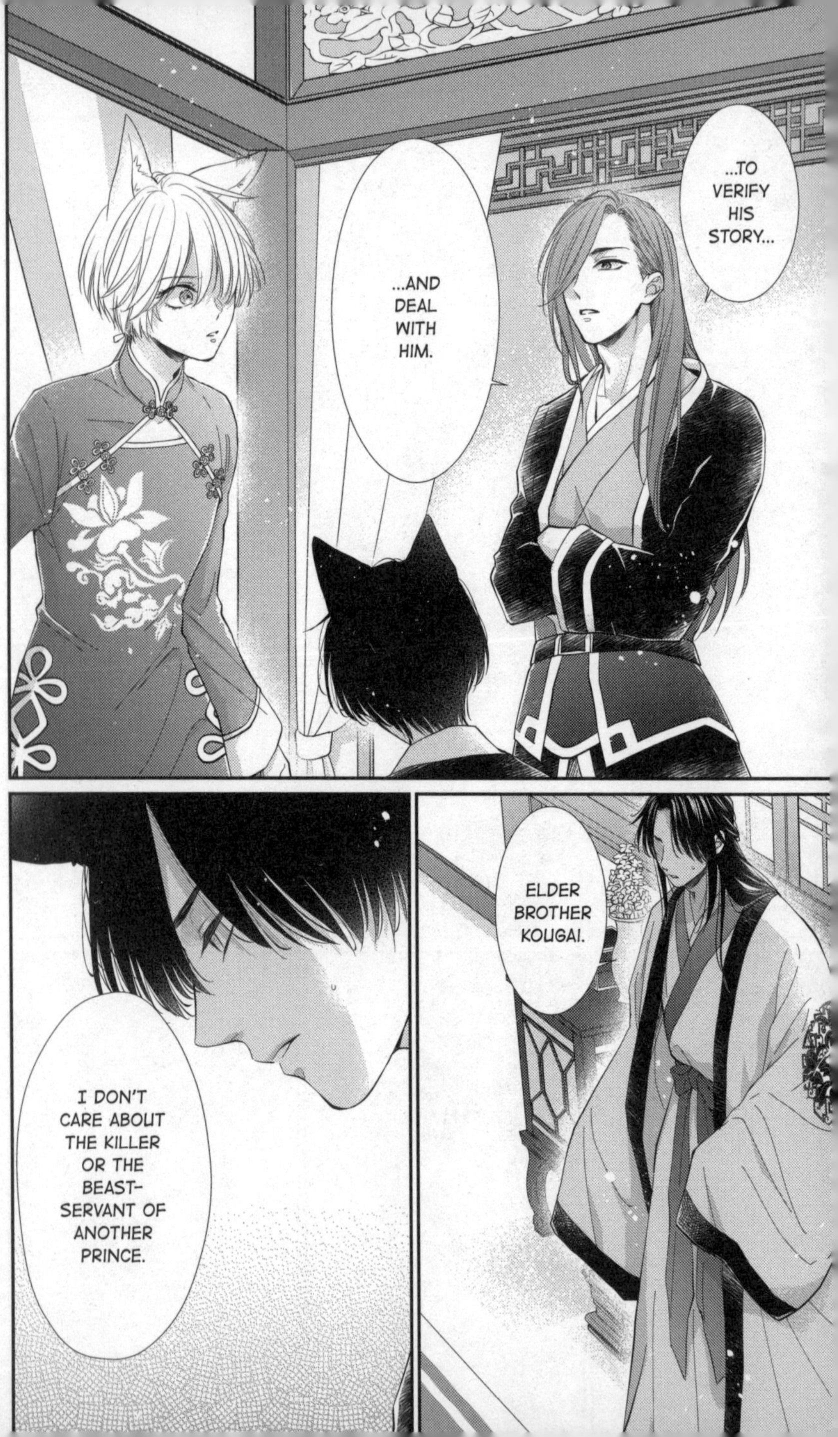
...TO VERIFY HIS STORY...
...AND DEAL WITH HIM.
ELDER BROTHER KOUGAI.
I DON'T CARE ABOUT THE KILLER OR THE BEAST-SERVANT OF ANOTHER PRINCE.

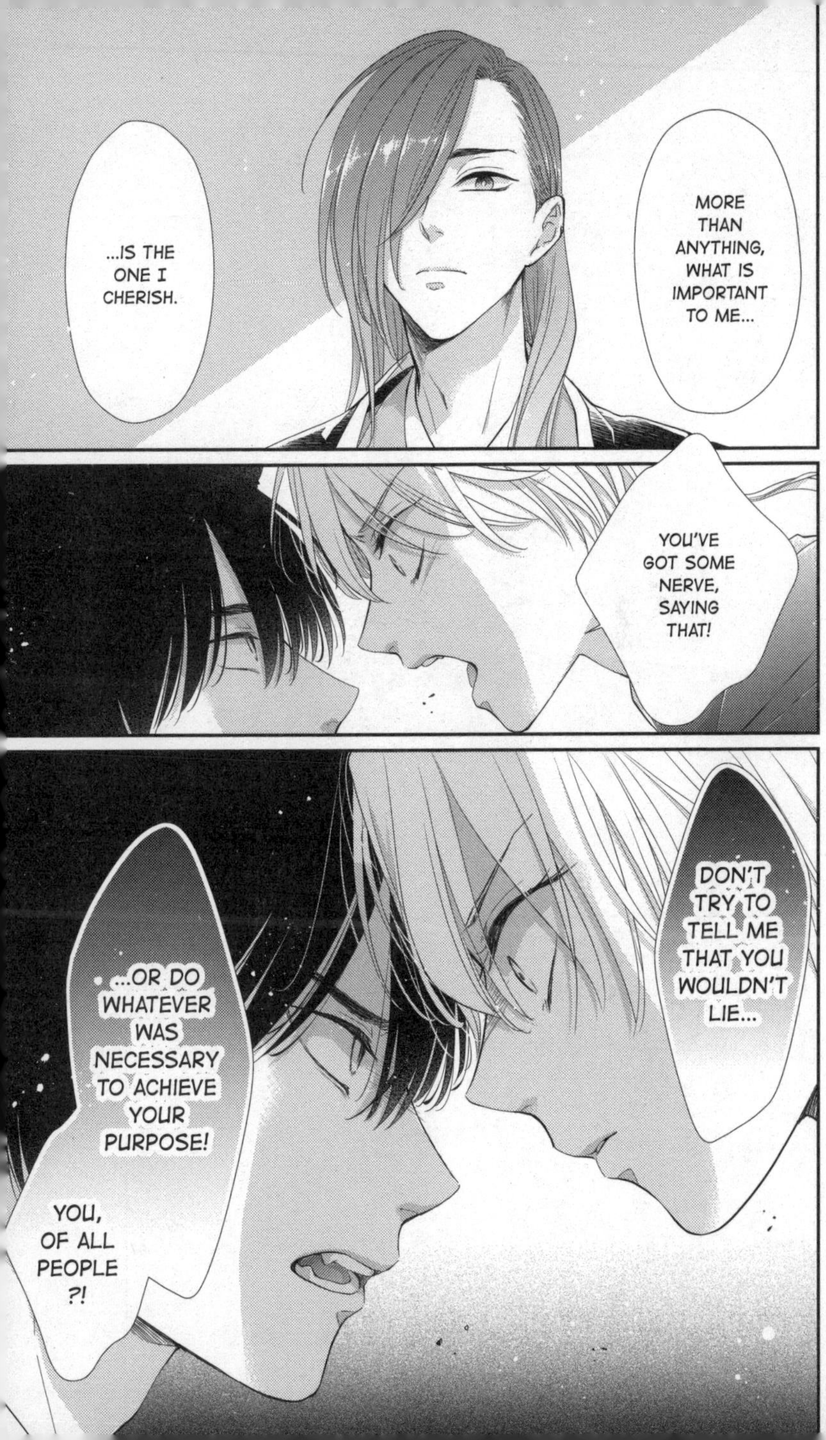
MORE THAN ANYTHING, WHAT IS IMPORTANT TO ME...
...IS THE ONE I CHERISH.
YOU'VE GOT SOME NERVE, SAYING THAT!
DON'T TRY TO TELL ME THAT YOU WOULDN'T LIE...
...OR DO WHATEVER WAS NECESSARY TO ACHIEVE YOUR PURPOSE!
YOU, OF ALL PEOPLE ?!

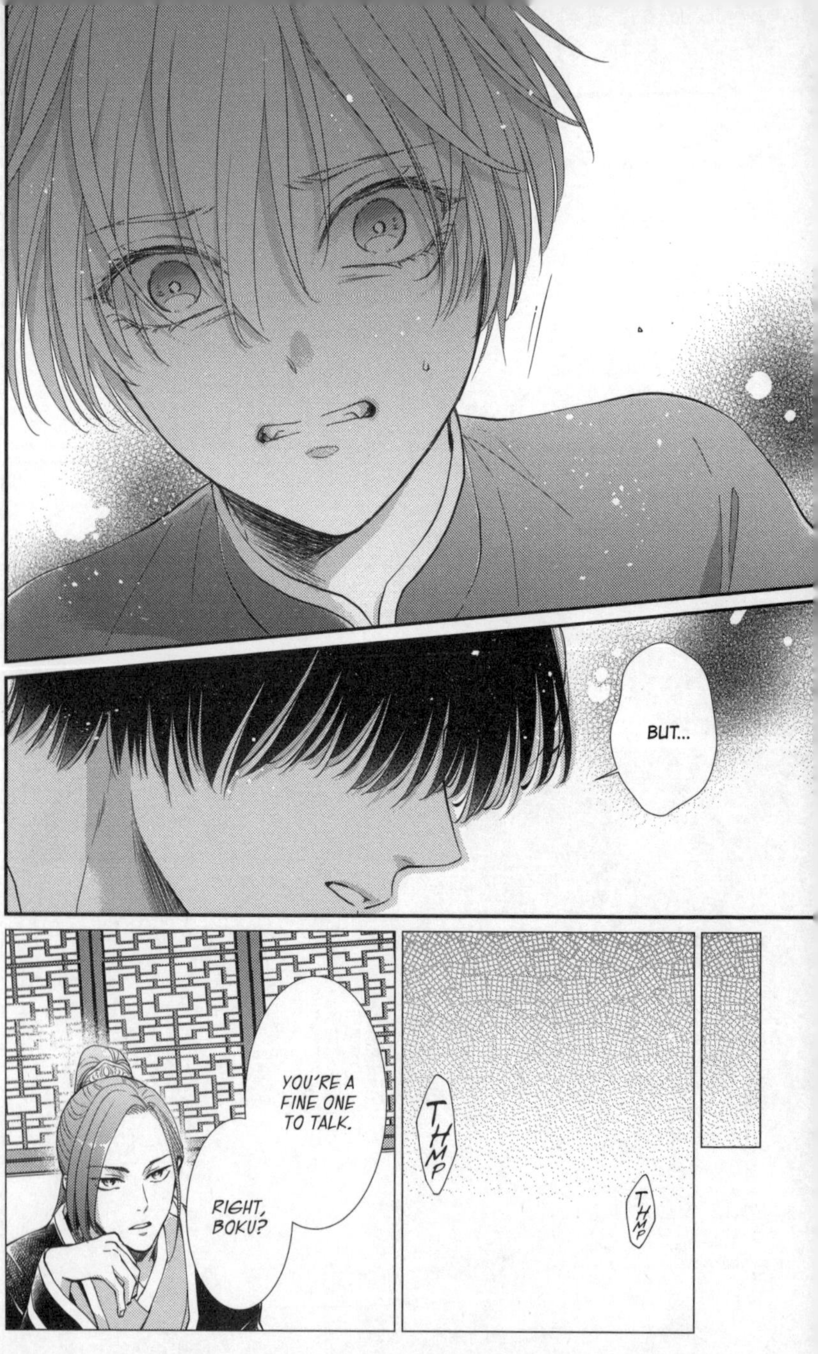
BUT...
THMP
THMP
YOU'RE A FINE ONE TO TALK.
RIGHT, BOKU?

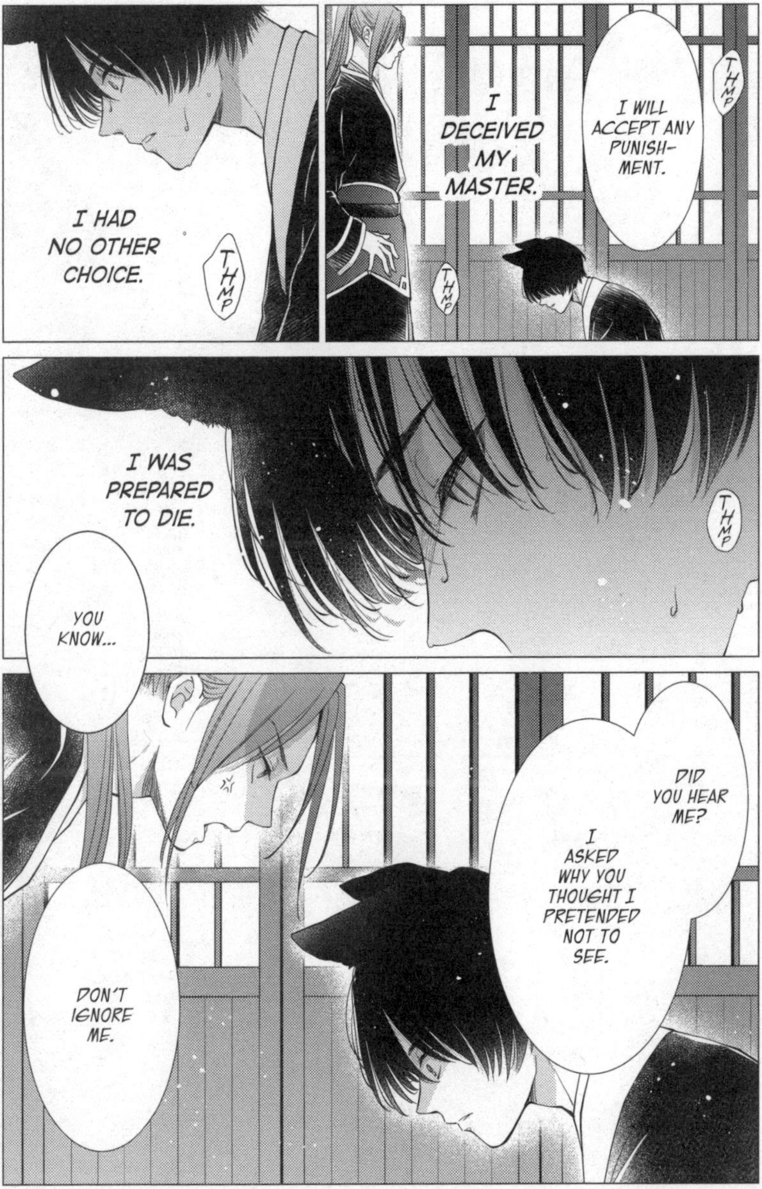
THMP
I WILL ACCEPT ANY PUNISH-MENT.
I DECEIVED MY MASTER.
THMP
I HAD NO OTHER CHOICE.
THMP
THMP
I WAS PREPARED TO DIE.
YOU KNOW...
DID YOU HEAR ME?
I ASKED WHY YOU THOUGHT I PRETENDED NOT TO SEE.
DON'T IGNORE ME.

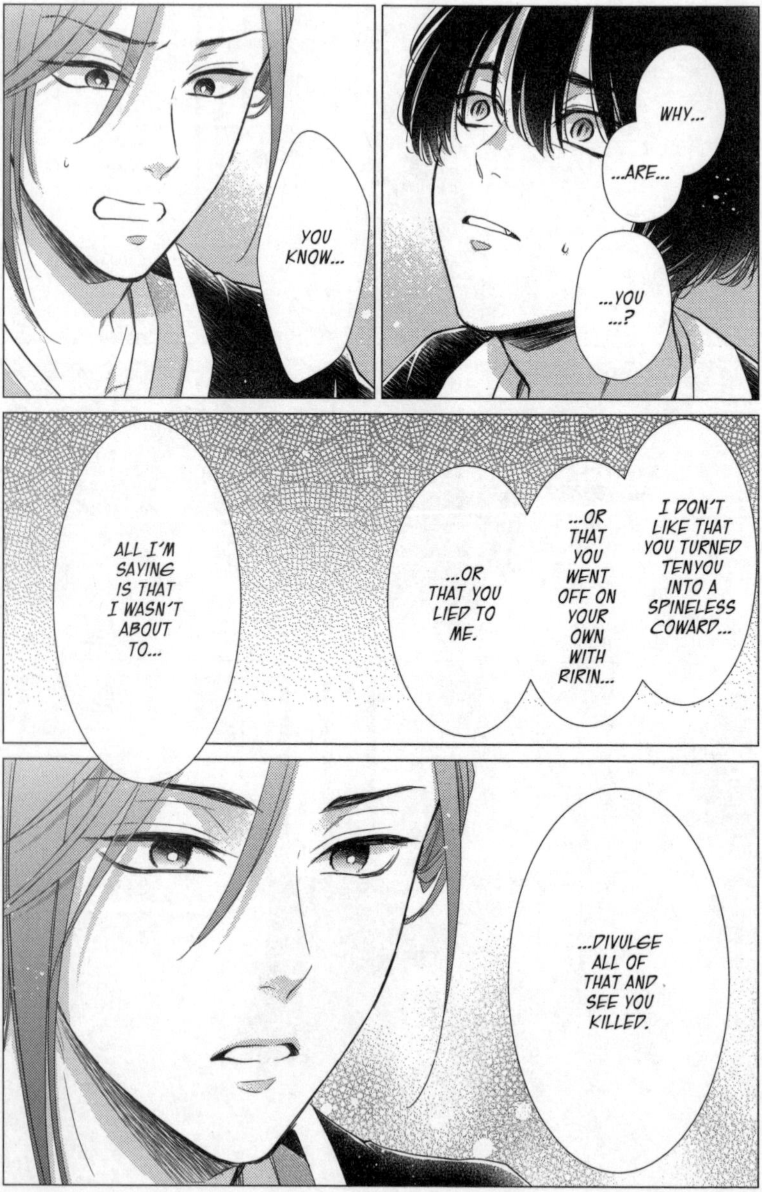
WHY...
...ARE...
...YOU ...?
YOU KNOW...
I DON'T LIKE THAT YOU TURNED TENYOU INTO A SPINELESS COWARD...
...OR THAT YOU WENT OFF ON YOUR OWN WITH RIRIN...
...OR THAT YOU LIED TO ME.
ALL I'M SAYING IS THAT I WASN'T ABOUT TO...
...DIVULGE ALL OF THAT AND SEE YOU KILLED.

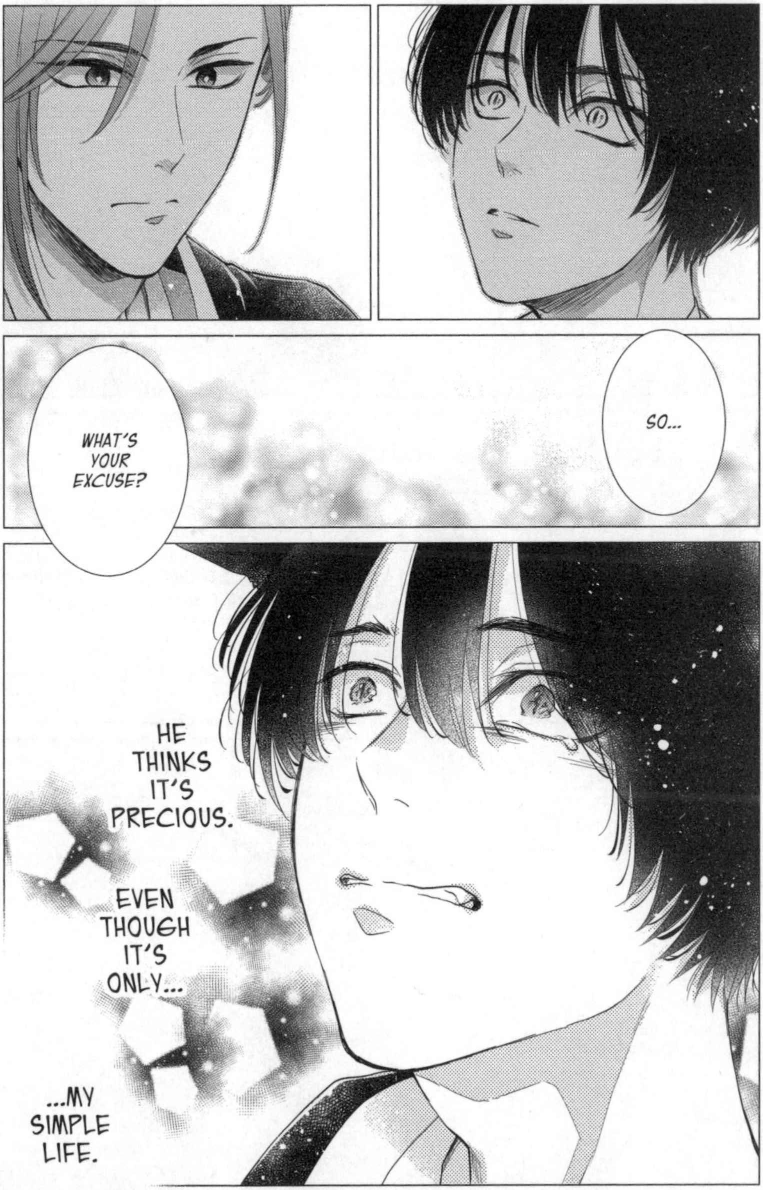
SO...
WHAT'S YOUR EXCUSE?
HE THINKS IT'S PRECIOUS.
EVEN THOUGH IT'S ONLY...
...MY SIMPLE LIFE.

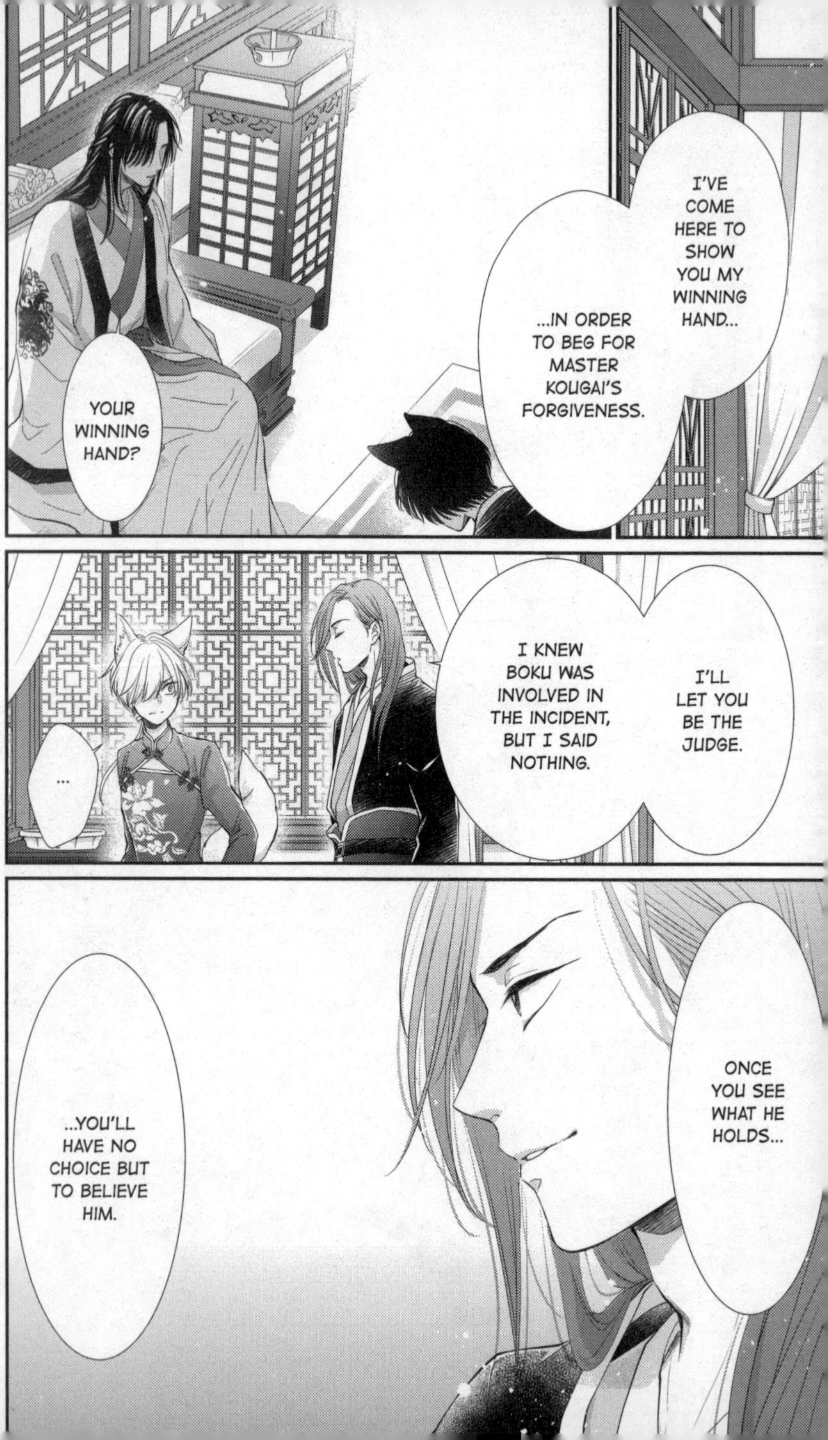
I'VE COME HERE TO SHOW YOU MY WINNING HAND...
...IN ORDER TO BEG FOR MASTER KOUGAI'S FORGIVENESS.
YOUR WINNING HAND?
I'LL LET YOU BE THE JUDGE.
I KNEW BOKU WAS INVOLVED IN THE INCIDENT, BUT I SAID NOTHING.
...
ONCE YOU SEE WHAT HE HOLDS...
...YOU'LL HAVE NO CHOICE BUT TO BELIEVE HIM.

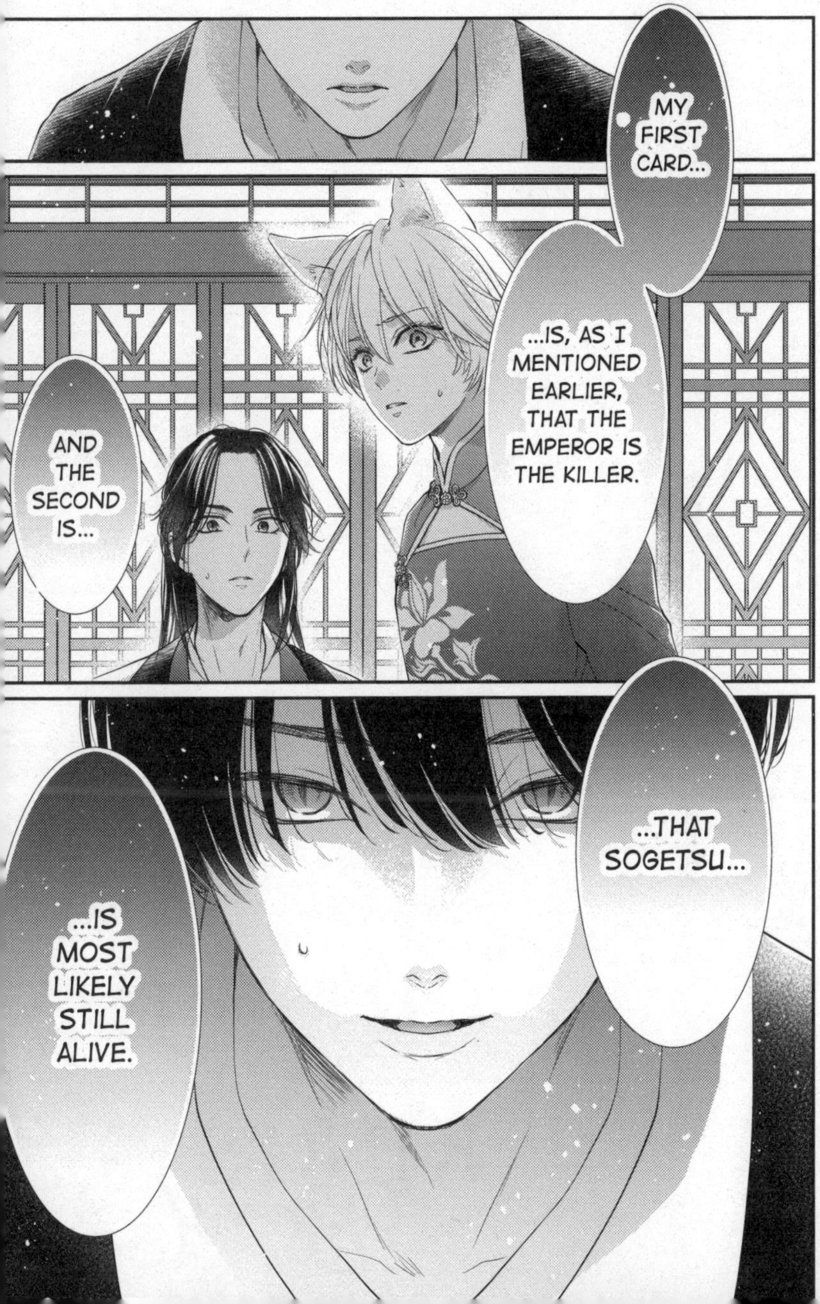
MY FIRST CARD...
...IS, AS I MENTIONED EARLIER, THAT THE EMPEROR IS THE KILLER.
AND THE SECOND IS...
...THAT SOGETSU...
...IS MOST LIKELY STILL ALIVE.

THE KING'S Beast 麗

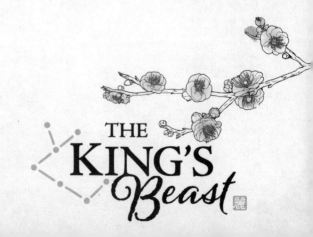

Chapter 25

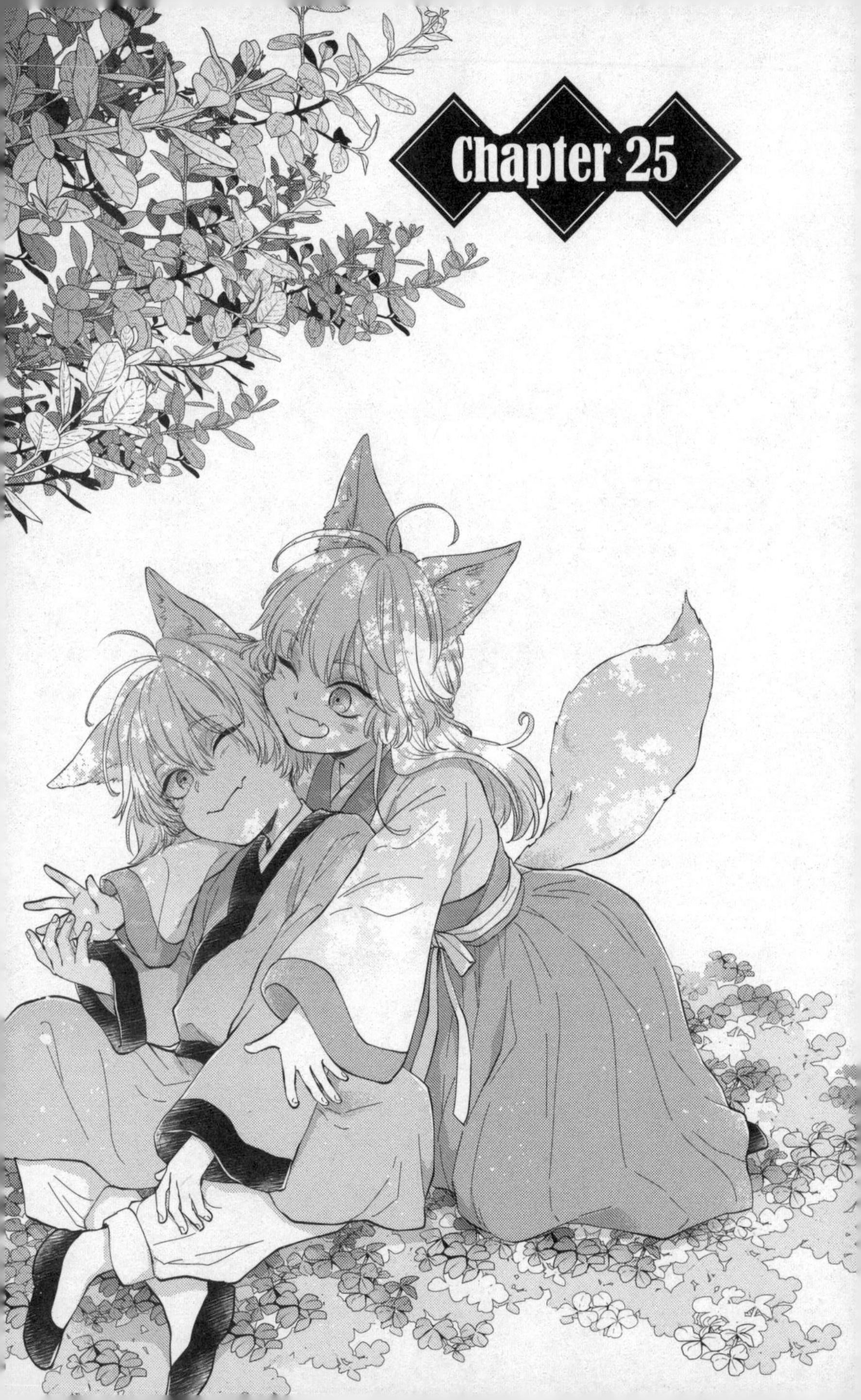

WHAT
IS
THAT...?

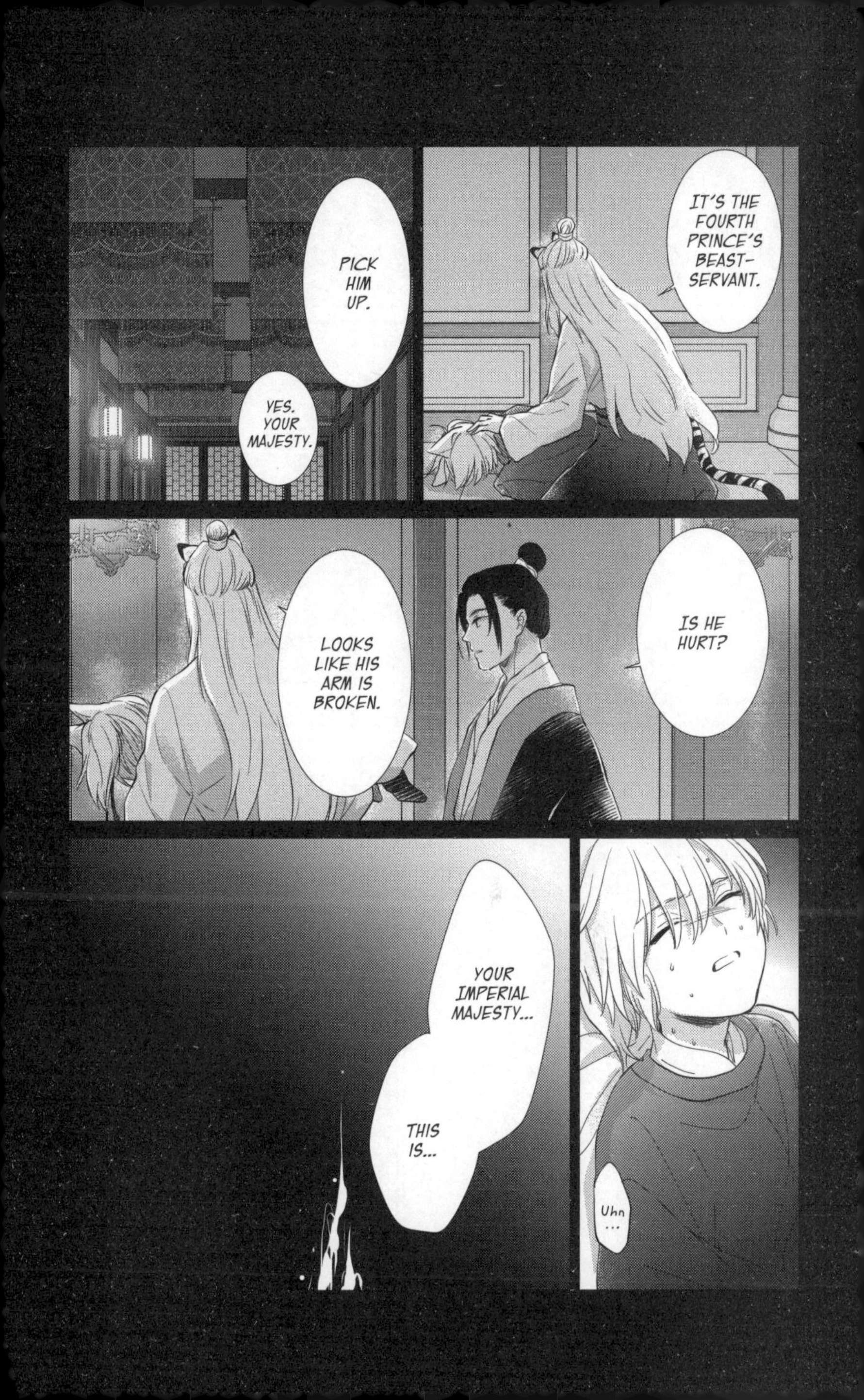
IT'S THE FOURTH PRINCE'S BEAST-SERVANT.
PICK HIM UP.
YES. YOUR MAJESTY.
IS HE HURT?
LOOKS LIKE HIS ARM IS BROKEN.
Uhn...
YOUR IMPERIAL MAJESTY...
THIS IS...

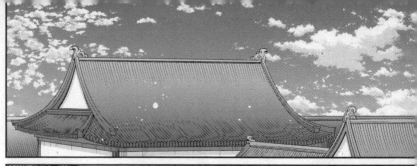

SOGETSU
...

...IS
ALIVE?

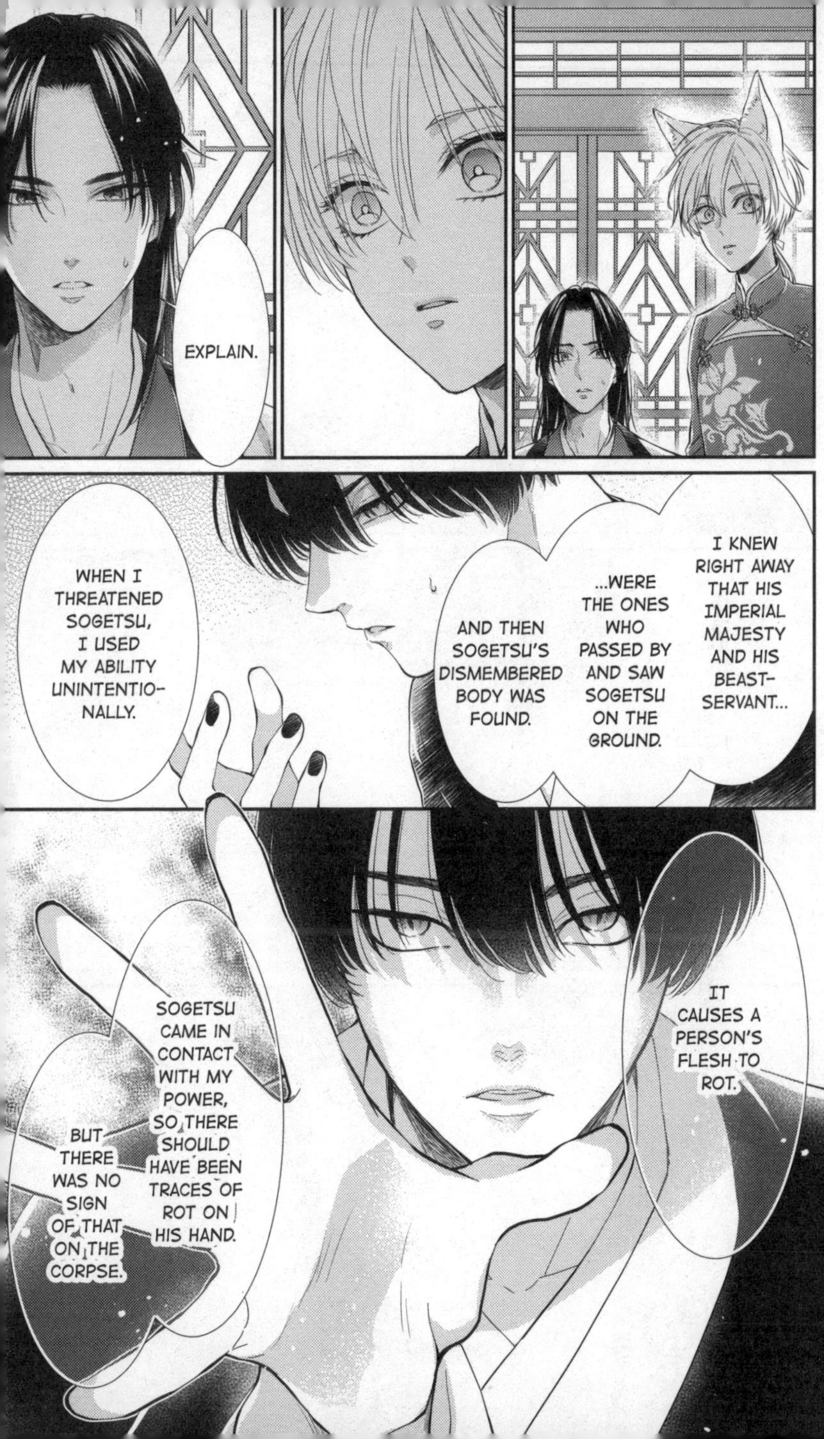
EXPLAIN.
I KNEW RIGHT AWAY THAT HIS IMPERIAL MAJESTY AND HIS BEAST-SERVANT...
...WERE THE ONES WHO PASSED BY AND SAW SOGETSU ON THE GROUND.
AND THEN SOGETSU'S DISMEMBERED BODY WAS FOUND.
WHEN I THREATENED SOGETSU, I USED MY ABILITY UNINTENTIONALLY.
IT CAUSES A PERSON'S FLESH TO ROT.
SOGETSU CAME IN CONTACT WITH MY POWER, SO THERE SHOULD HAVE BEEN TRACES OF ROT ON HIS HAND.
BUT THERE WAS NO SIGN OF THAT ON THE CORPSE.

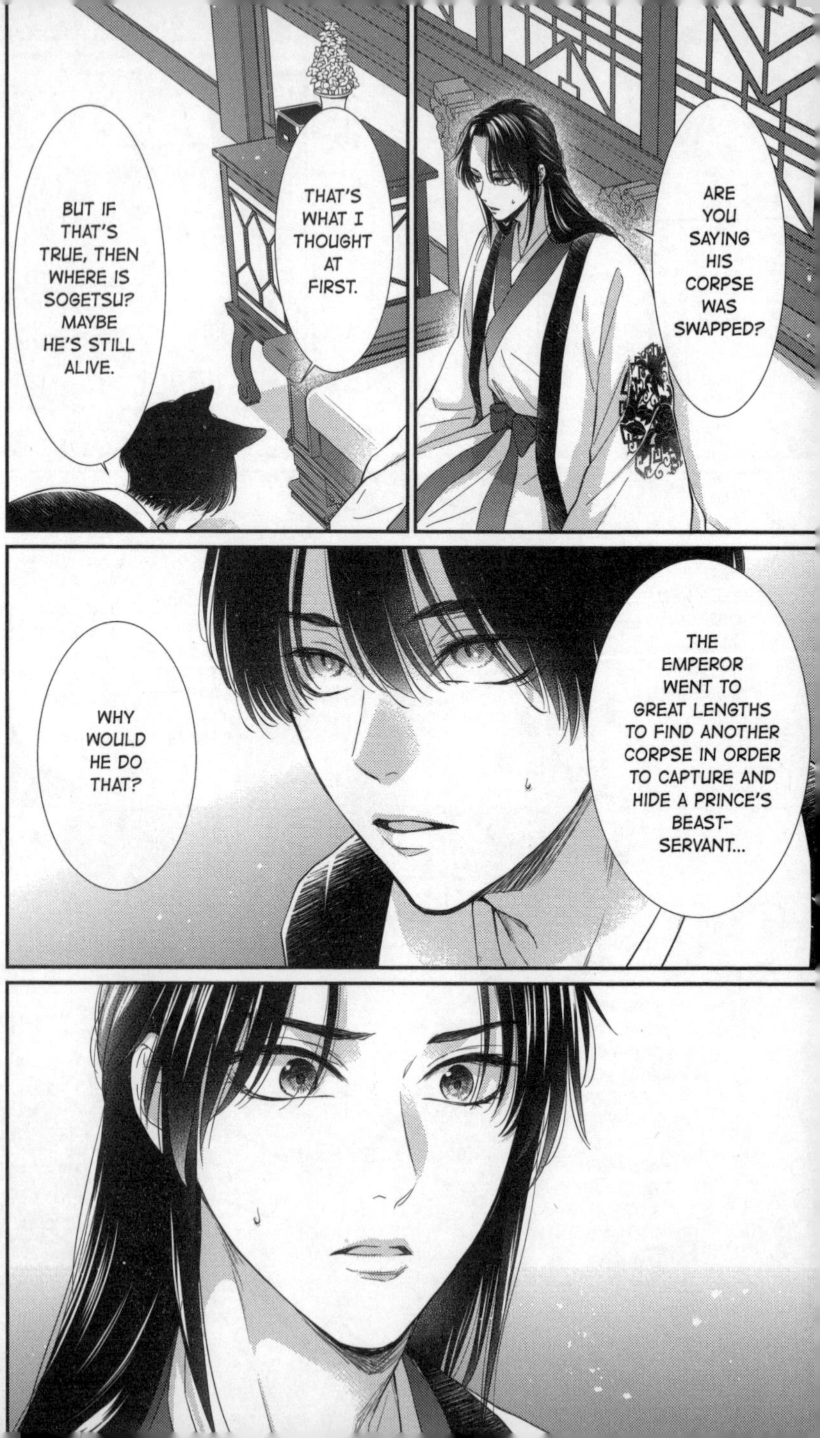
ARE YOU SAYING HIS CORPSE WAS SWAPPED?
THAT'S WHAT I THOUGHT AT FIRST.
BUT IF THAT'S TRUE, THEN WHERE IS SOGETSU? MAYBE HE'S STILL ALIVE.
THE EMPEROR WENT TO GREAT LENGTHS TO FIND ANOTHER CORPSE IN ORDER TO CAPTURE AND HIDE A PRINCE'S BEAST-SERVANT...
WHY WOULD HE DO THAT?

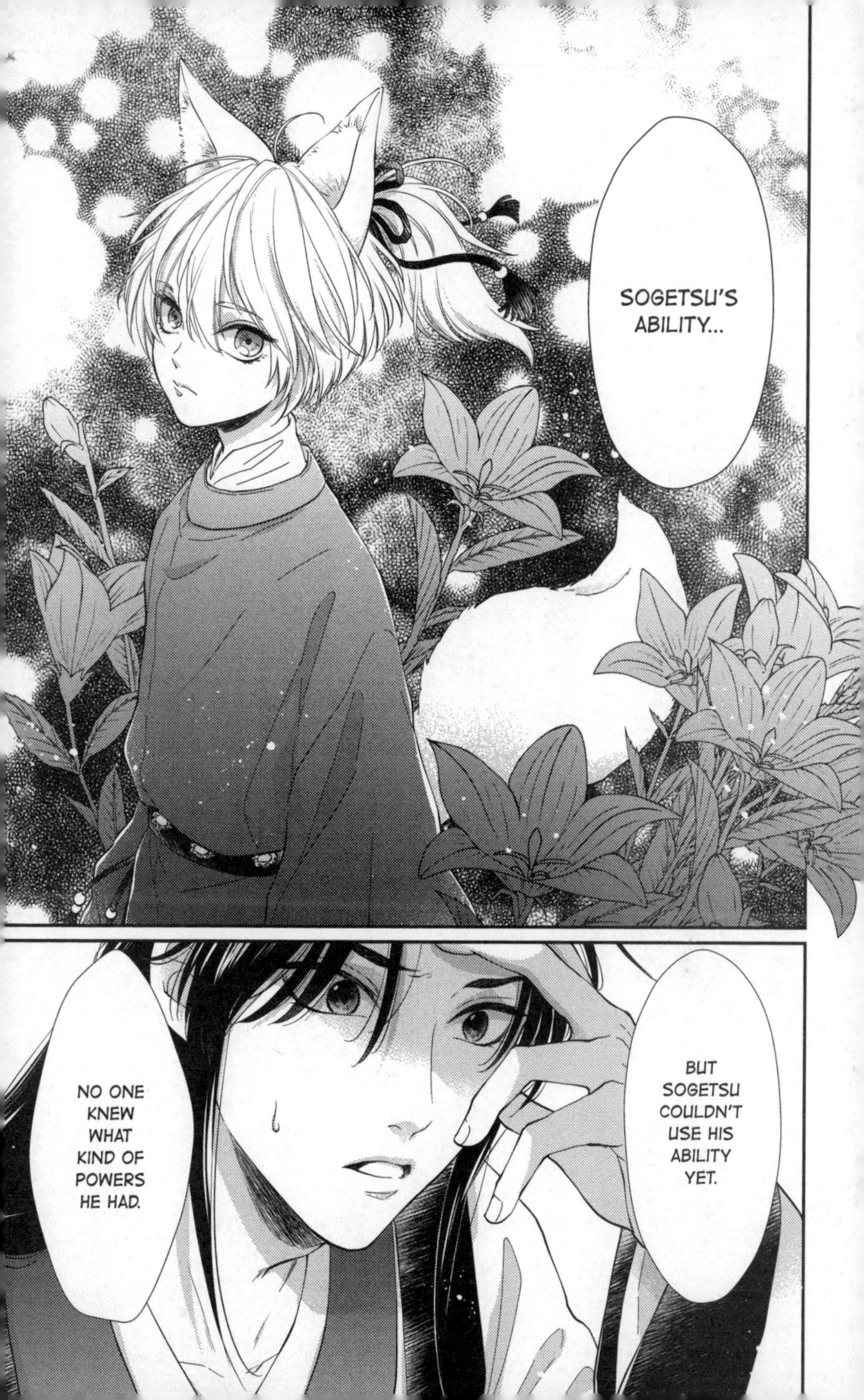
SOGETSU'S ABILITY...
BUT SOGETSU COULDN'T USE HIS ABILITY YET.
NO ONE KNEW WHAT KIND OF POWERS HE HAD.

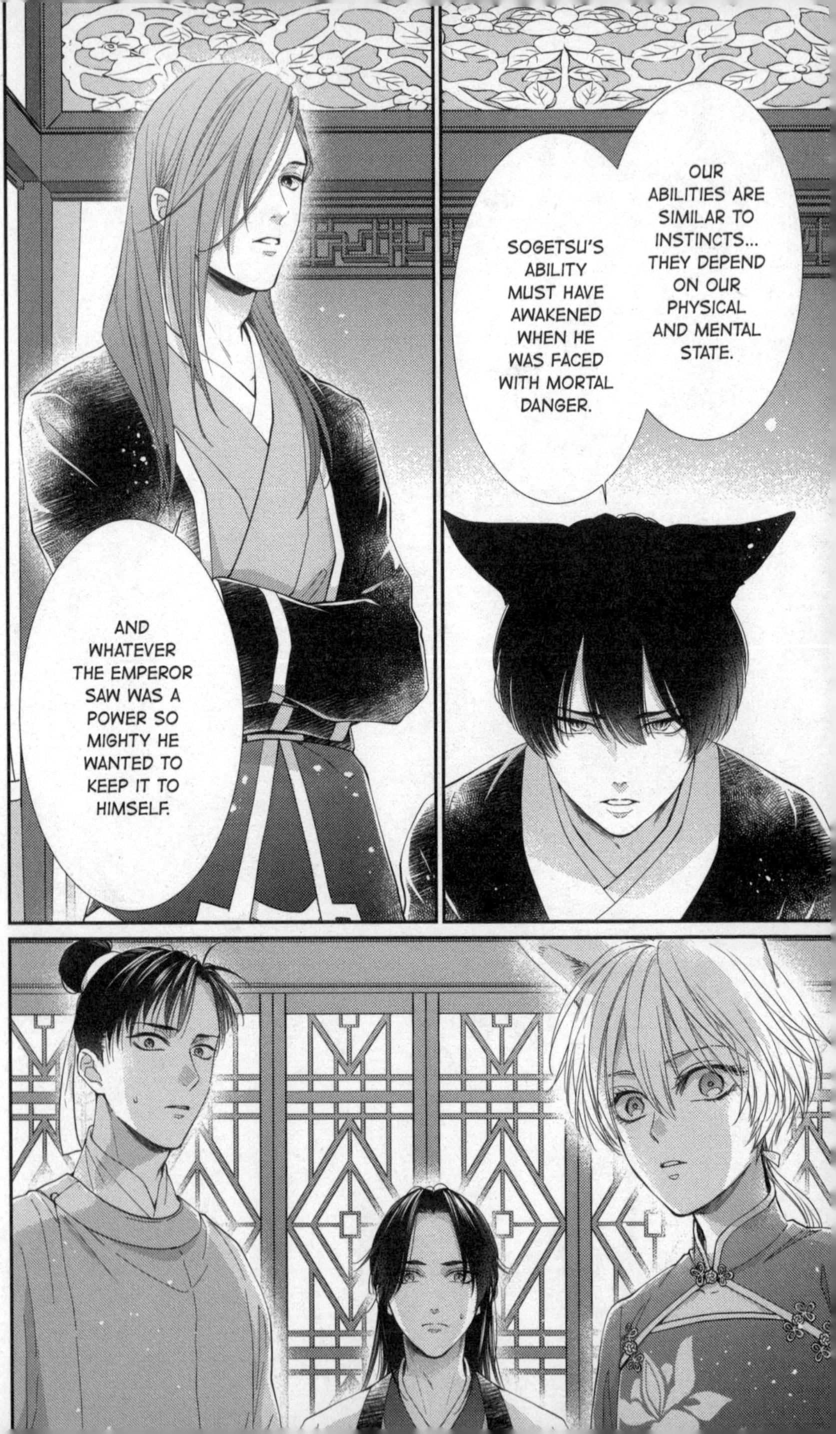
OUR ABILITIES ARE SIMILAR TO INSTINCTS... THEY DEPEND ON OUR PHYSICAL AND MENTAL STATE.
SOGETSU'S ABILITY MUST HAVE AWAKENED WHEN HE WAS FACED WITH MORTAL DANGER.
AND WHATEVER THE EMPEROR SAW WAS A POWER SO MIGHTY HE WANTED TO KEEP IT TO HIMSELF.

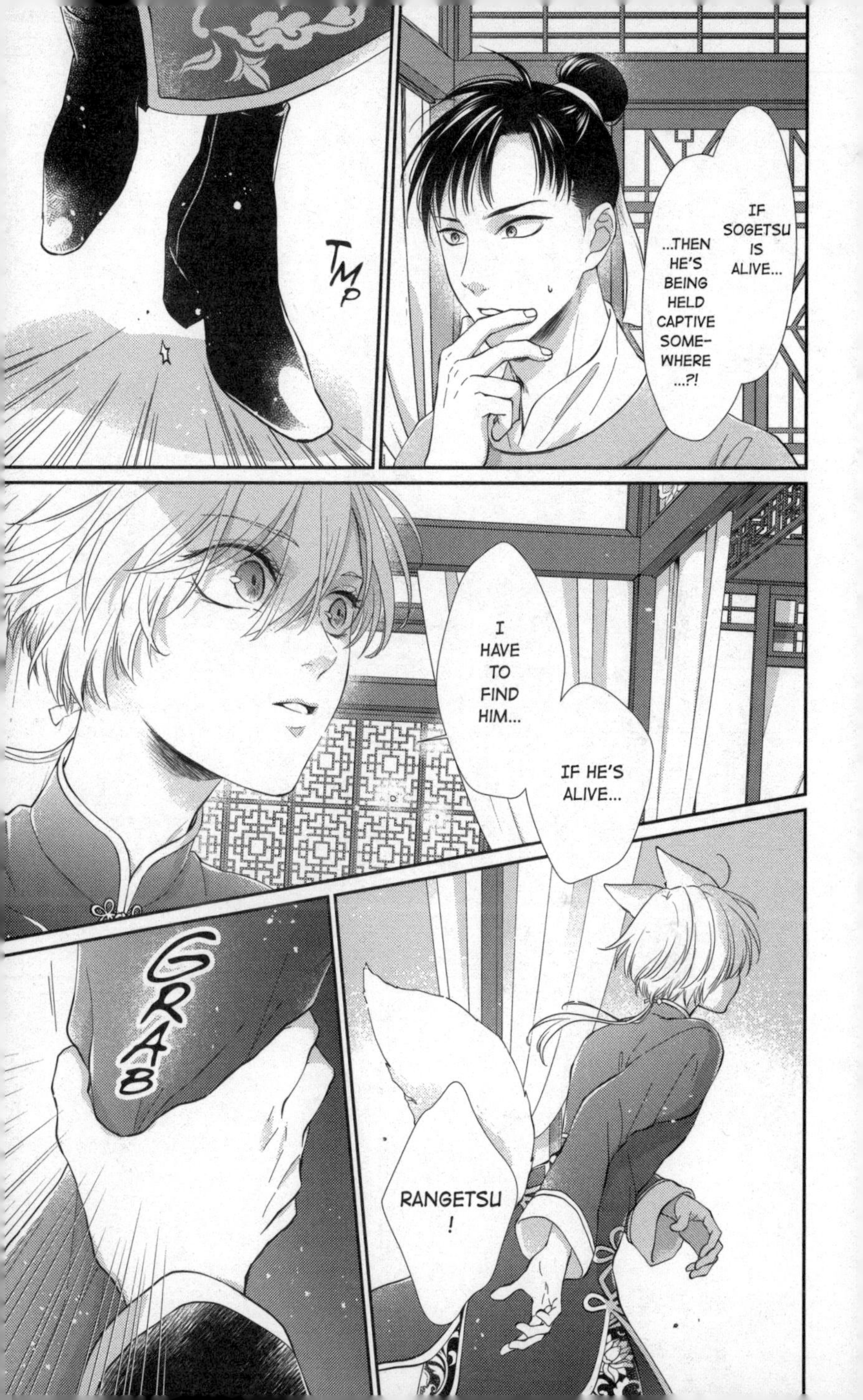
IF SOGETSU IS ALIVE...
...THEN HE'S BEING HELD CAPTIVE SOME-WHERE ...?!
TMP
I HAVE TO FIND HIM...
IF HE'S ALIVE...
RANGETSU!
GRAB

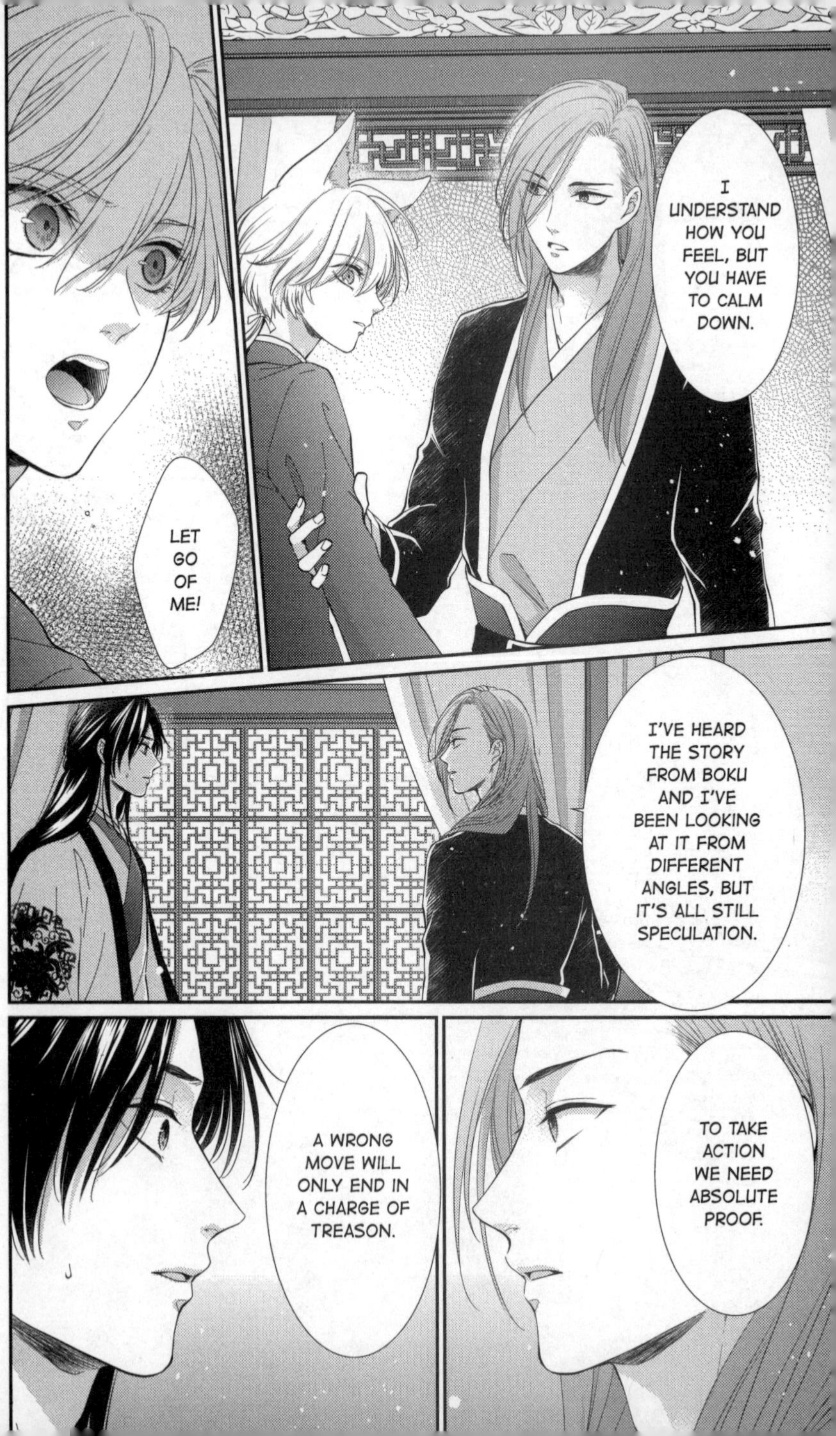
I UNDERSTAND HOW YOU FEEL, BUT YOU HAVE TO CALM DOWN.
LET GO OF ME!
I'VE HEARD THE STORY FROM BOKU AND I'VE BEEN LOOKING AT IT FROM DIFFERENT ANGLES, BUT IT'S ALL STILL SPECULATION.
TO TAKE ACTION WE NEED ABSOLUTE PROOF.
A WRONG MOVE WILL ONLY END IN A CHARGE OF TREASON.

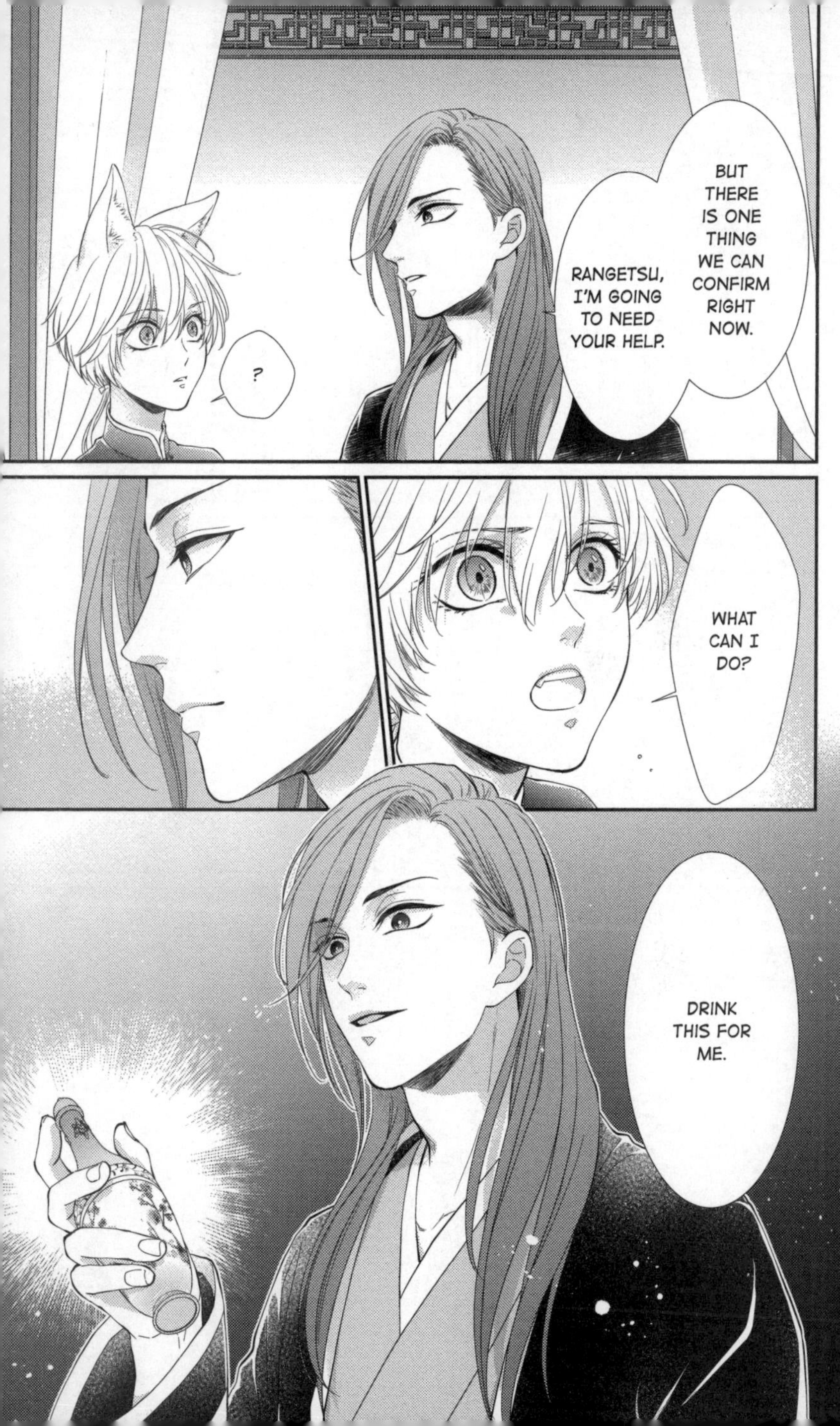
BUT THERE IS ONE THING WE CAN CONFIRM RIGHT NOW.
RANGETSU, I'M GOING TO NEED YOUR HELP.
?
WHAT CAN I DO?
DRINK THIS FOR ME.

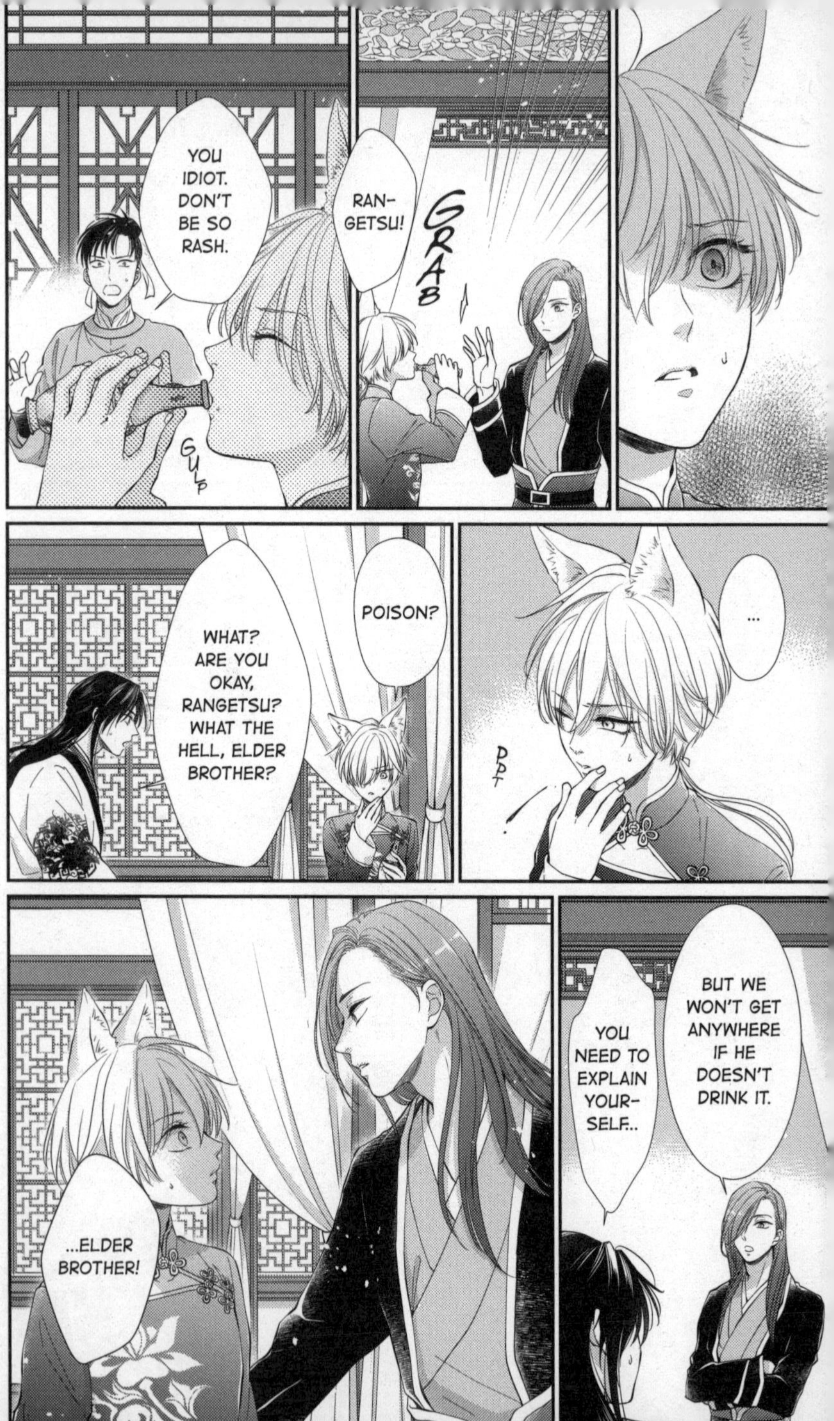
RAN-GETSU!
GRAB
YOU IDIOT. DON'T BE SO RASH.
GULP
...
PPT
POISON?
WHAT? ARE YOU OKAY, RANGETSU? WHAT THE HELL, ELDER BROTHER?
BUT WE WON'T GET ANYWHERE IF HE DOESN'T DRINK IT.
YOU NEED TO EXPLAIN YOUR-SELF...
...ELDER BROTHER!

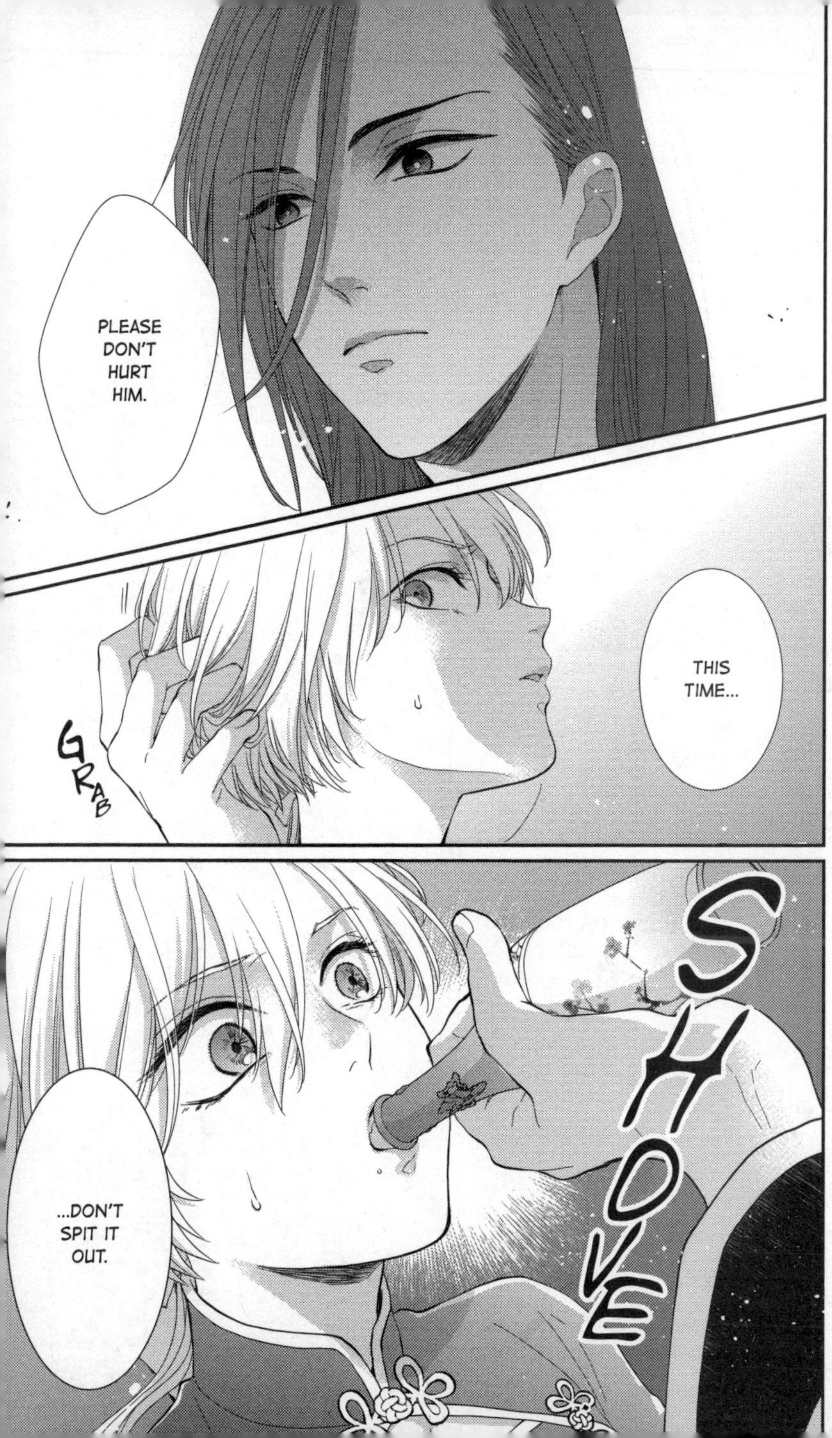
PLEASE DON'T HURT HIM.
THIS TIME...
GRAB
SHOVE
...DON'T SPIT IT OUT.

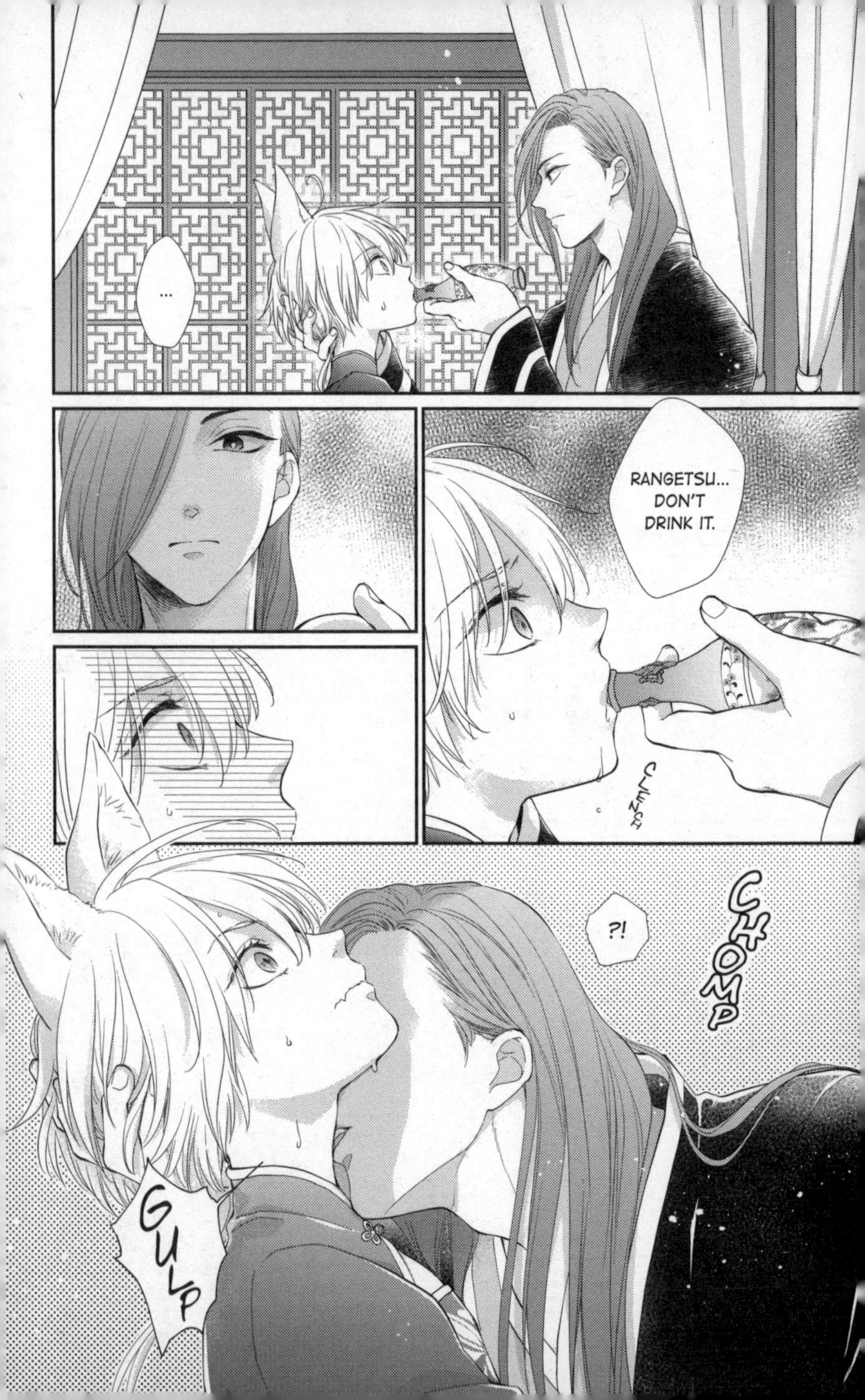
...
RANGETSU... DON'T DRINK IT.
CLENCH
CHOMP
?!
GULP

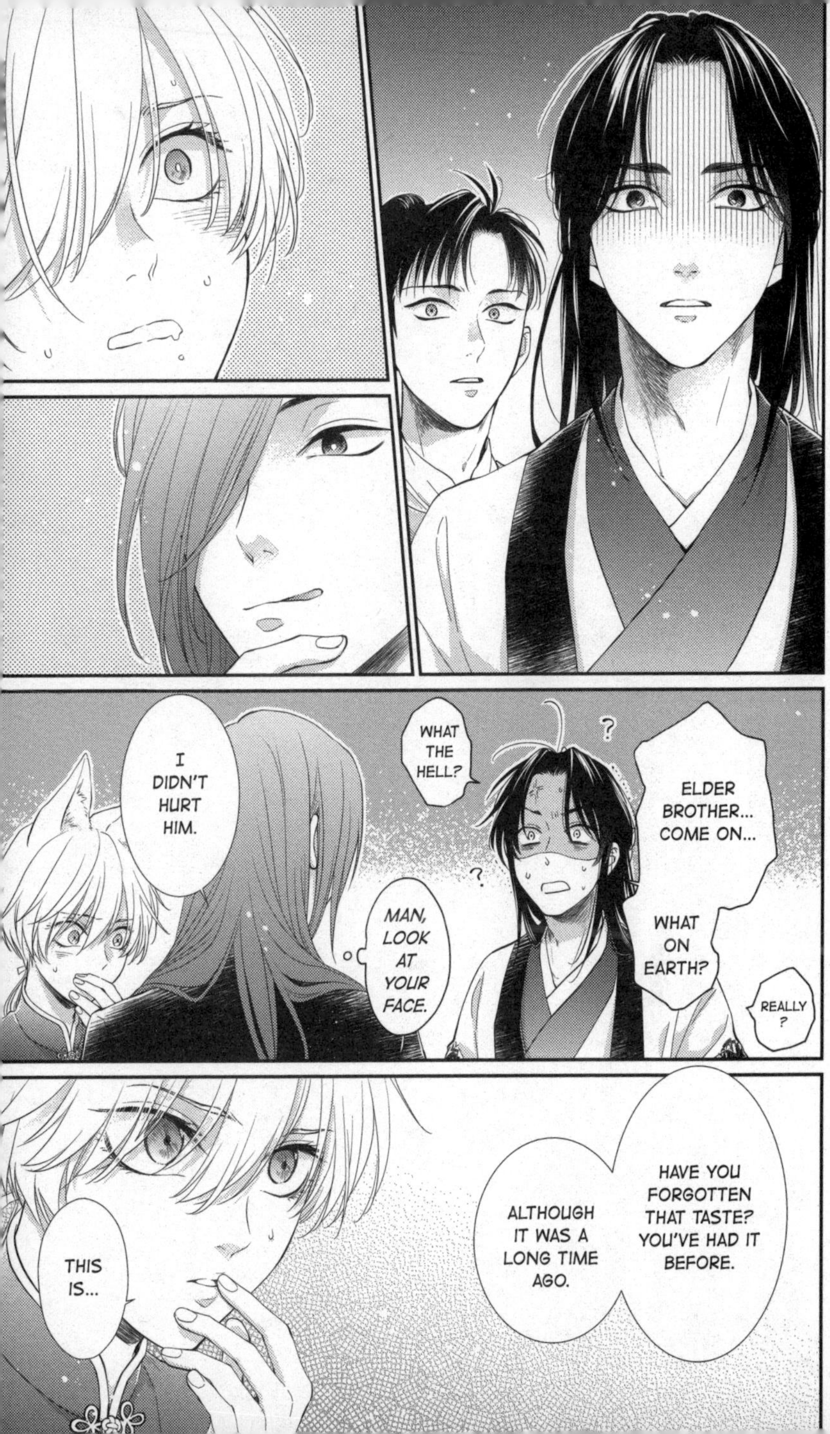
ELDER BROTHER... COME ON...
WHAT ON EARTH?
REALLY?
WHAT THE HELL?
MAN, LOOK AT YOUR FACE.
I DIDN'T HURT HIM.
HAVE YOU FORGOTTEN THAT TASTE? YOU'VE HAD IT BEFORE.
ALTHOUGH IT WAS A LONG TIME AGO.
THIS IS...

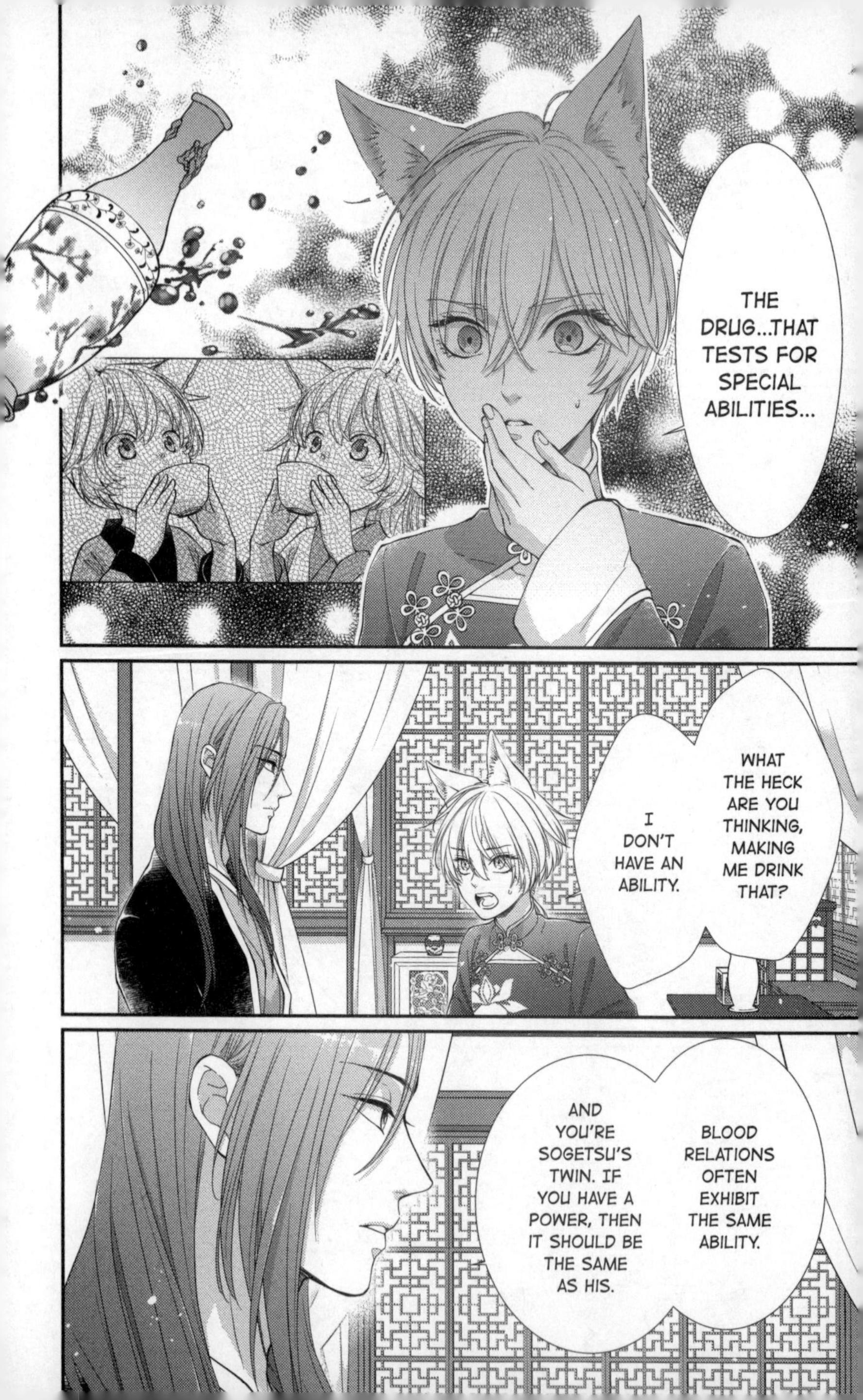
THE DRUG...THAT TESTS FOR SPECIAL ABILITIES...
WHAT THE HECK ARE YOU THINKING, MAKING ME DRINK THAT?
I DON'T HAVE AN ABILITY.
BLOOD RELATIONS OFTEN EXHIBIT THE SAME ABILITY.
AND YOU'RE SOGETSU'S TWIN. IF YOU HAVE A POWER, THEN IT SHOULD BE THE SAME AS HIS.

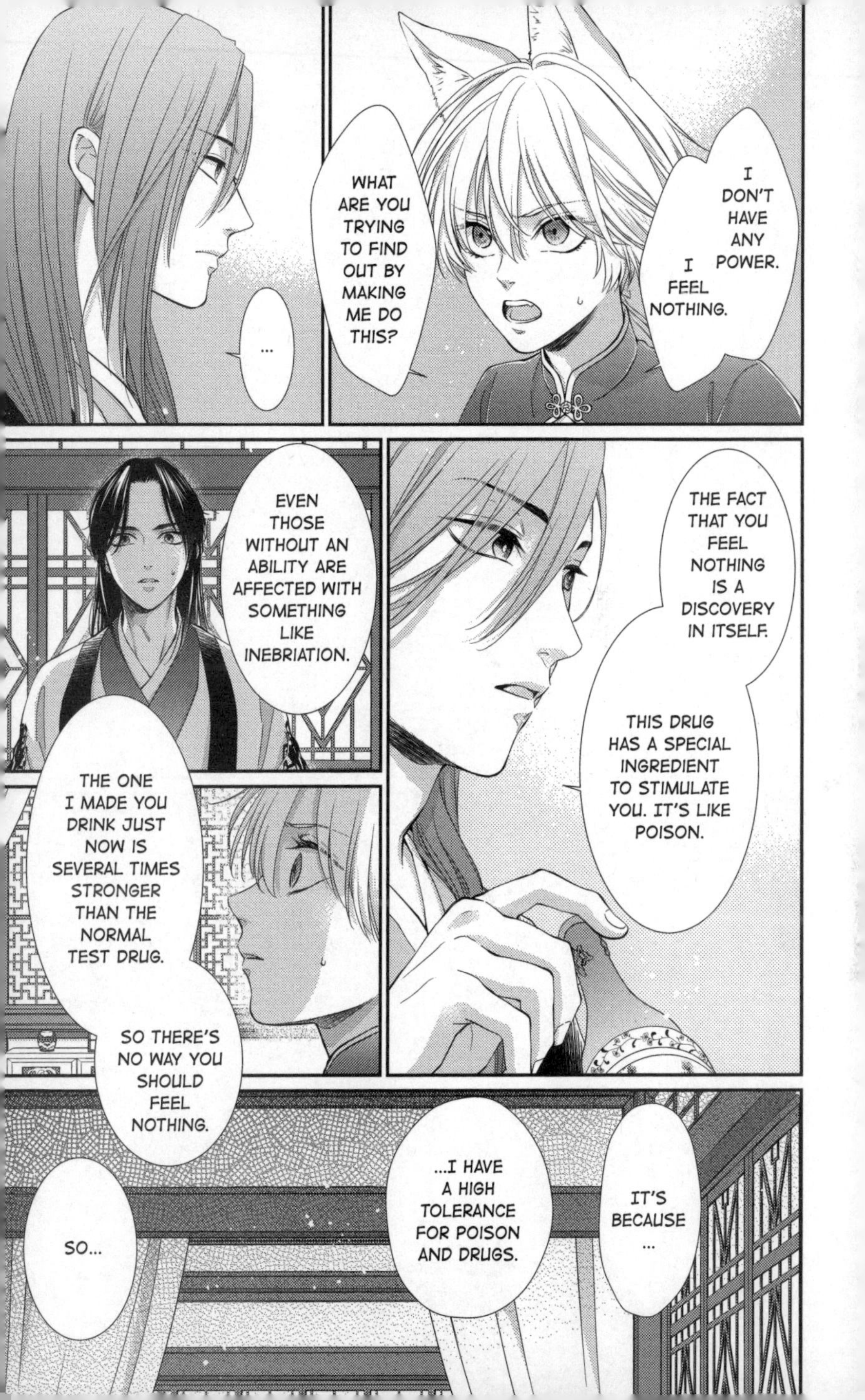
I DON'T HAVE ANY POWER.
I FEEL NOTHING.
WHAT ARE YOU TRYING TO FIND OUT BY MAKING ME DO THIS?
...
THE FACT THAT YOU FEEL NOTHING IS A DISCOVERY IN ITSELF.
THIS DRUG HAS A SPECIAL INGREDIENT TO STIMULATE YOU. IT'S LIKE POISON.
EVEN THOSE WITHOUT AN ABILITY ARE AFFECTED WITH SOMETHING LIKE INEBRIATION.
THE ONE I MADE YOU DRINK JUST NOW IS SEVERAL TIMES STRONGER THAN THE NORMAL TEST DRUG.
SO THERE'S NO WAY YOU SHOULD FEEL NOTHING.
IT'S BECAUSE ...
...I HAVE A HIGH TOLERANCE FOR POISON AND DRUGS.
SO...

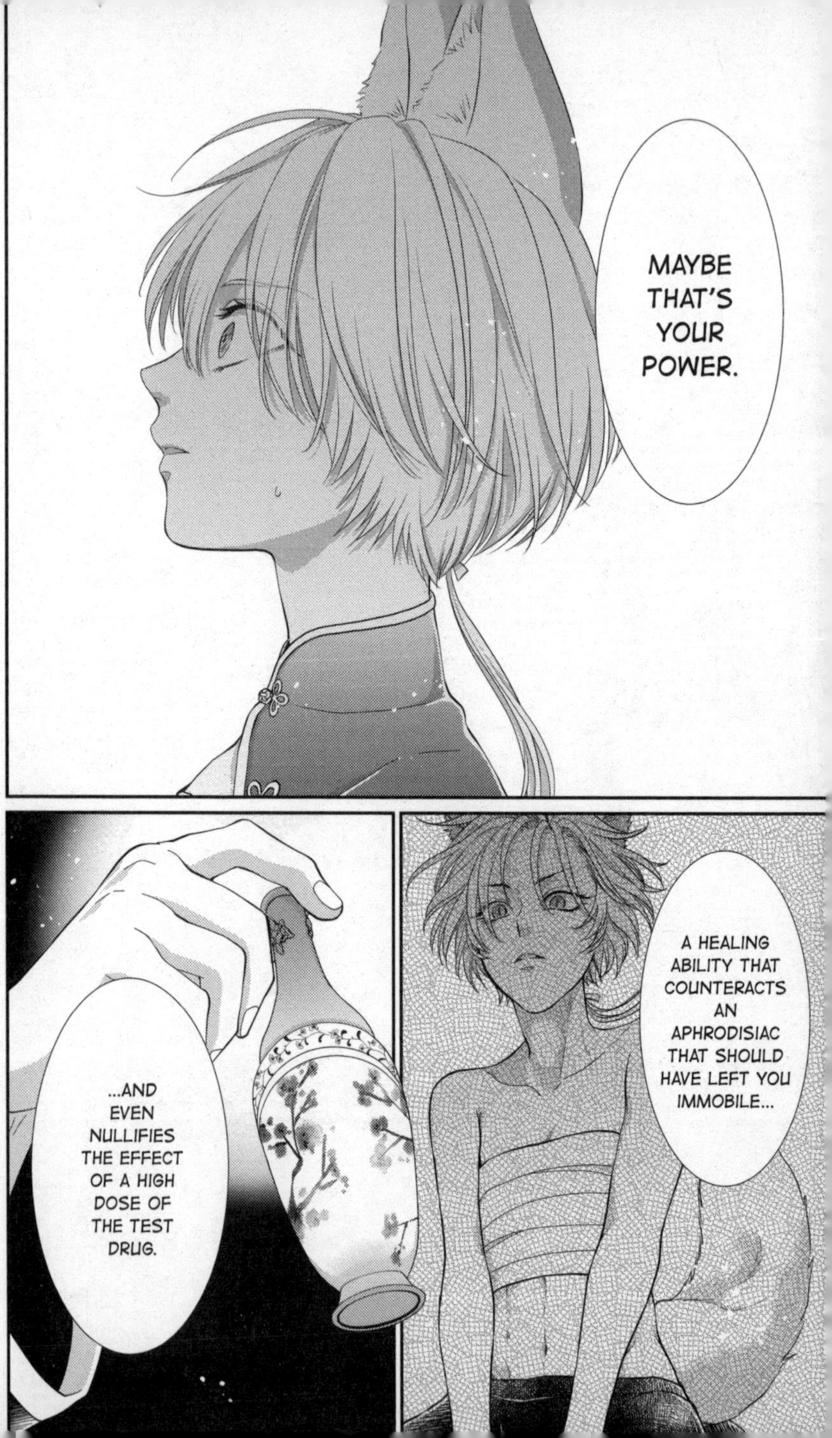
MAYBE THAT'S YOUR POWER.
A HEALING ABILITY THAT COUNTERACTS AN APHRODISIAC THAT SHOULD HAVE LEFT YOU IMMOBILE...
...AND EVEN NULLIFIES THE EFFECT OF A HIGH DOSE OF THE TEST DRUG.

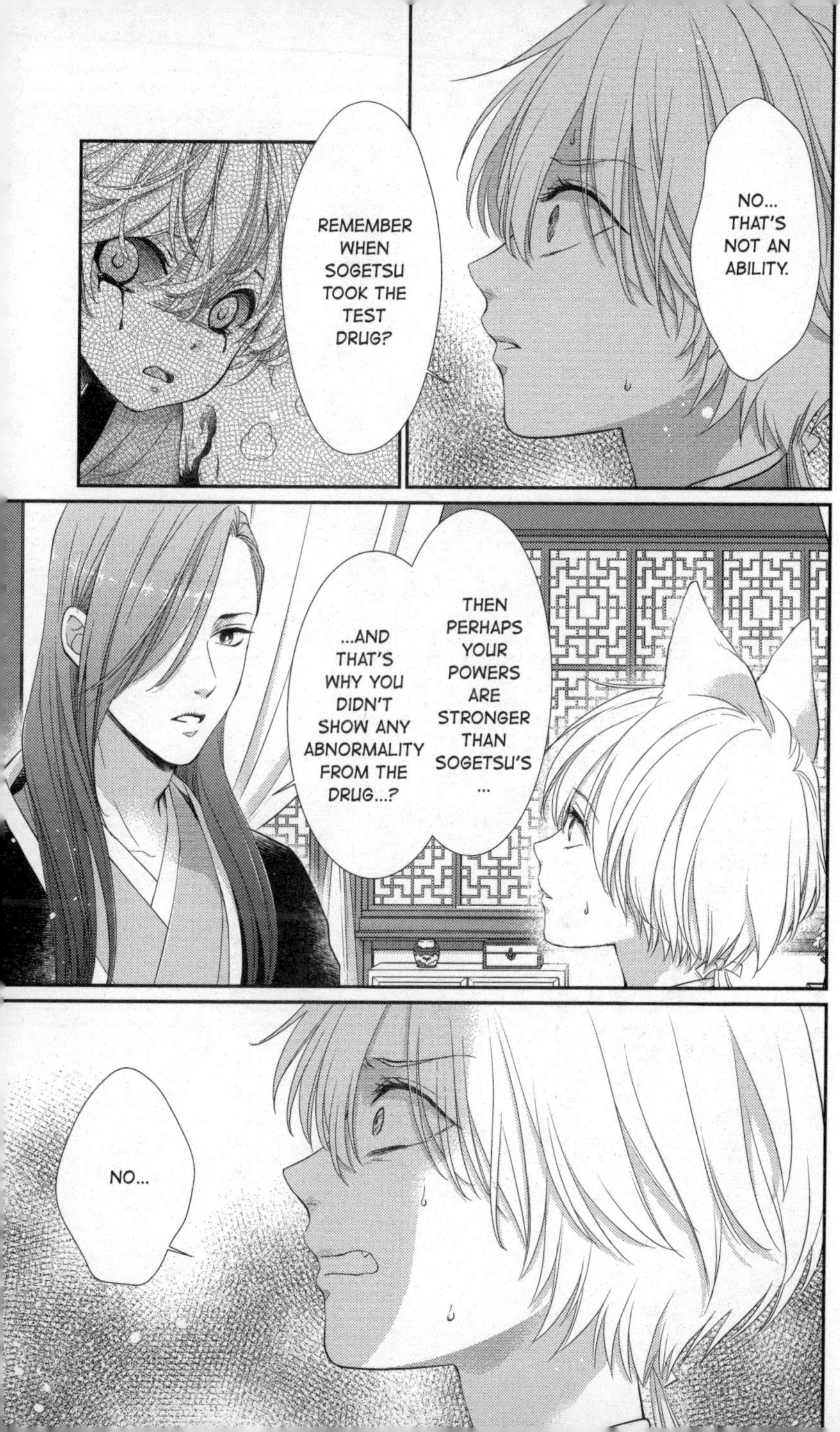
NO... THAT'S NOT AN ABILITY.
REMEMBER WHEN SOGETSU TOOK THE TEST DRUG?
THEN PERHAPS YOUR POWERS ARE STRONGER THAN SOGETSU'S ...
...AND THAT'S WHY YOU DIDN'T SHOW ANY ABNORMALITY FROM THE DRUG...?
NO...

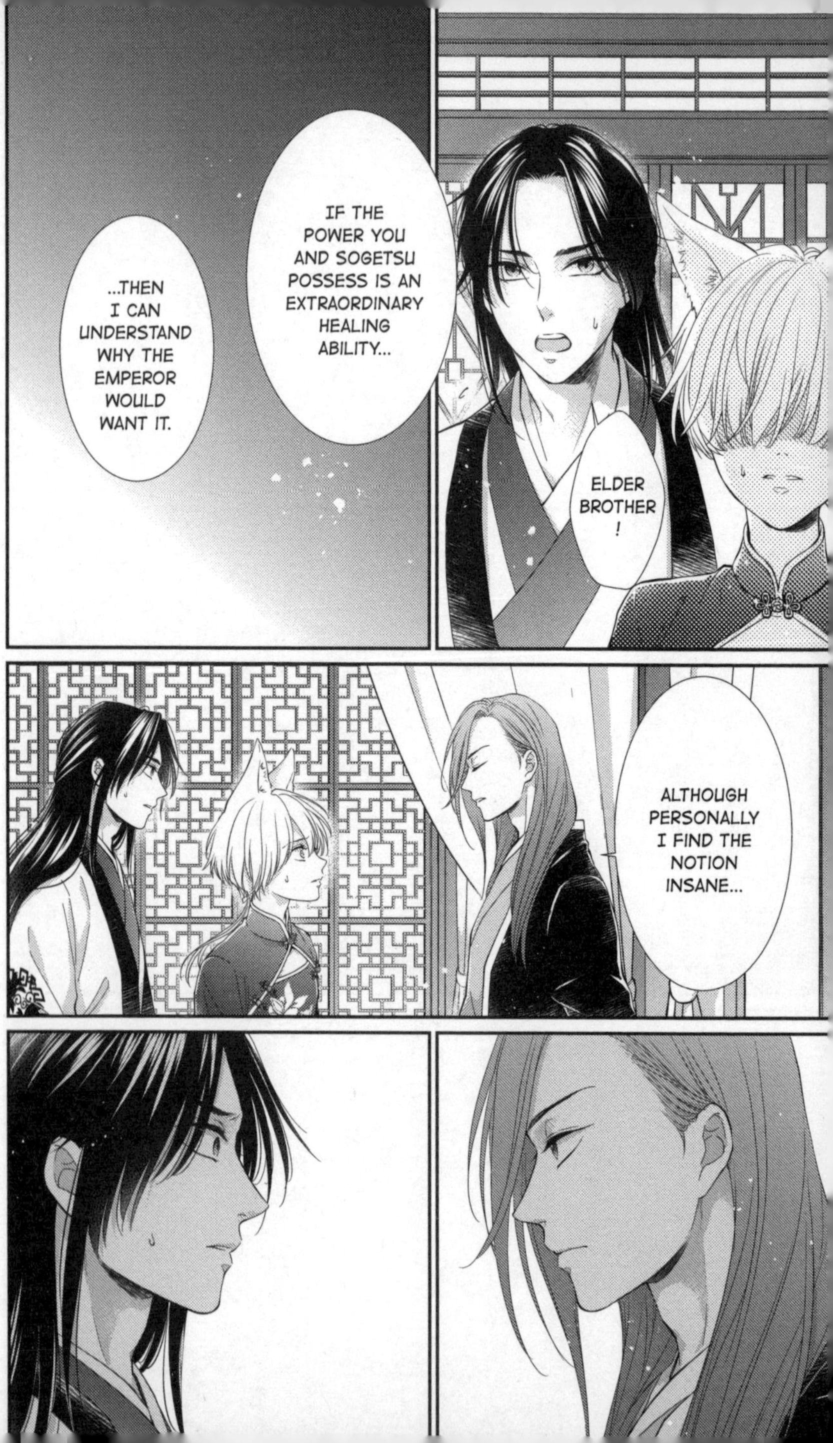
ELDER BROTHER!
IF THE POWER YOU AND SOGETSU POSSESS IS AN EXTRAORDINARY HEALING ABILITY...
...THEN I CAN UNDERSTAND WHY THE EMPEROR WOULD WANT IT.
ALTHOUGH PERSONALLY I FIND THE NOTION INSANE...

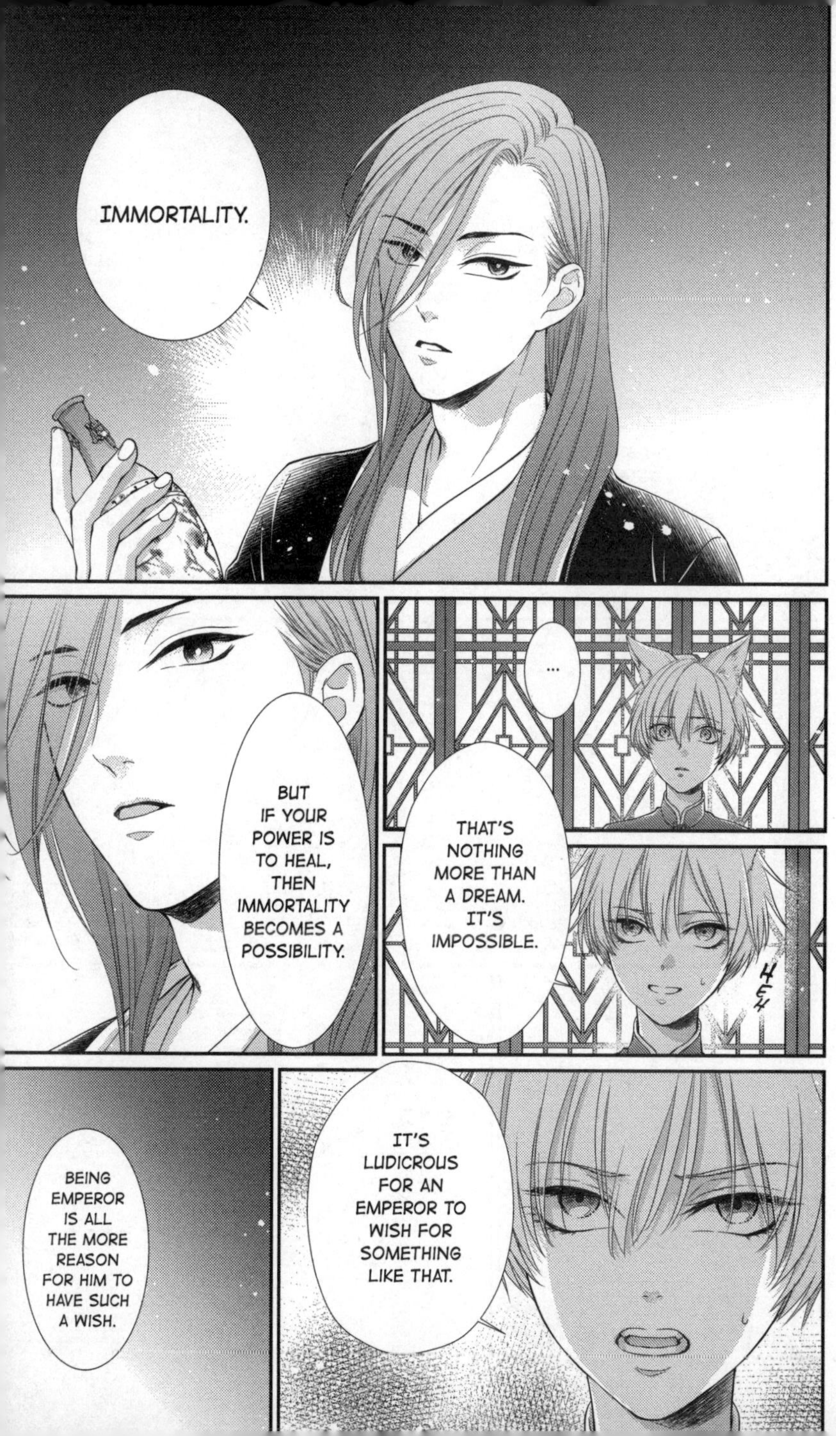
IMMORTALITY.
...
THAT'S NOTHING MORE THAN A DREAM. IT'S IMPOSSIBLE.
HEH
BUT IF YOUR POWER IS TO HEAL, THEN IMMORTALITY BECOMES A POSSIBILITY.
IT'S LUDICROUS FOR AN EMPEROR TO WISH FOR SOMETHING LIKE THAT.
BEING EMPEROR IS ALL THE MORE REASON FOR HIM TO HAVE SUCH A WISH.

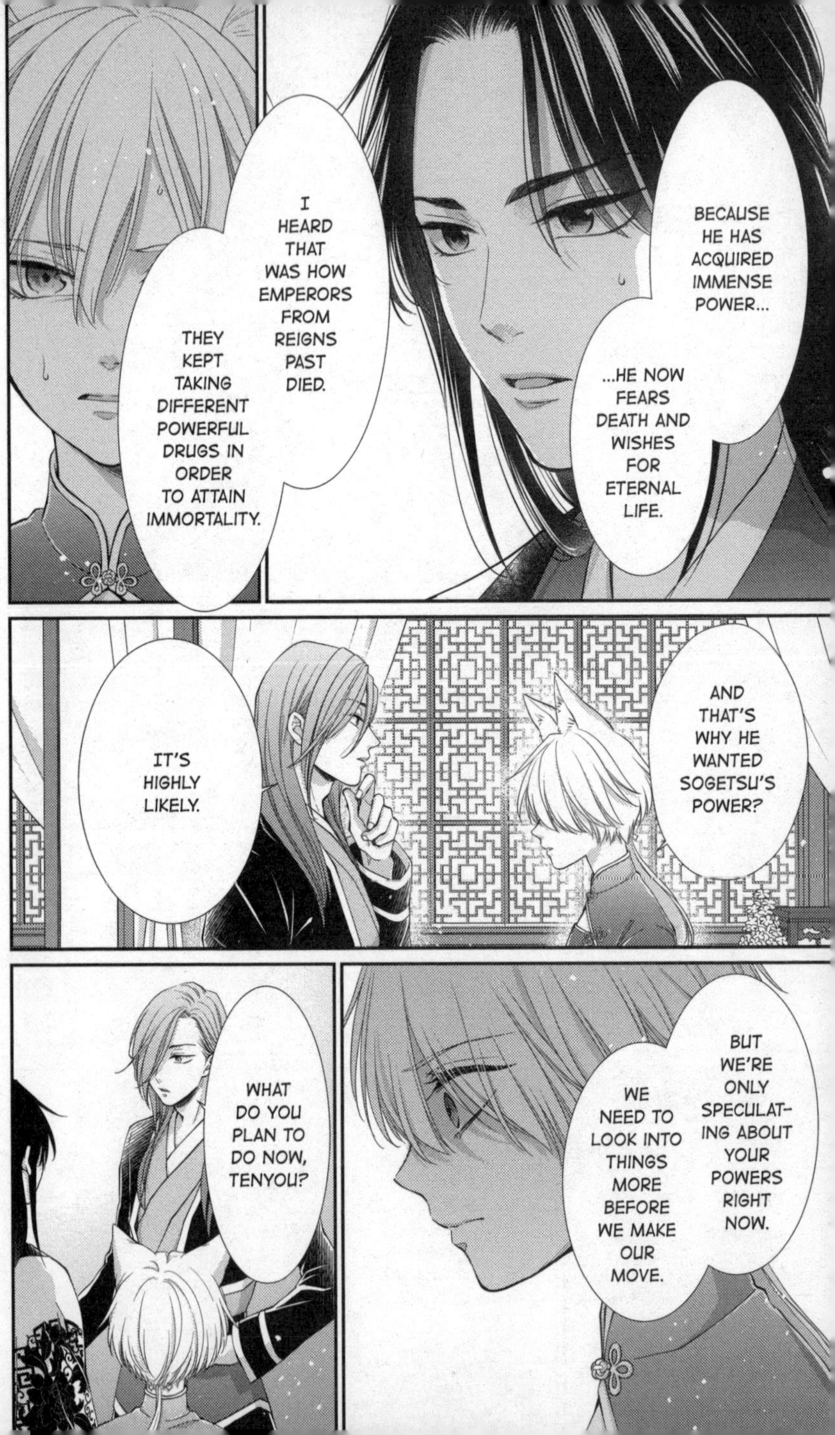
BECAUSE HE HAS ACQUIRED IMMENSE POWER...
...HE NOW FEARS DEATH AND WISHES FOR ETERNAL LIFE.
I HEARD THAT WAS HOW EMPERORS FROM REIGNS PAST DIED.
THEY KEPT TAKING DIFFERENT POWERFUL DRUGS IN ORDER TO ATTAIN IMMORTALITY.
AND THAT'S WHY HE WANTED SOGETSU'S POWER?
IT'S HIGHLY LIKELY.
BUT WE'RE ONLY SPECULAT-ING ABOUT YOUR POWERS RIGHT NOW.
WE NEED TO LOOK INTO THINGS MORE BEFORE WE MAKE OUR MOVE.
WHAT DO YOU PLAN TO DO NOW, TENYOU?

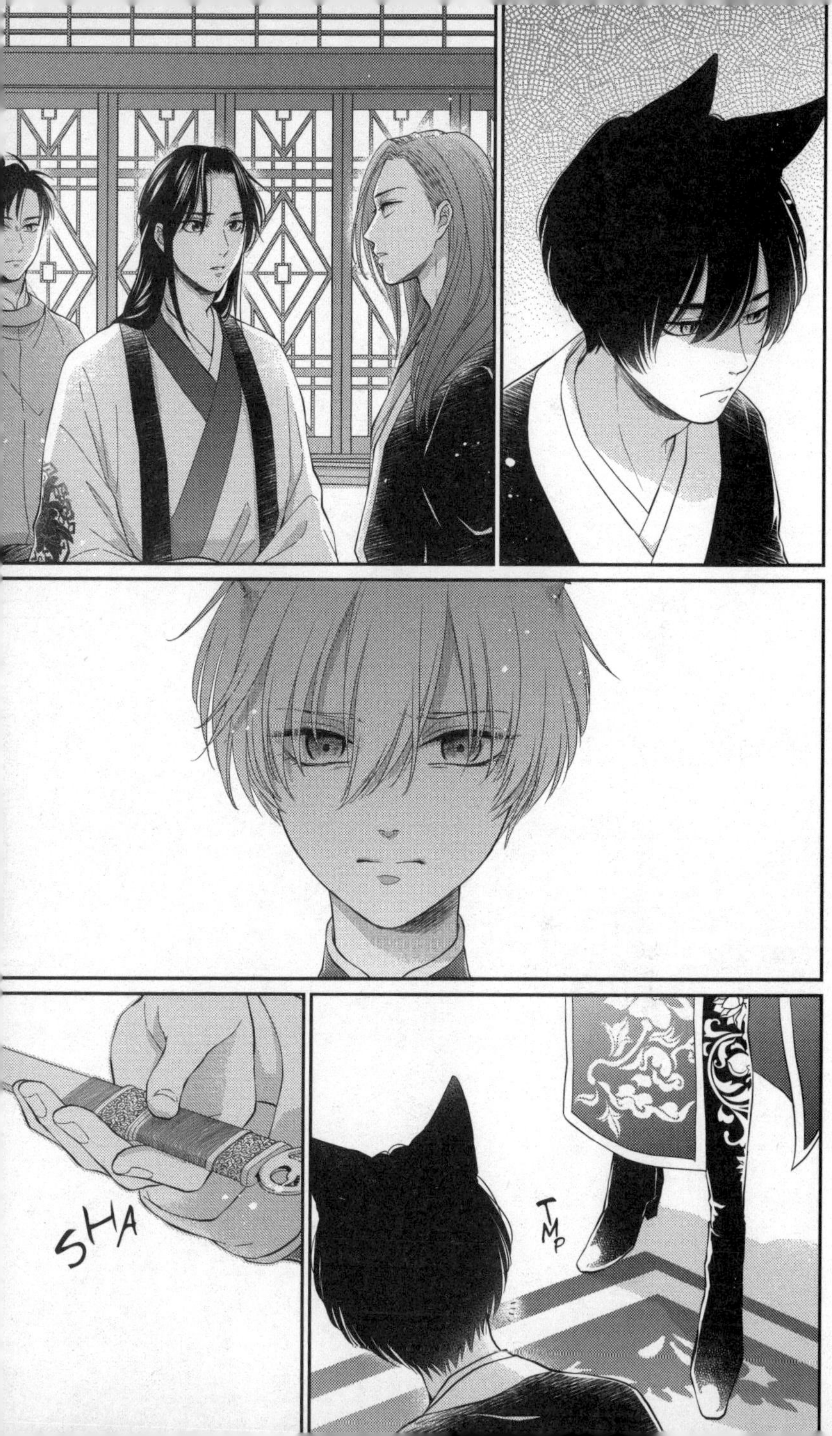
TMP
SHA

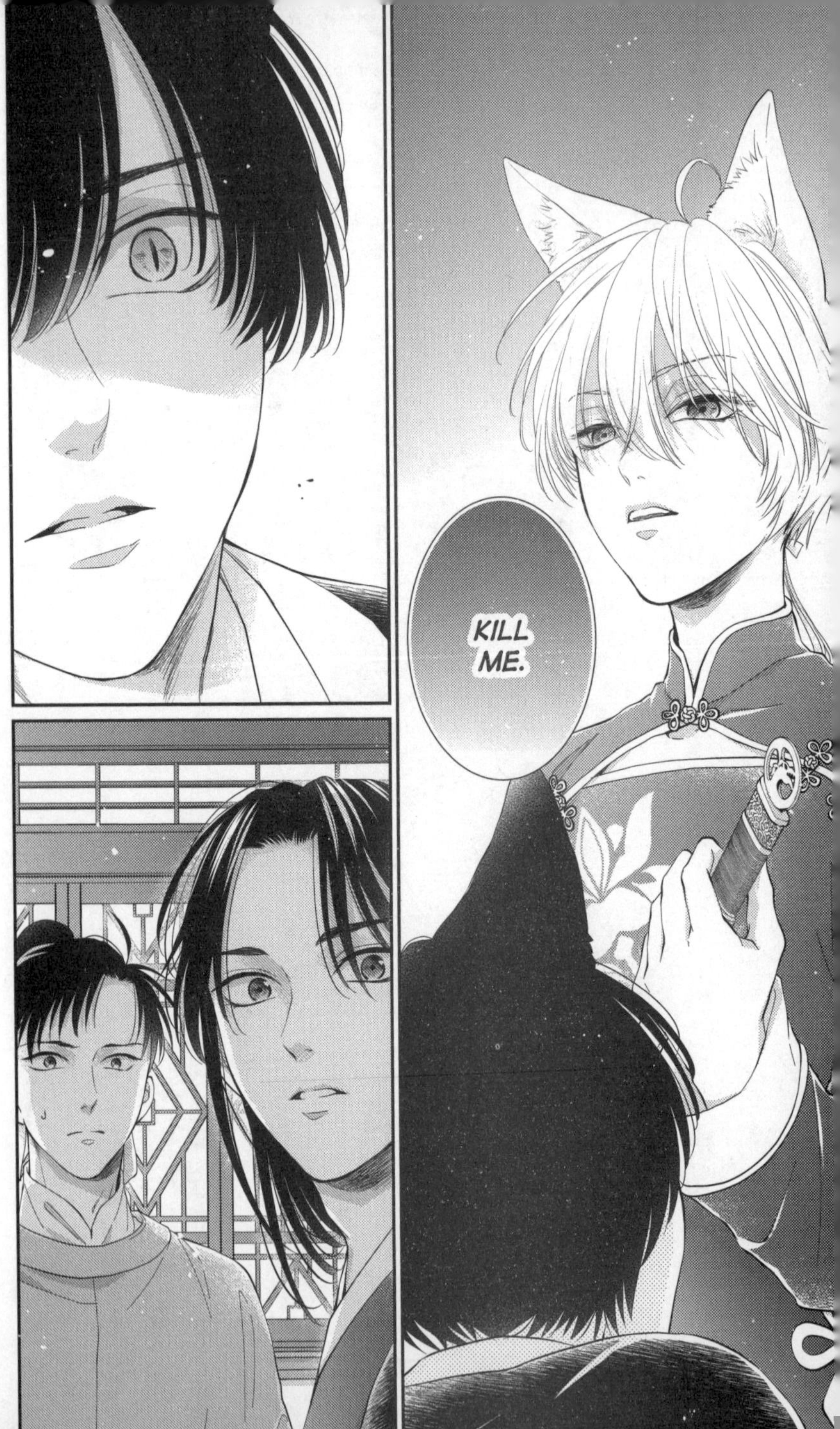
KILL ME.

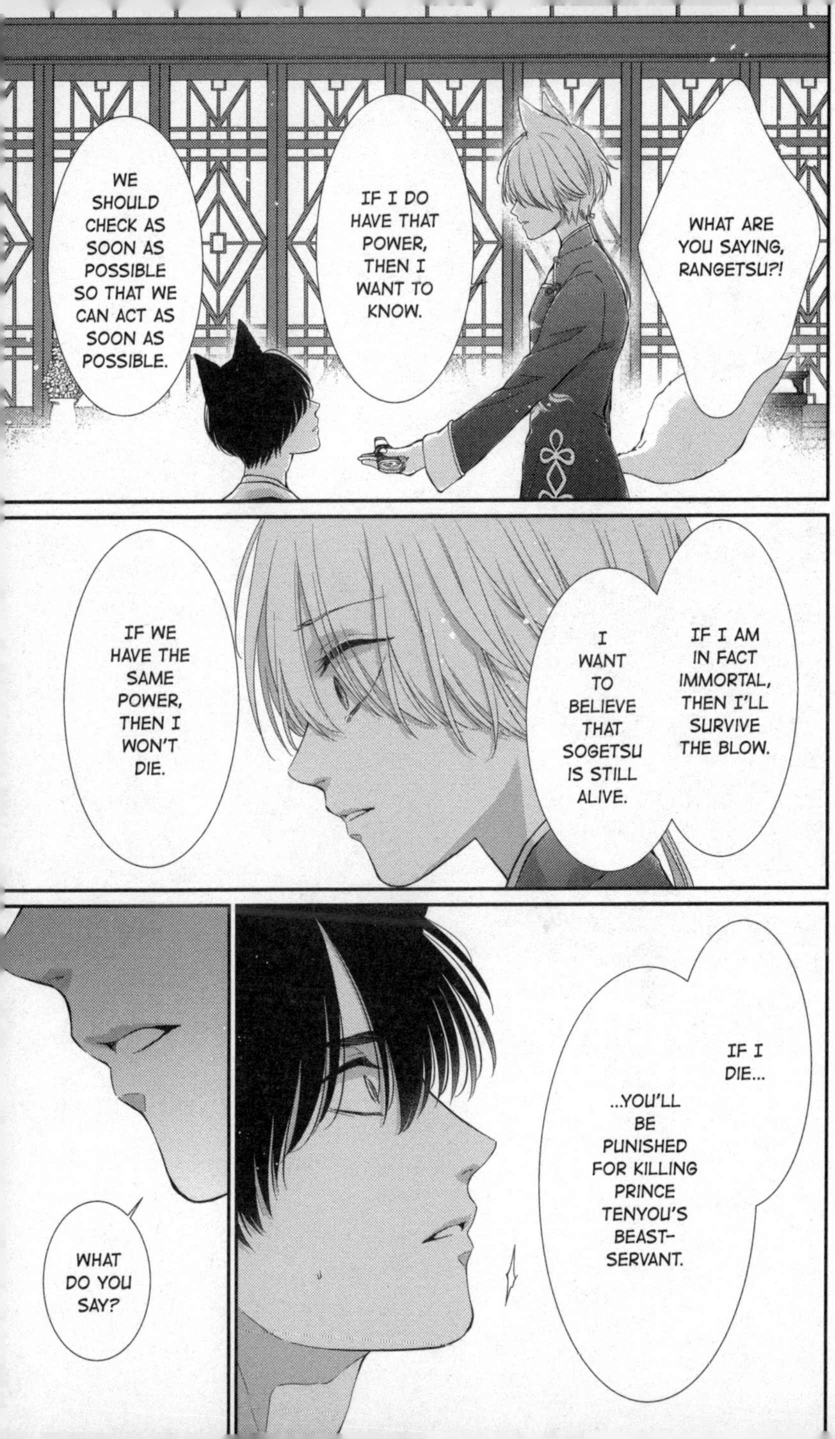
WHAT ARE YOU SAYING, RANGETSU?!
IF I DO HAVE THAT POWER, THEN I WANT TO KNOW.
WE SHOULD CHECK AS SOON AS POSSIBLE SO THAT WE CAN ACT AS SOON AS POSSIBLE.
IF I AM IN FACT IMMORTAL, THEN I'LL SURVIVE THE BLOW.
I WANT TO BELIEVE THAT SOGETSU IS STILL ALIVE.
IF WE HAVE THE SAME POWER, THEN I WON'T DIE.
IF I DIE...
...YOU'LL BE PUNISHED FOR KILLING PRINCE TENYOU'S BEAST-SERVANT.
WHAT DO YOU SAY?

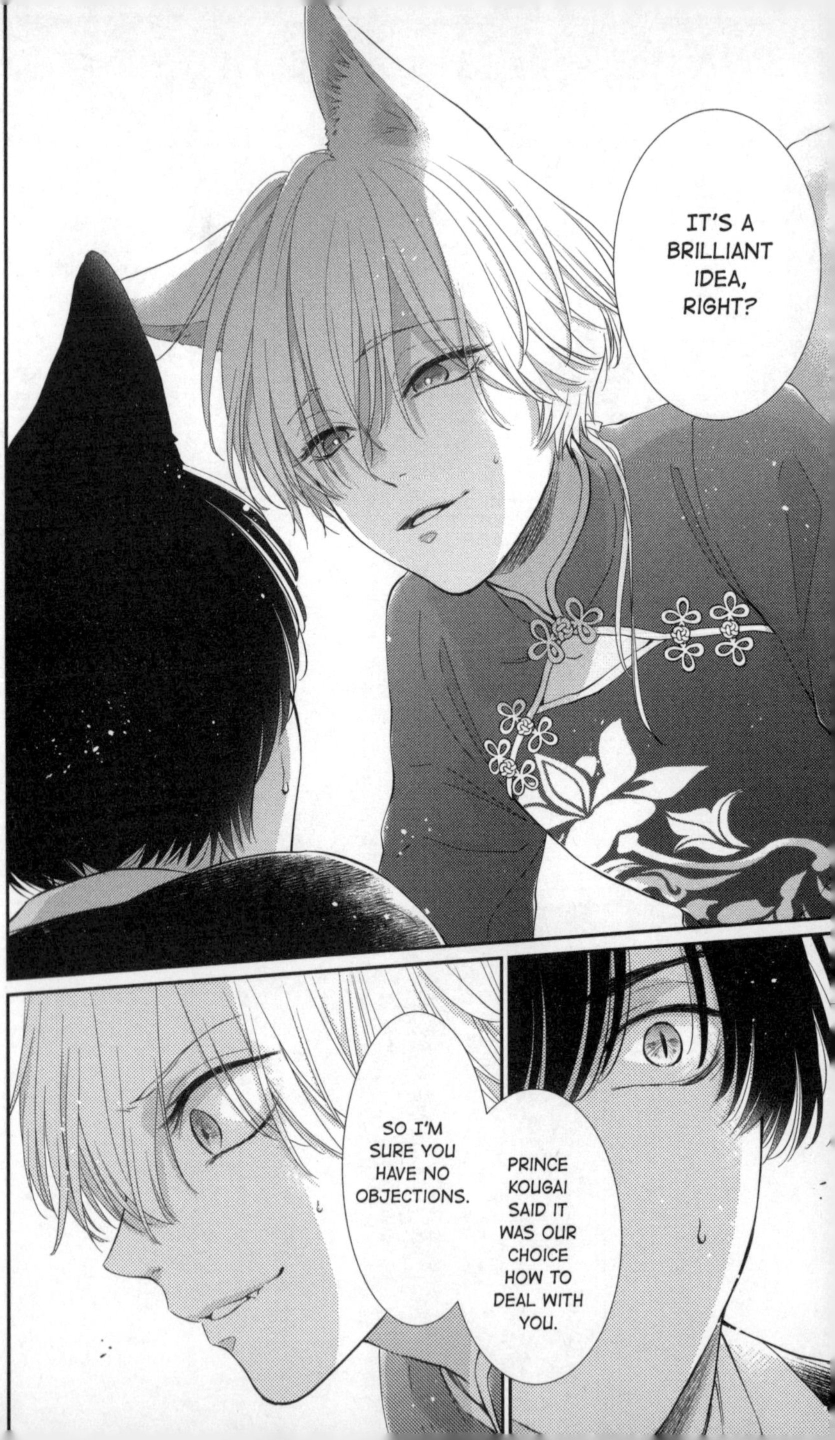
IT'S A BRILLIANT IDEA, RIGHT?
PRINCE KOUGAI SAID IT WAS OUR CHOICE HOW TO DEAL WITH YOU.
SO I'M SURE YOU HAVE NO OBJECTIONS.

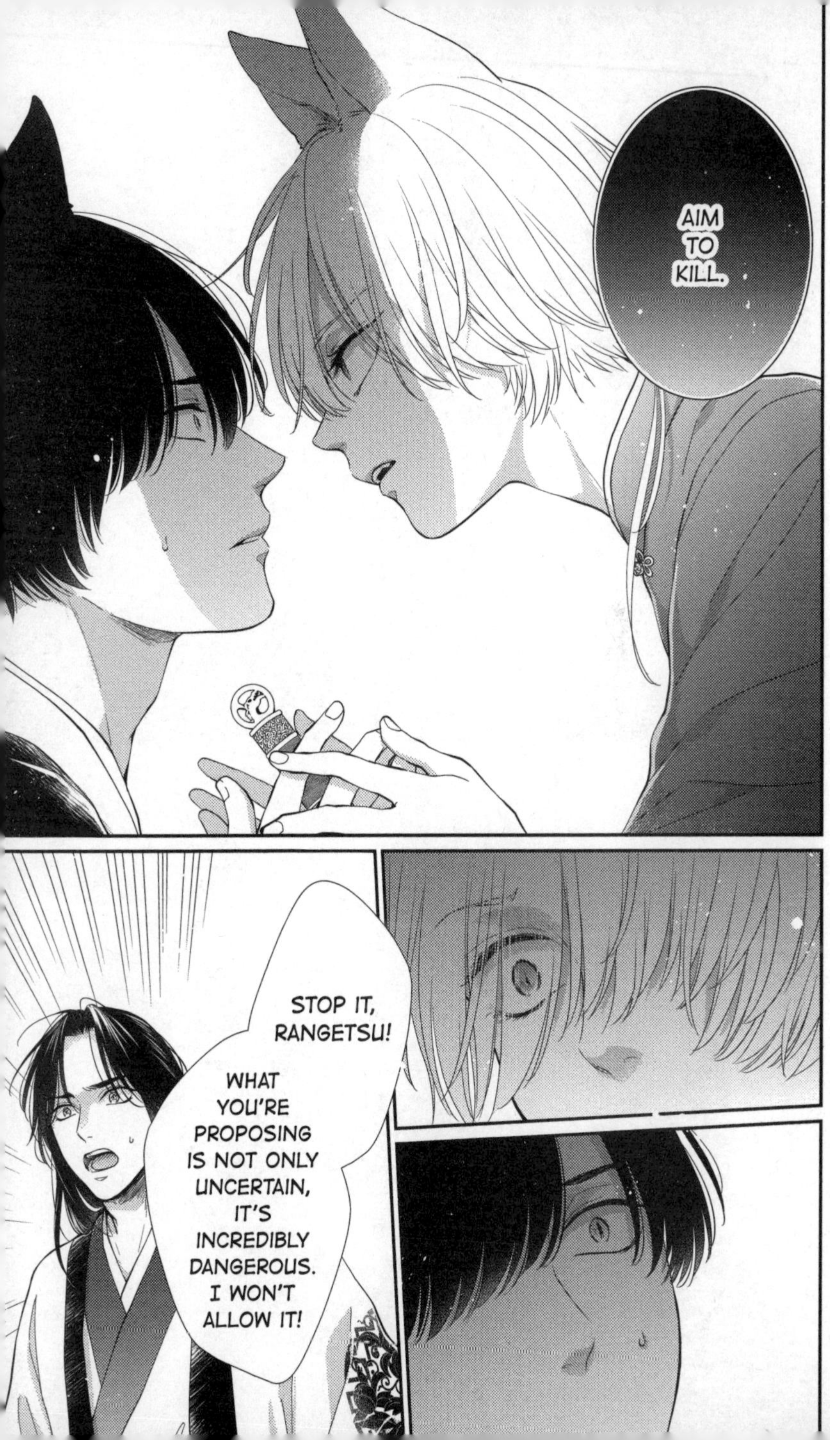
AIM TO KILL.
STOP IT, RANGETSU!
WHAT YOU'RE PROPOSING IS NOT ONLY UNCERTAIN, IT'S INCREDIBLY DANGEROUS. I WON'T ALLOW IT!

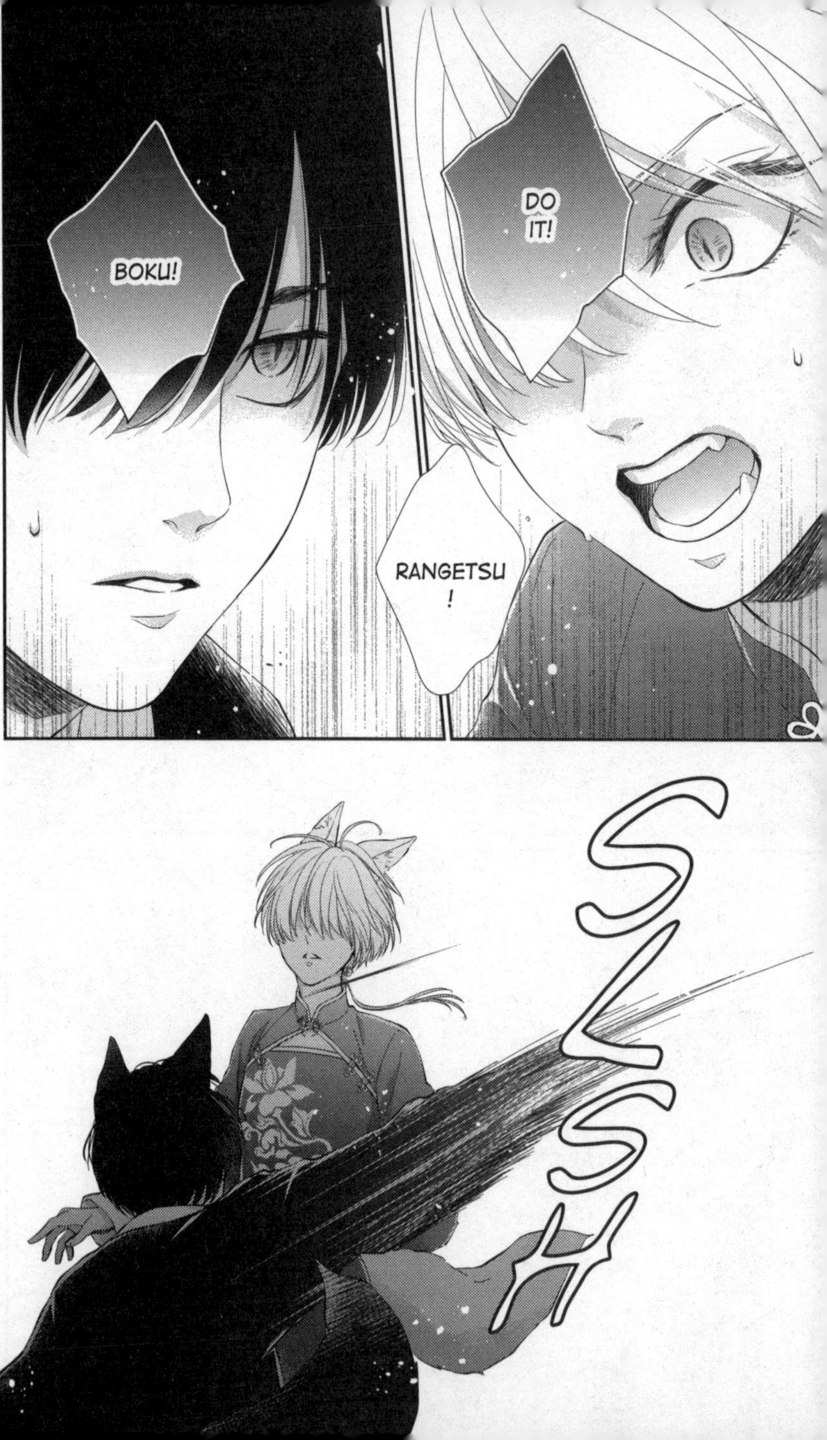
DO IT!
RANGETSU!
BOKU!
SLSH

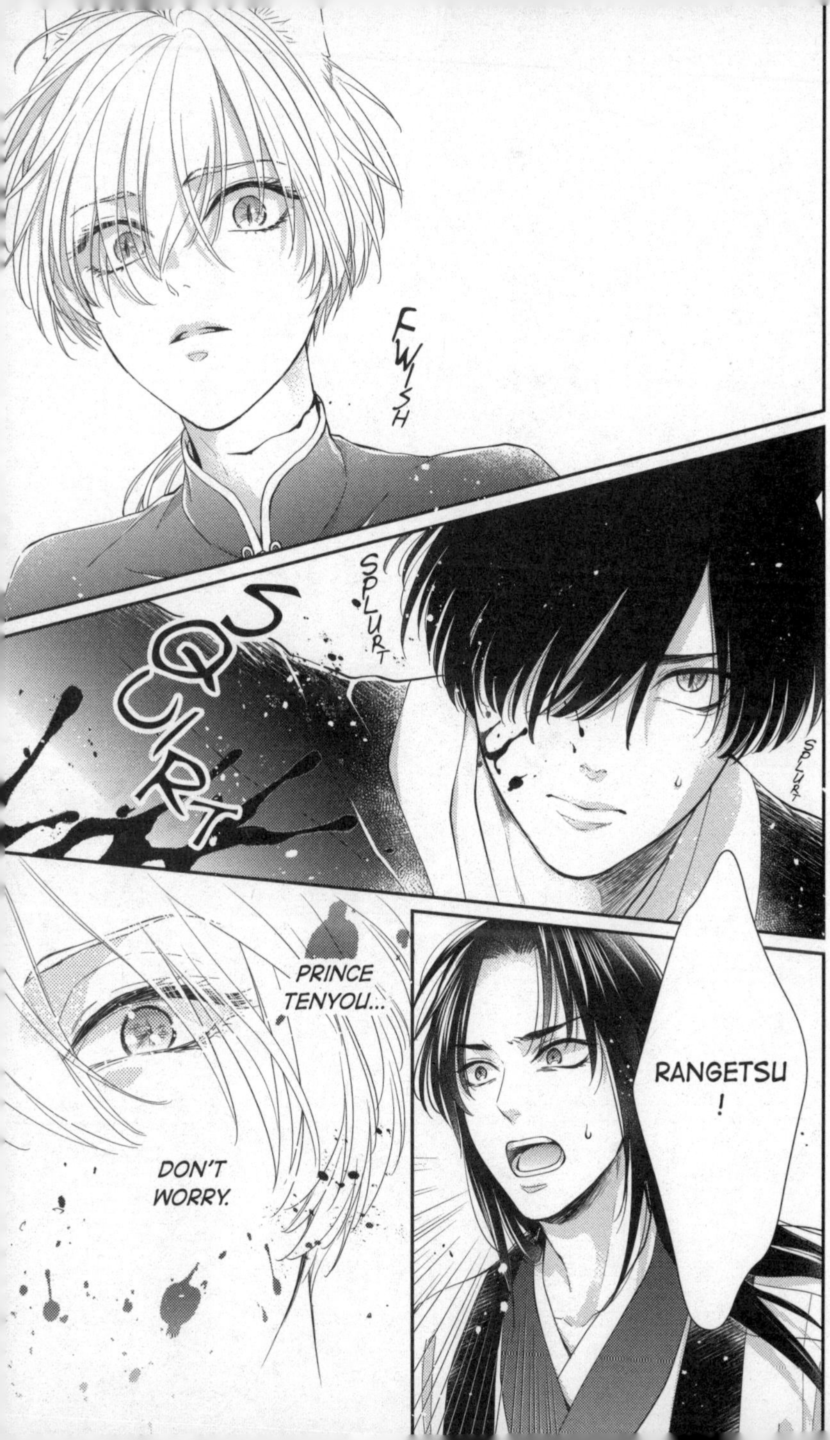
FWISH
SPLURT
SPLURT
SQUIRT
RANGETSU!
PRINCE TENYOU...
DON'T WORRY.

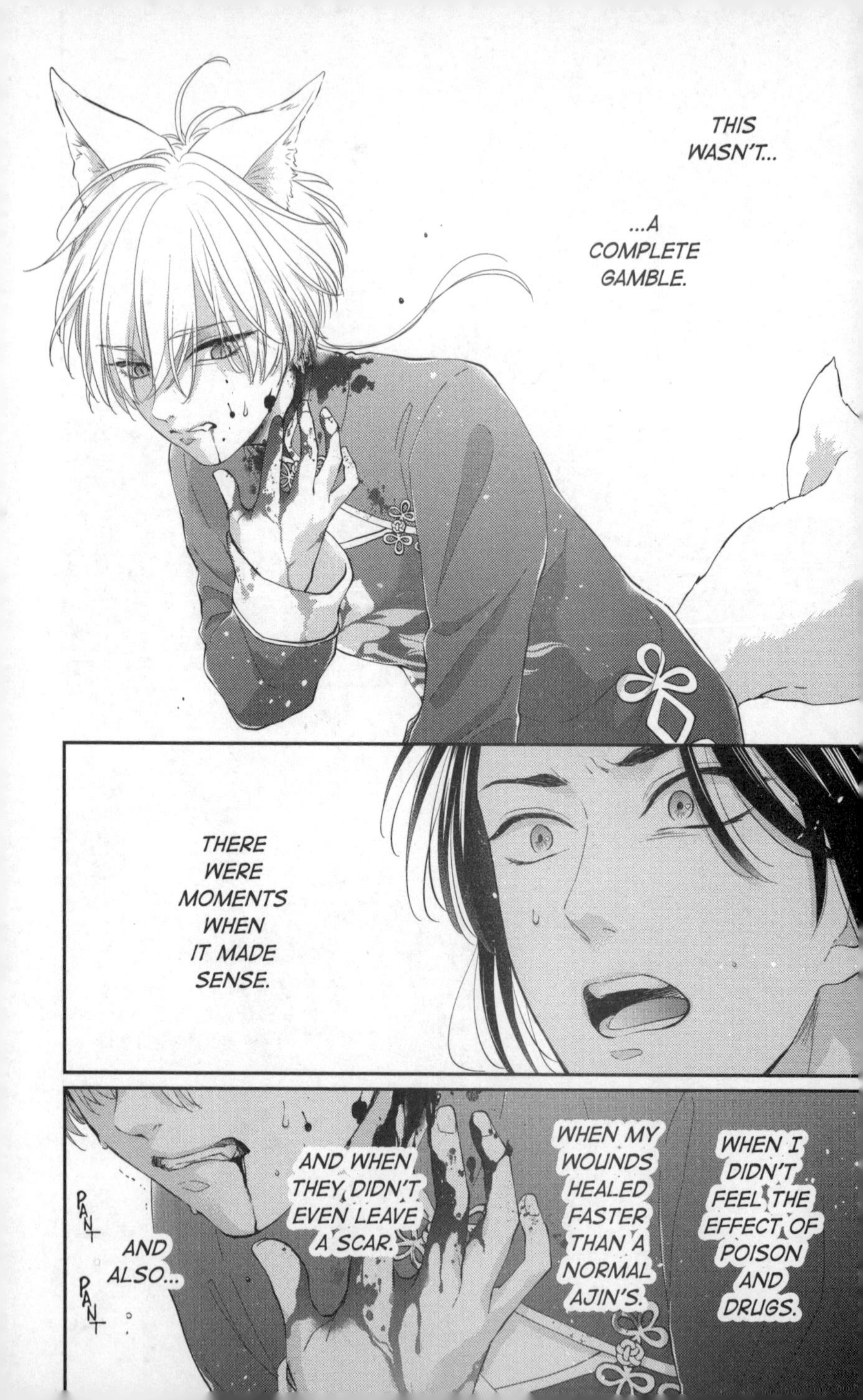
THIS WASN'T...
...A COMPLETE GAMBLE.
THERE WERE MOMENTS WHEN IT MADE SENSE.
WHEN I DIDN'T FEEL THE EFFECT OF POISON AND DRUGS.
WHEN MY WOUNDS HEALED FASTER THAN A NORMAL AJIN'S.
AND WHEN THEY DIDN'T EVEN LEAVE A SCAR.
AND ALSO...
PANT PANT

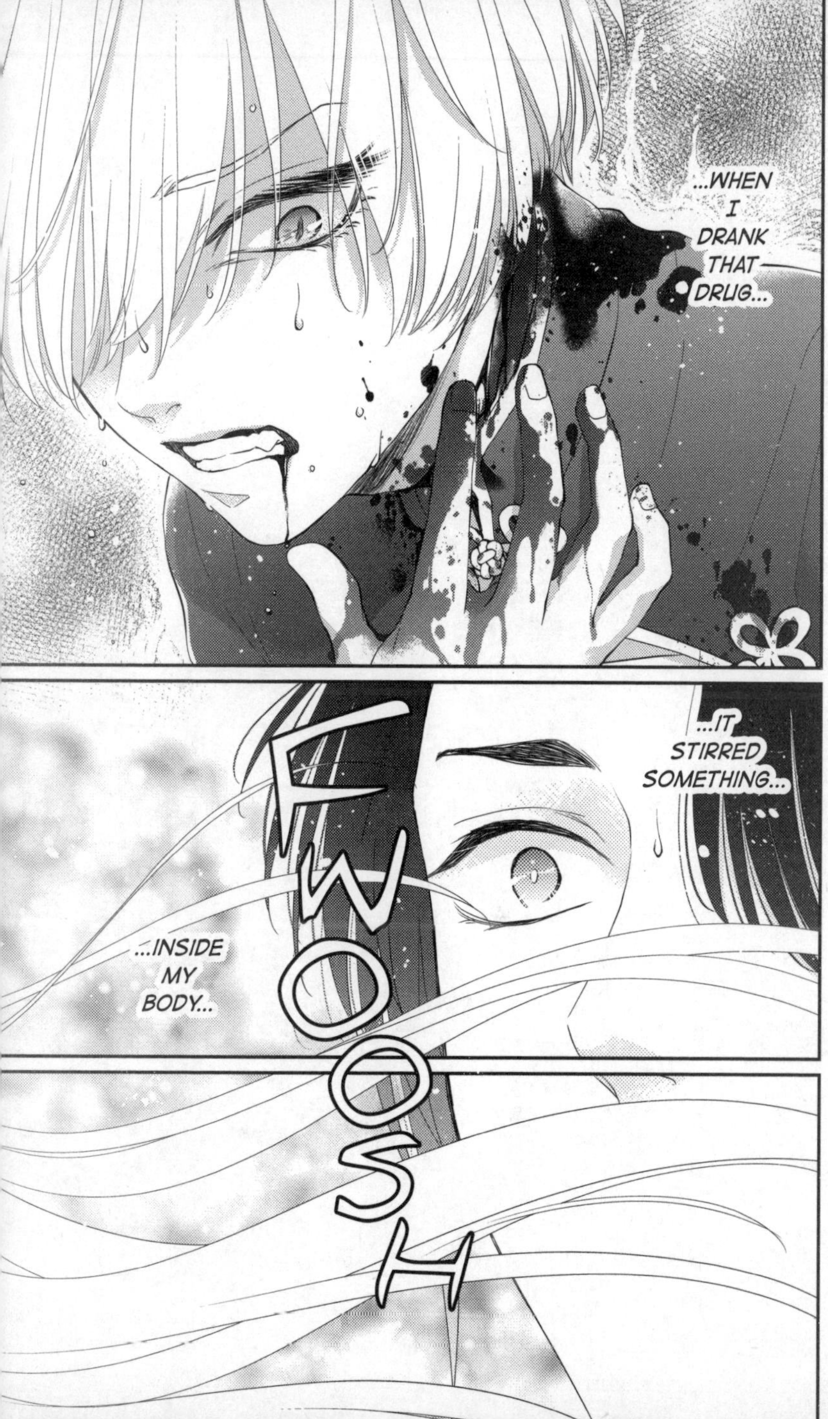
...WHEN I DRANK THAT DRUG...
...IT STIRRED SOMETHING...
...INSIDE MY BODY...
FWOOSH

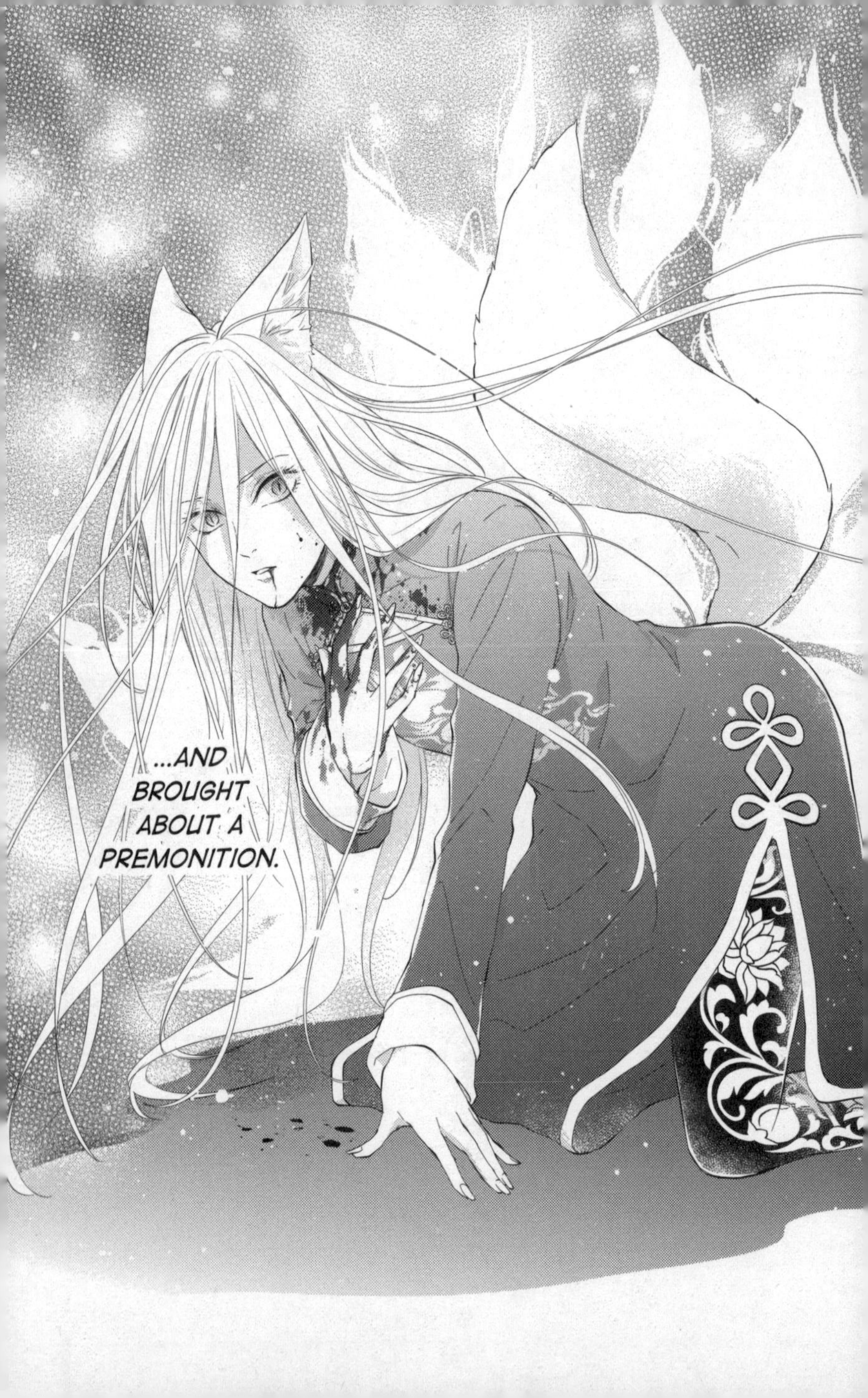
...AND BROUGHT ABOUT A PREMONITION.

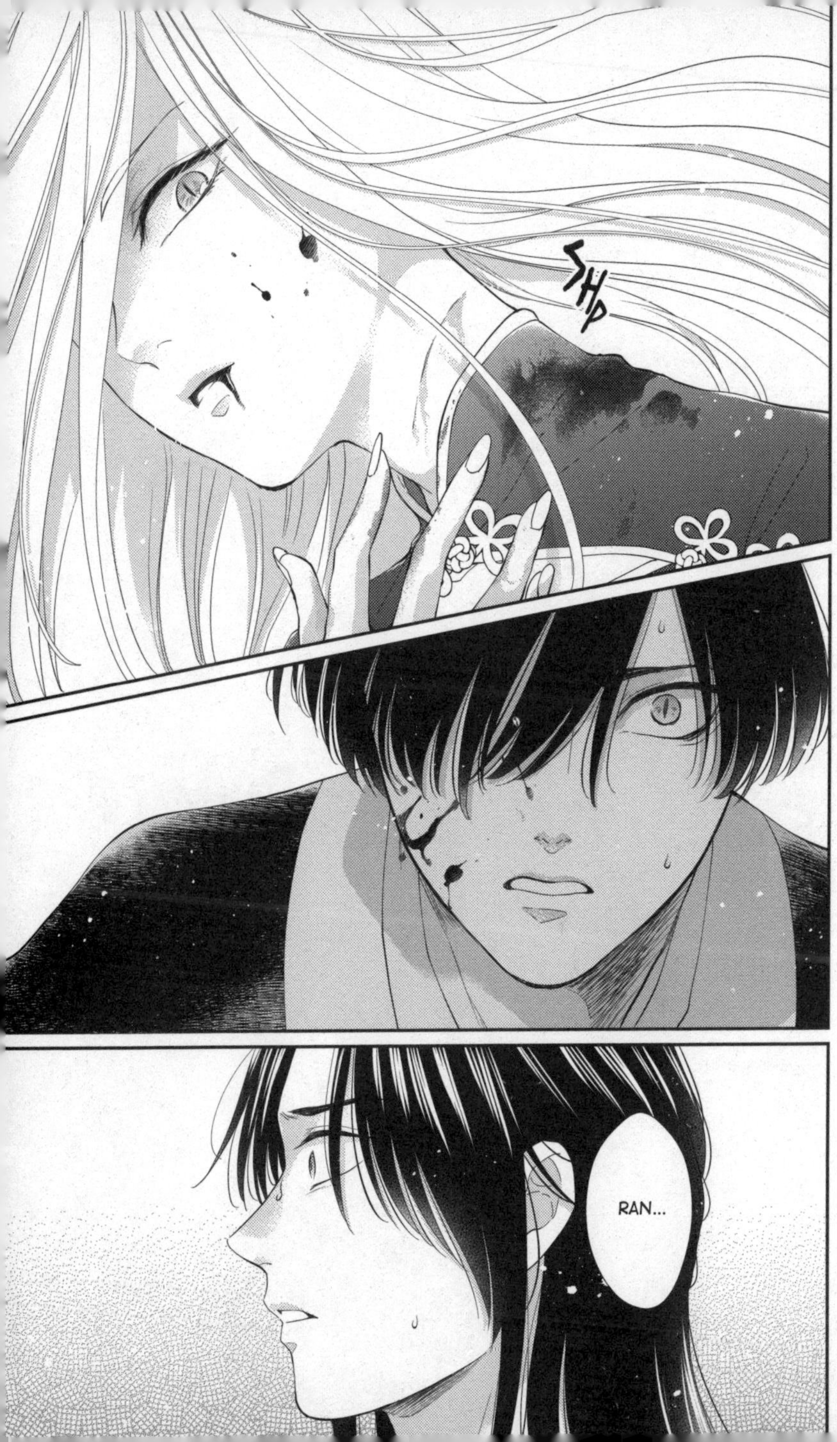
SHP
RAN...

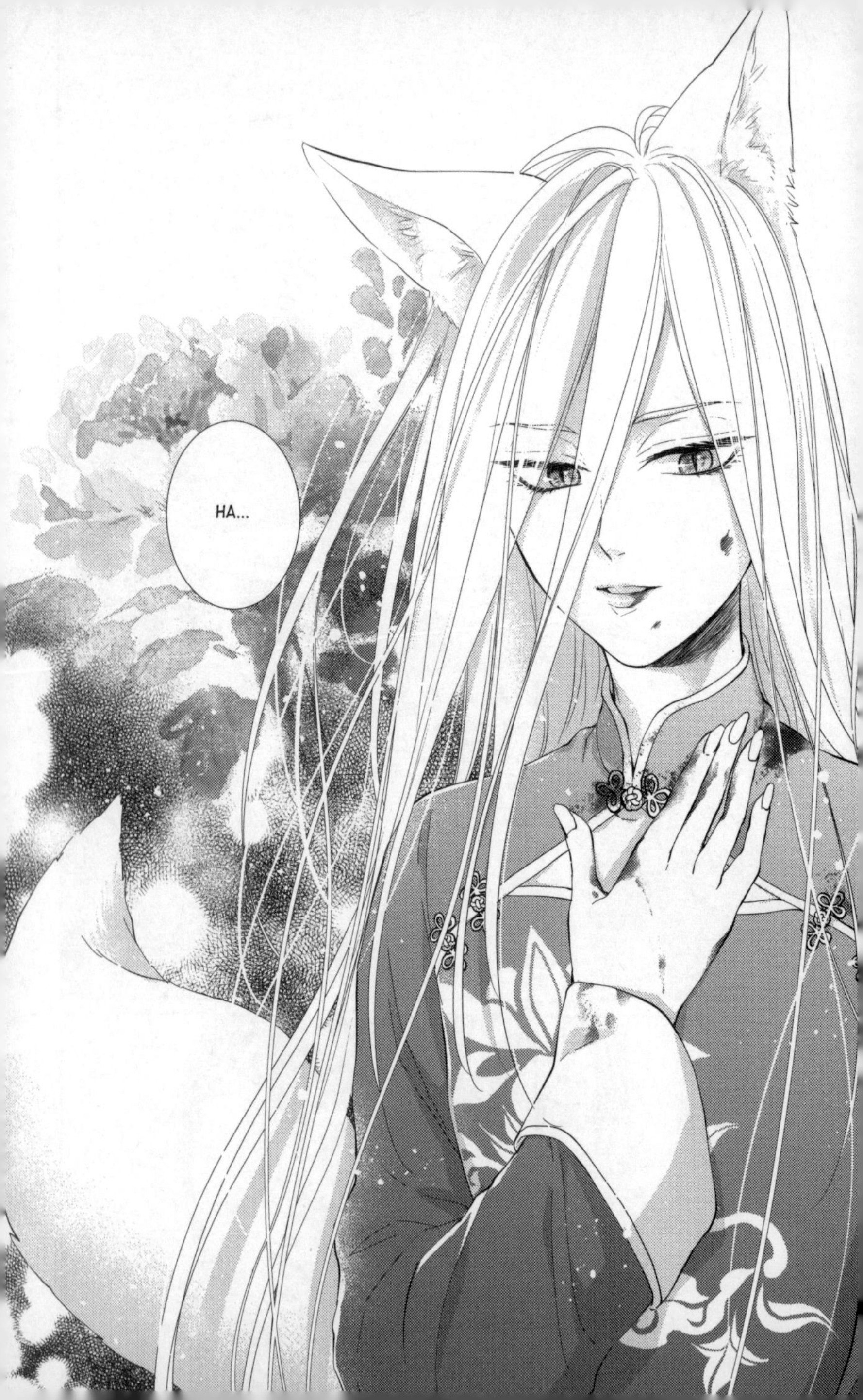
HA...

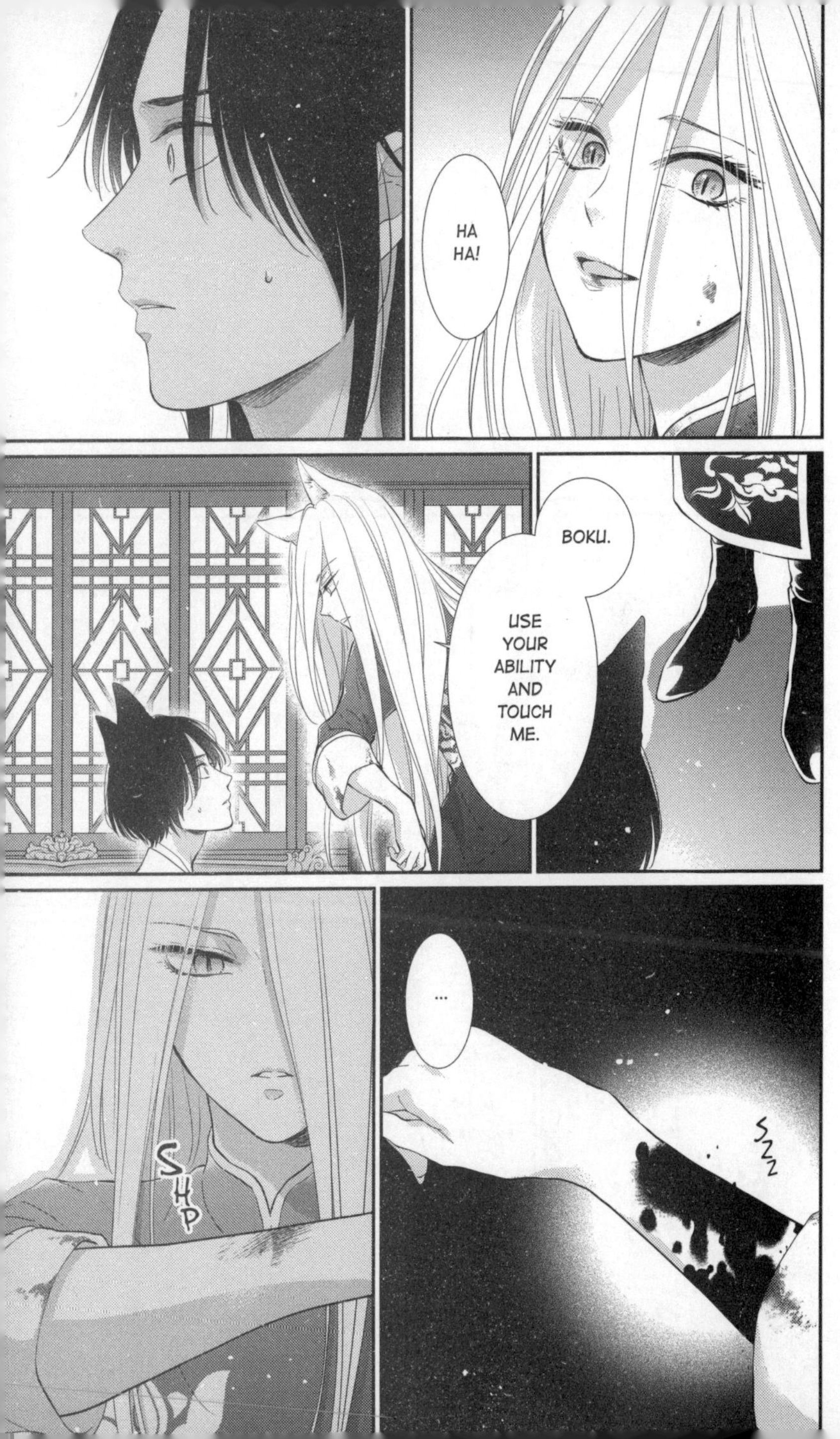
HA HA!
BOKU.
USE YOUR ABILITY AND TOUCH ME.
...
SZZ
SHP

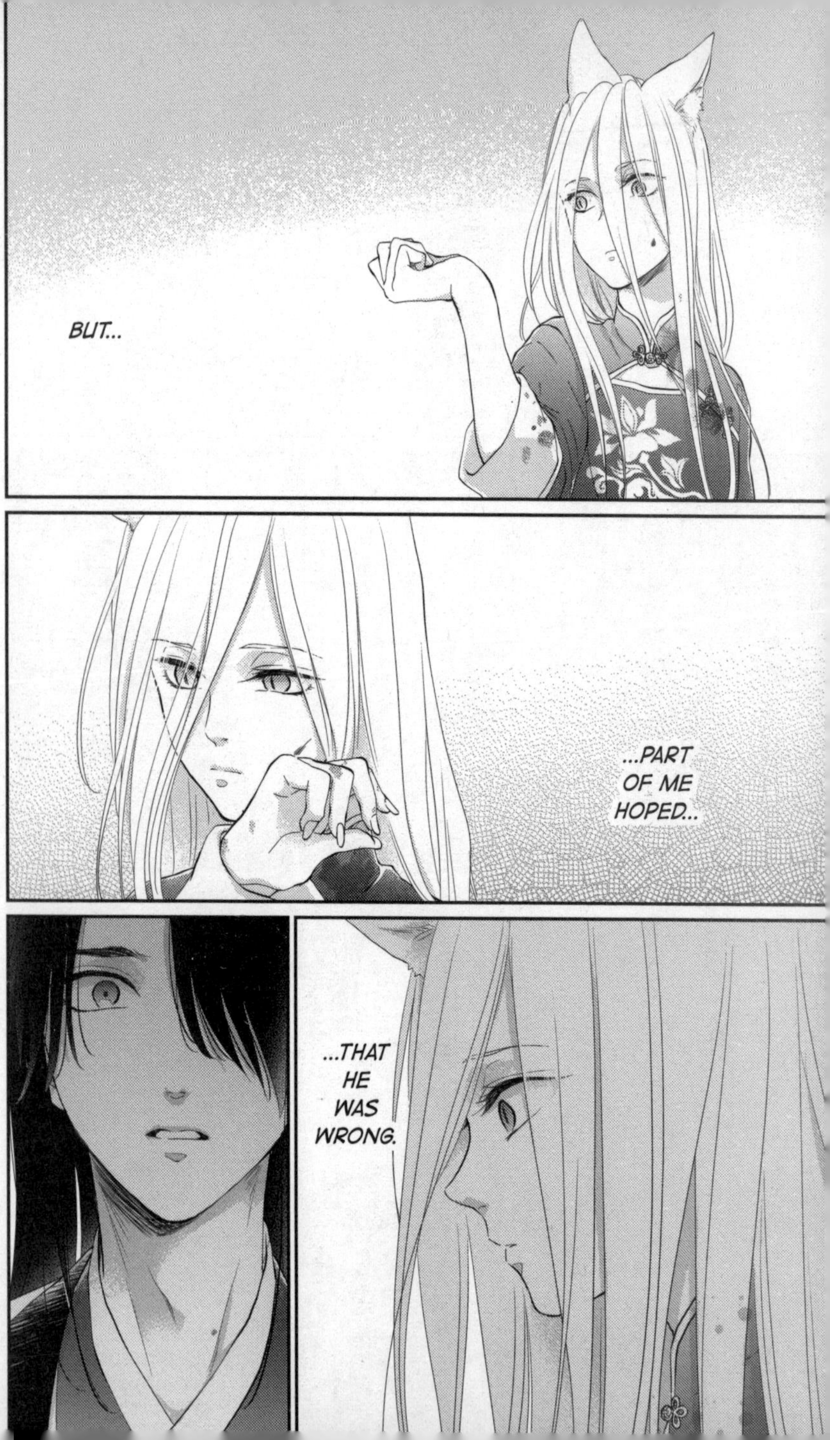
BUT...
...PART OF ME HOPED...
...THAT HE WAS WRONG.

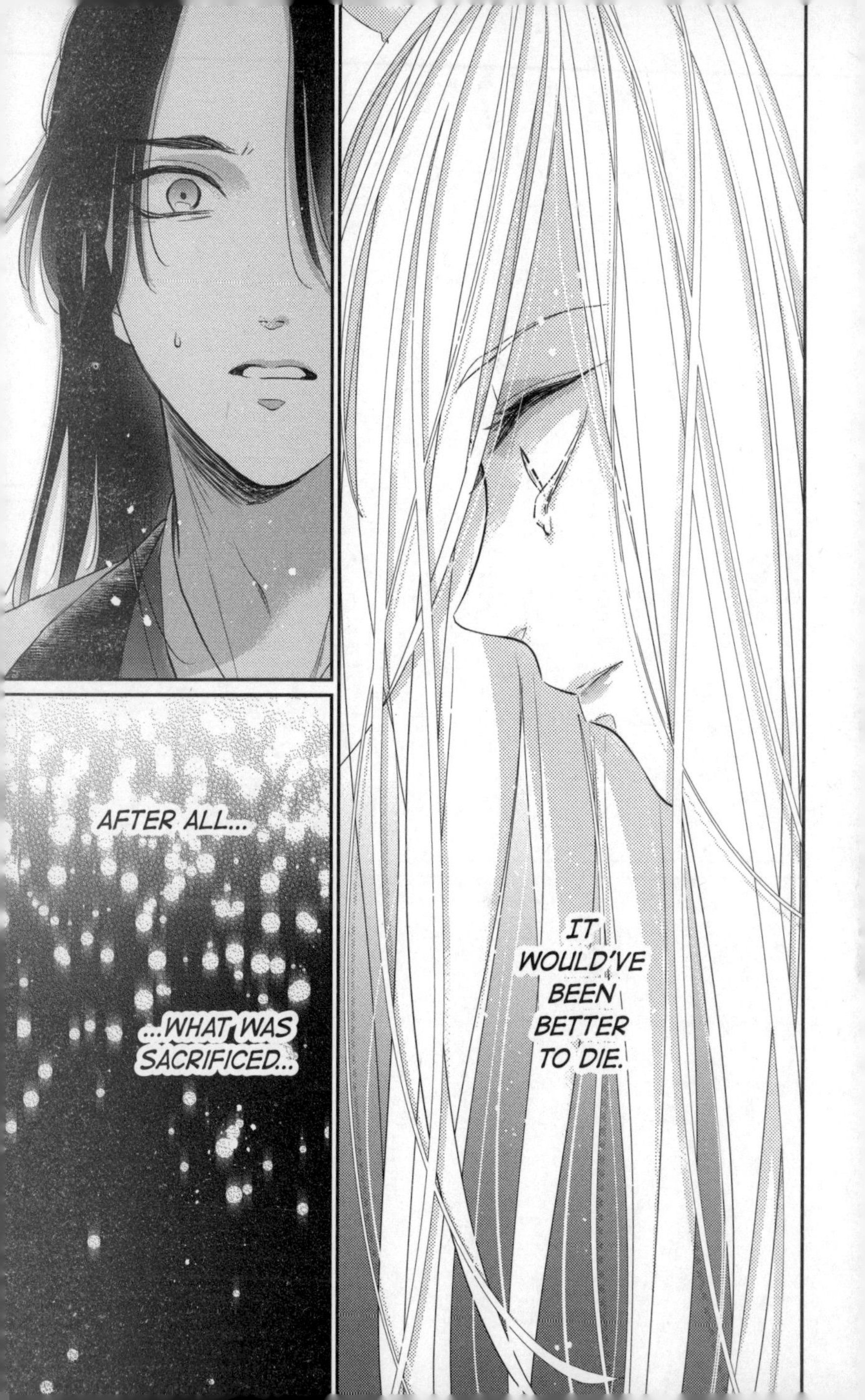
IT WOULD'VE BEEN BETTER TO DIE.
AFTER ALL...
...WHAT WAS SACRIFICED...

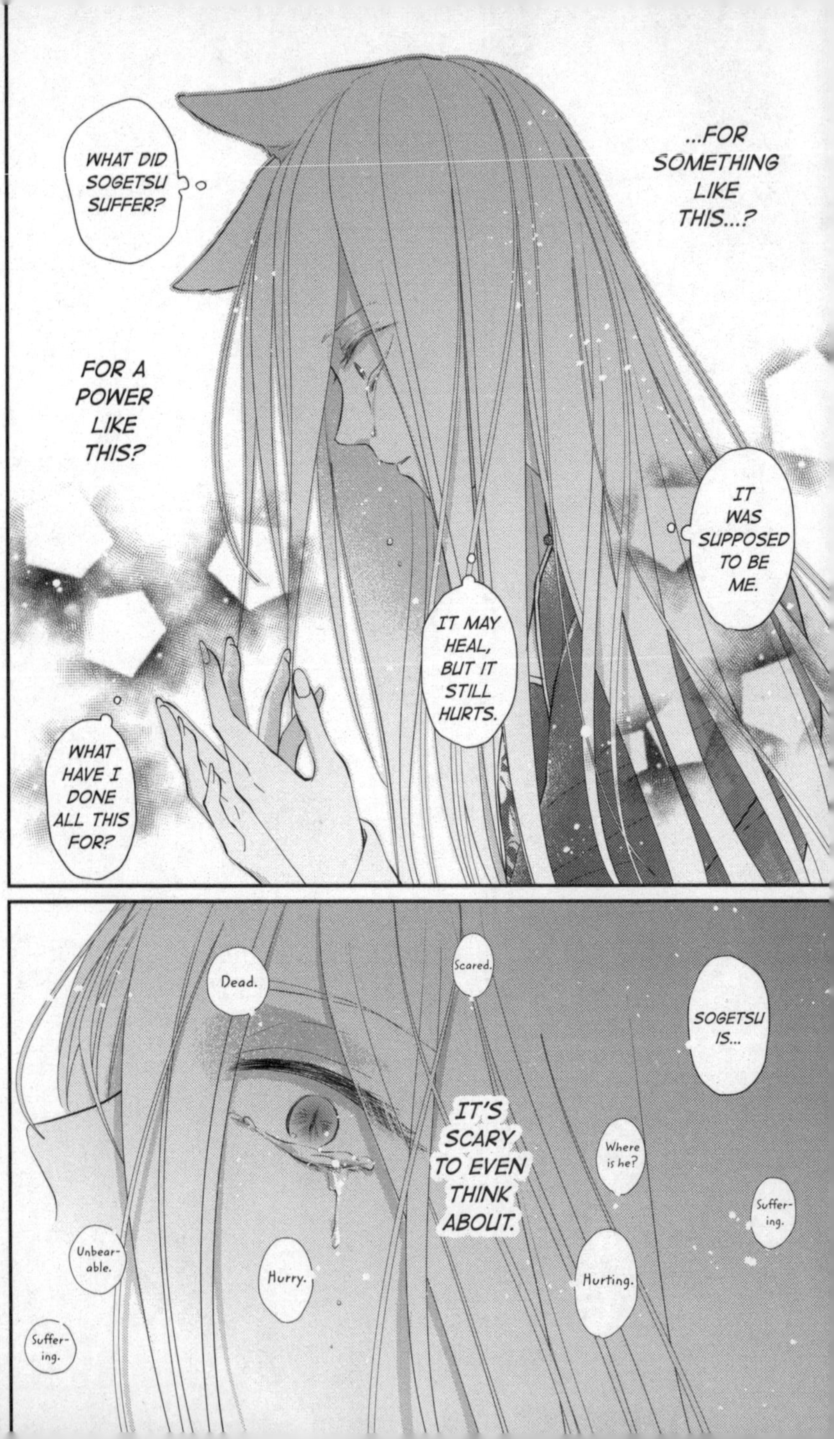
...FOR SOMETHING LIKE THIS...?
WHAT DID SOGETSU SUFFER?
IT WAS SUPPOSED TO BE ME.
IT MAY HEAL, BUT IT STILL HURTS.
FOR A POWER LIKE THIS?
WHAT HAVE I DONE ALL THIS FOR?
SOGETSU IS...
Scared.
Dead.
Where is he?
IT'S SCARY TO EVEN THINK ABOUT.
Suffer-ing.
Hurting.
Hurry.
Unbear-able.
Suffer-ing.

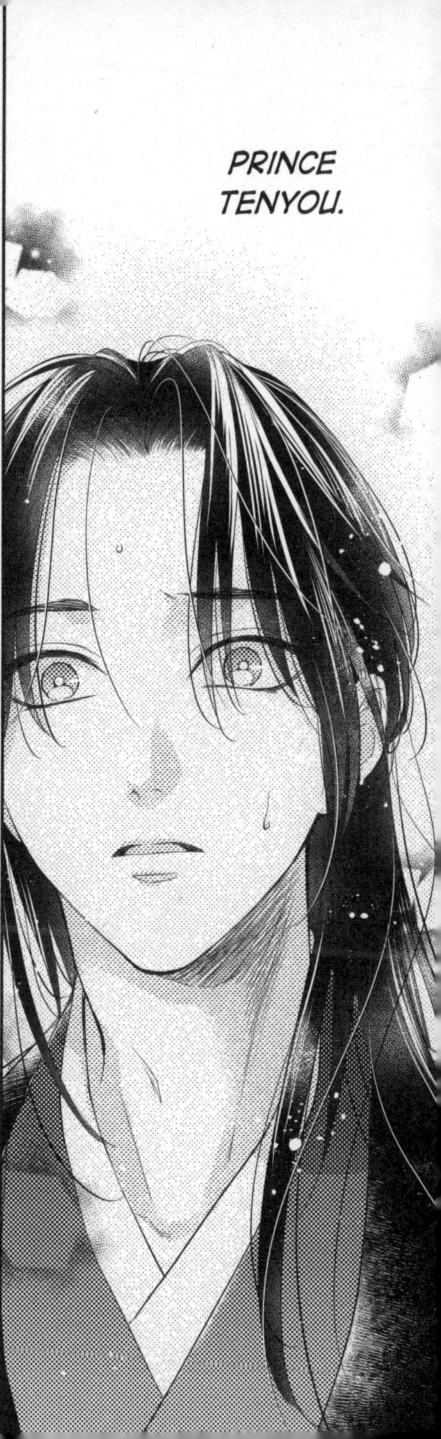
PRINCE TENYOU.
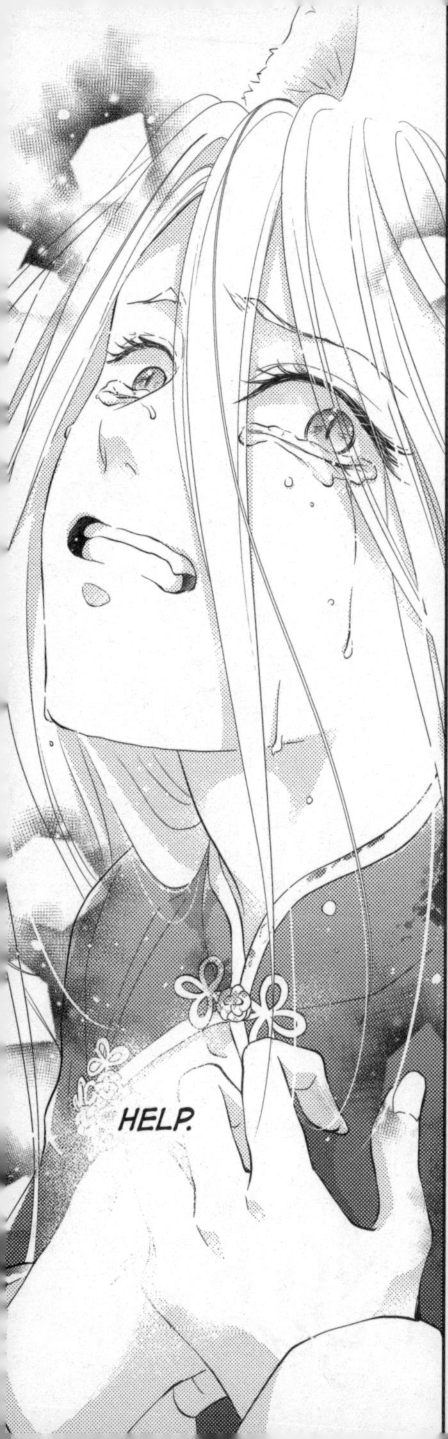
HELP.

THE KING'S *Beast*

麗

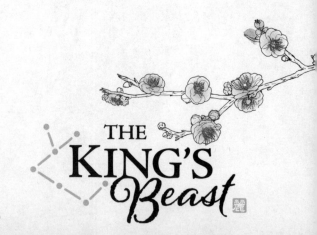

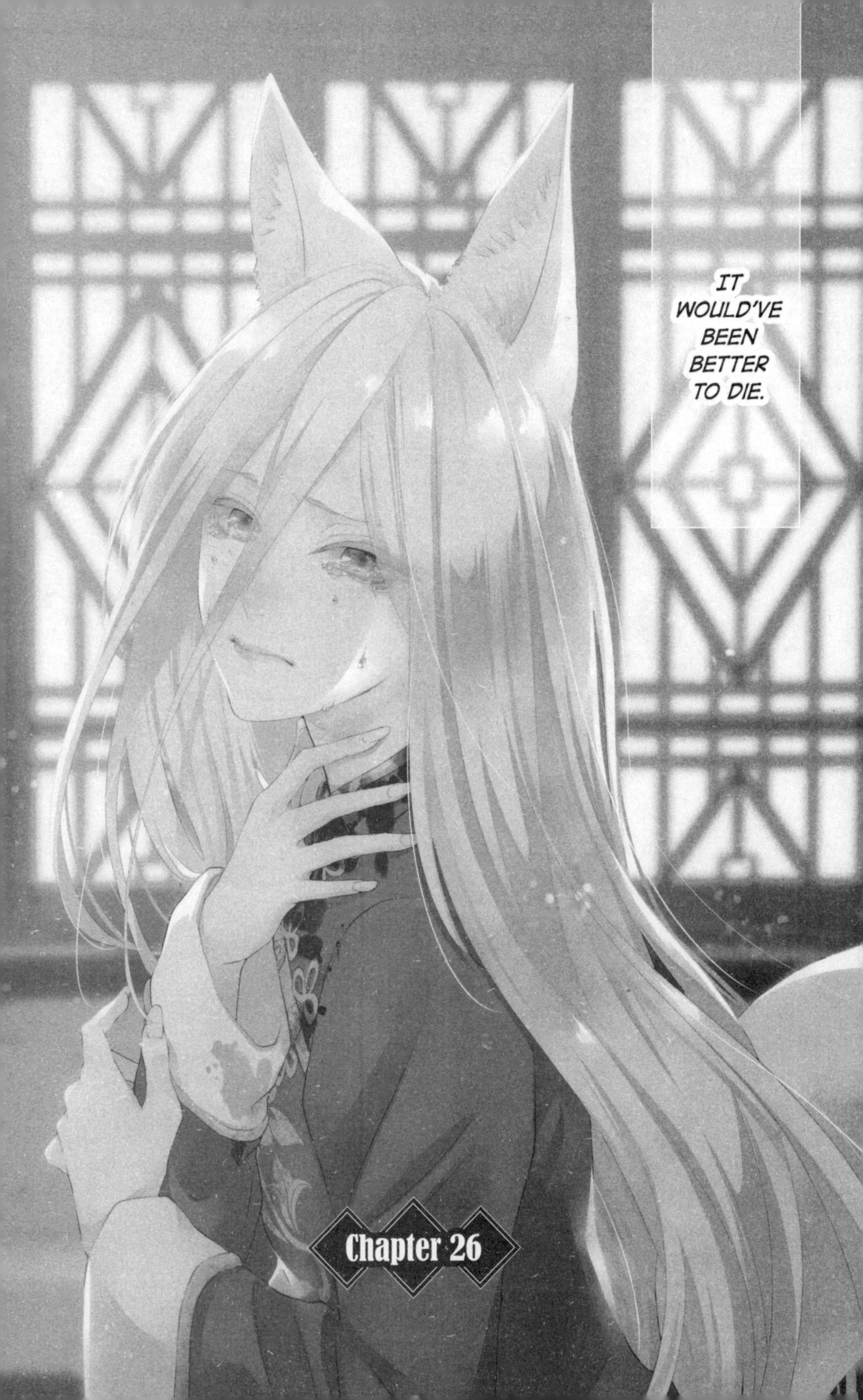
IT WOULD'VE BEEN BETTER TO DIE.
Chapter 26

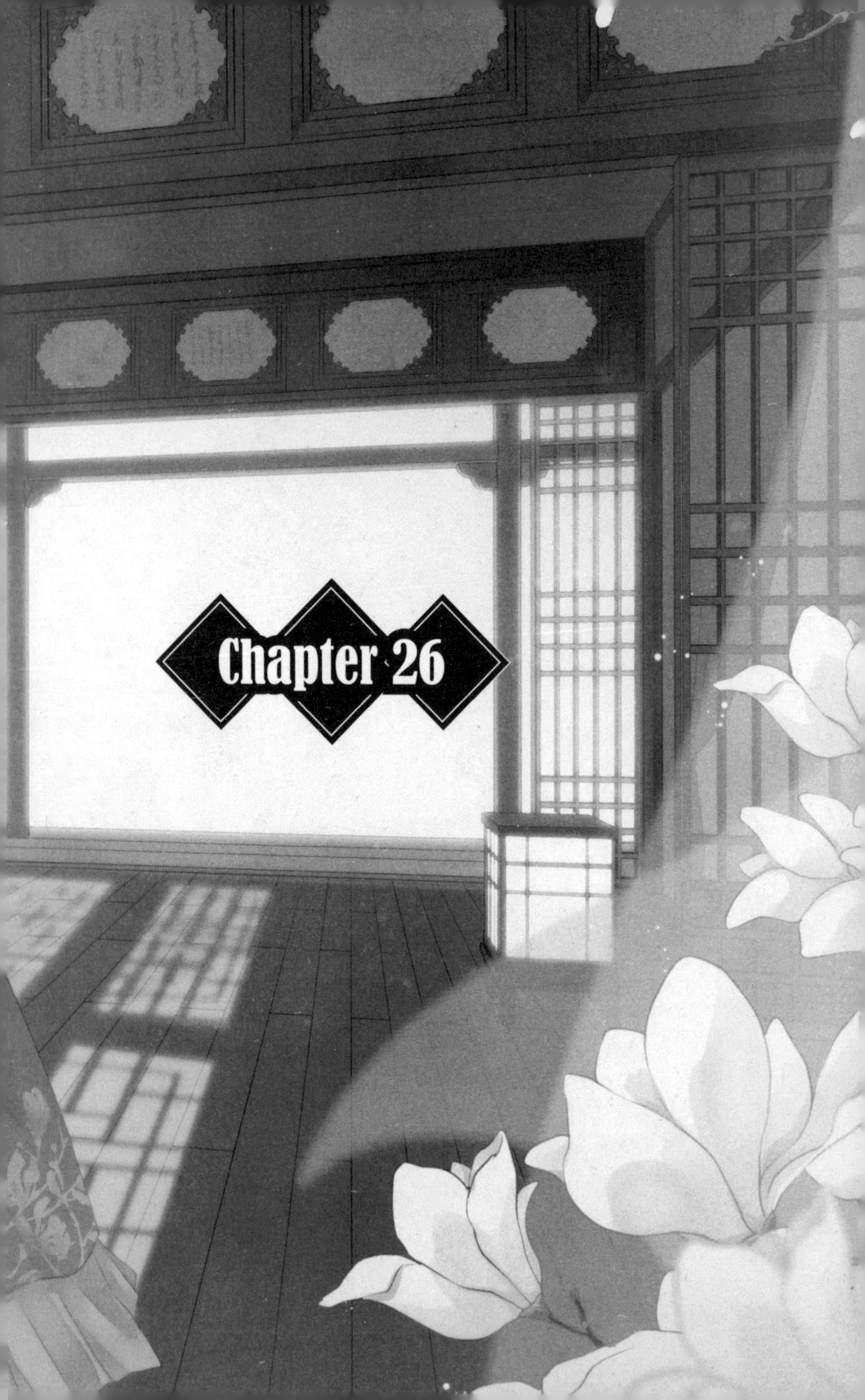
Chapter 26

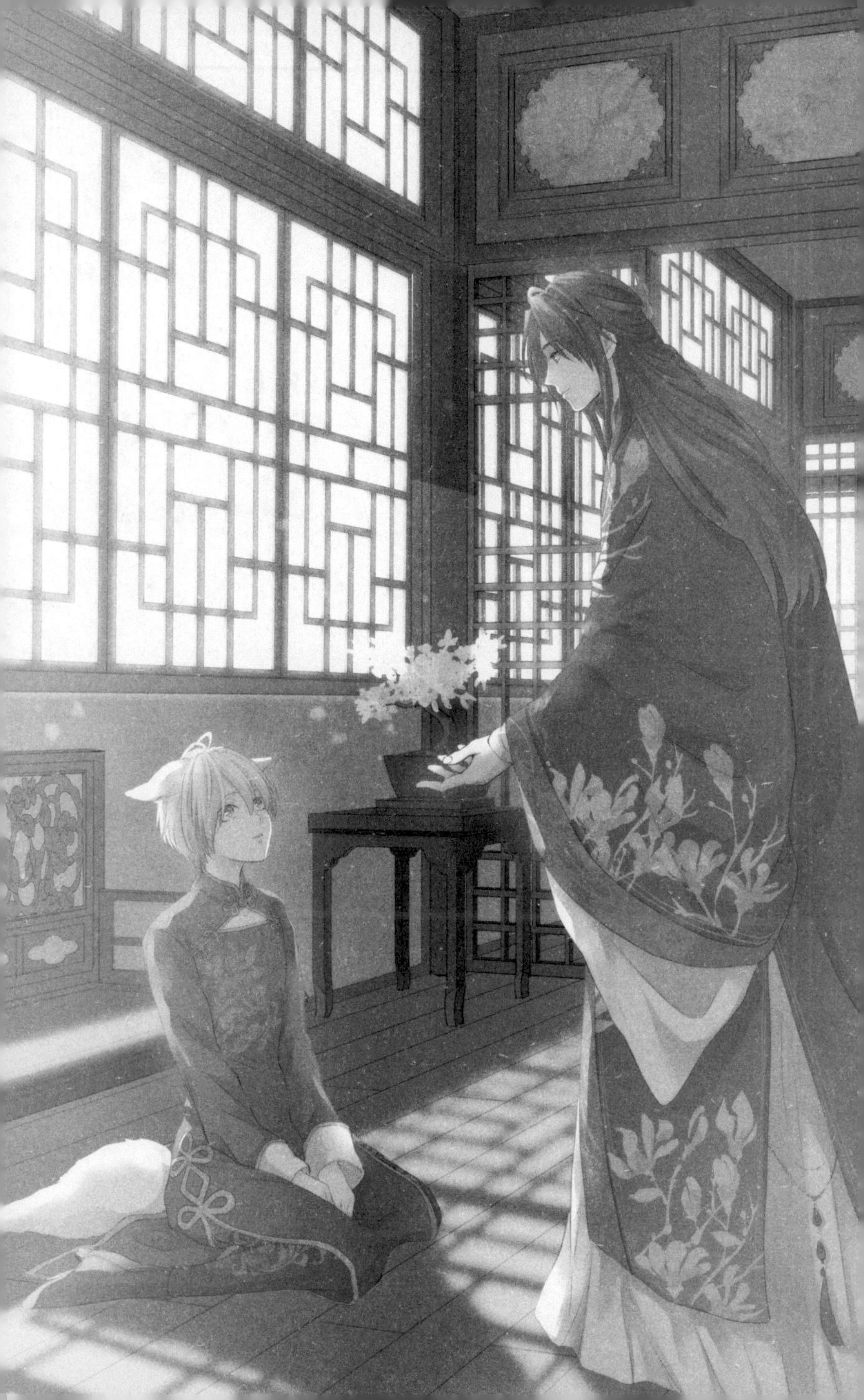

THE KING'S Beast

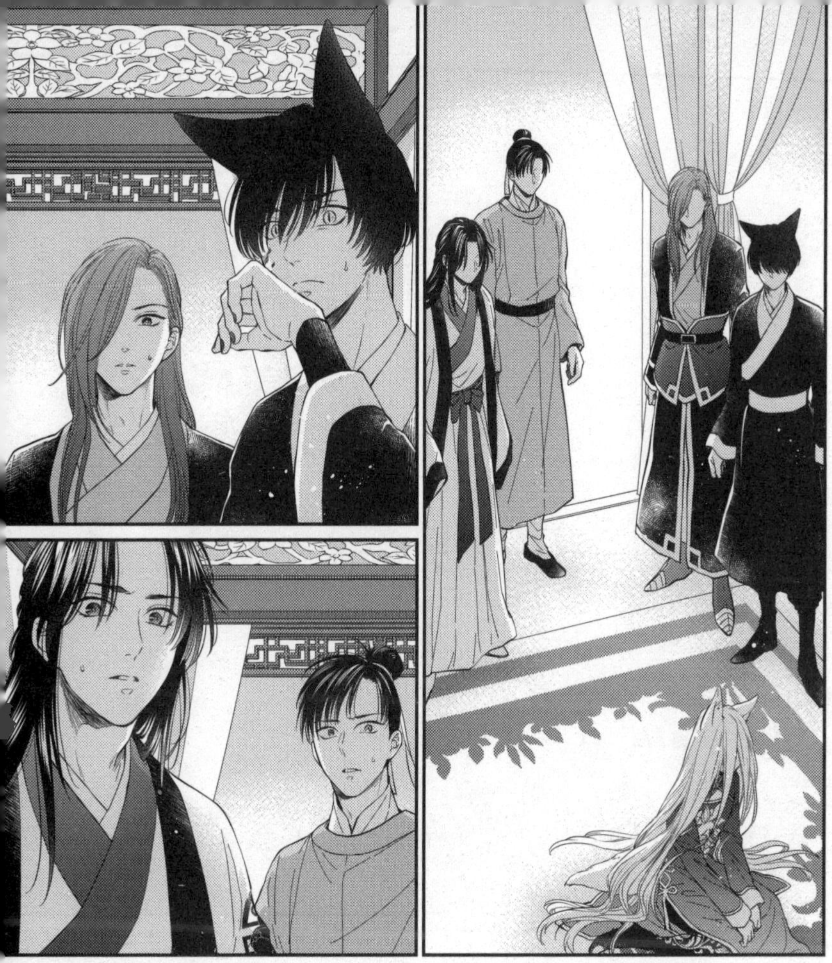

THE KING'S *Beast*

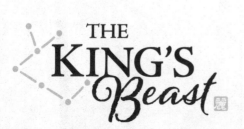

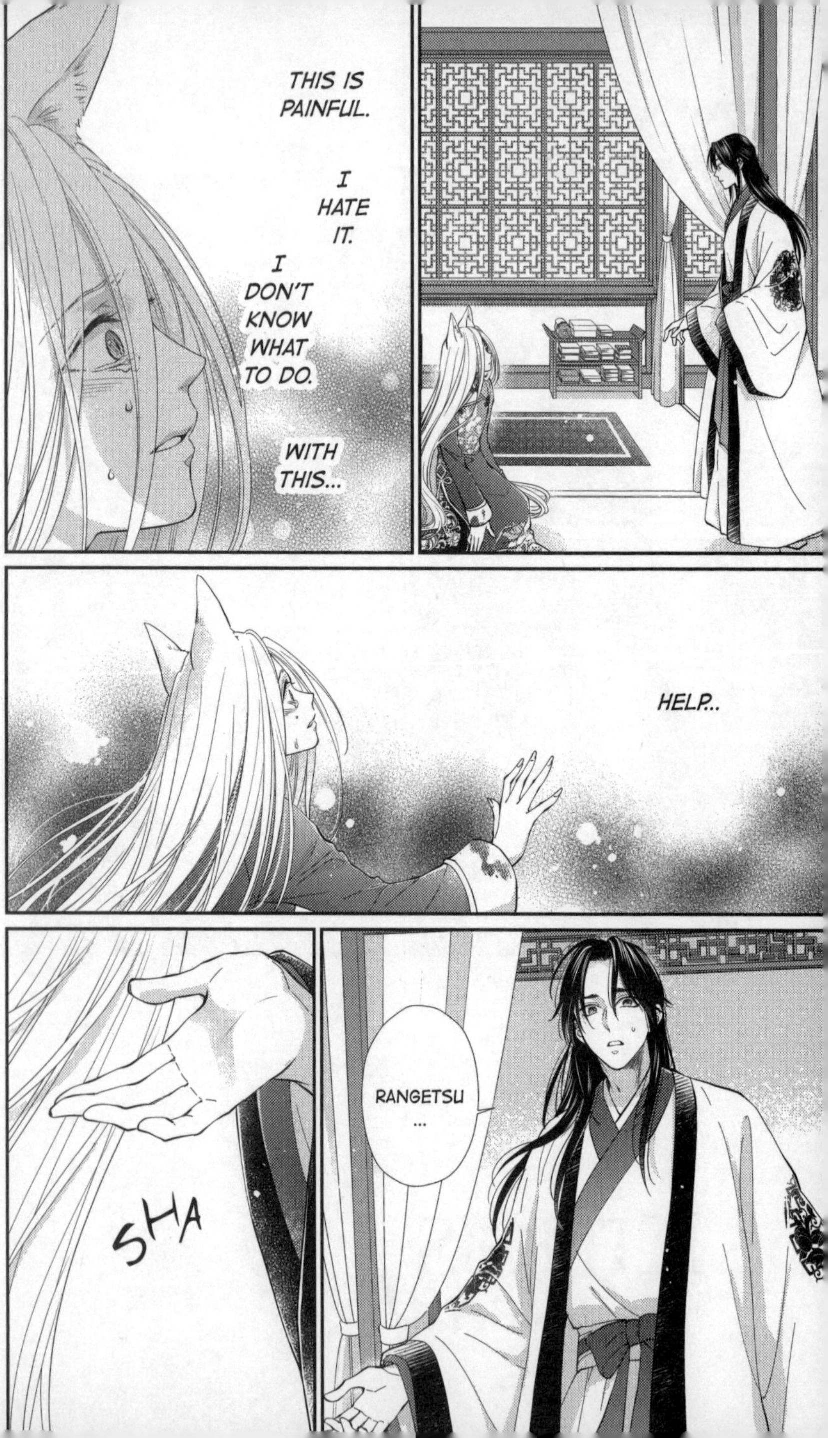
THIS IS PAINFUL.
I HATE IT.
I DON'T KNOW WHAT TO DO.
WITH THIS...
HELP...
RANGETSU ...
SHA

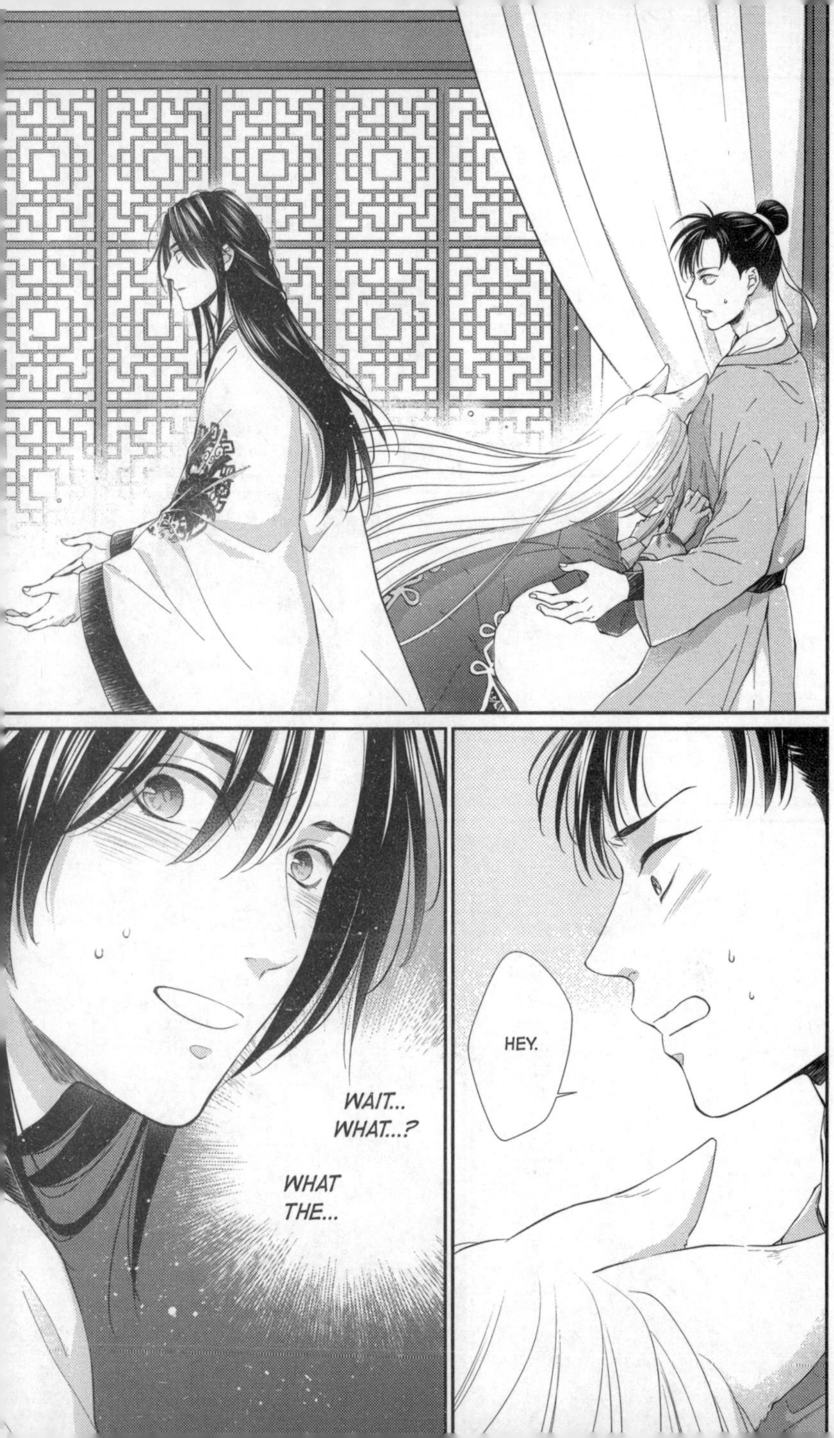
HEY.
WAIT... WHAT...?
WHAT THE...

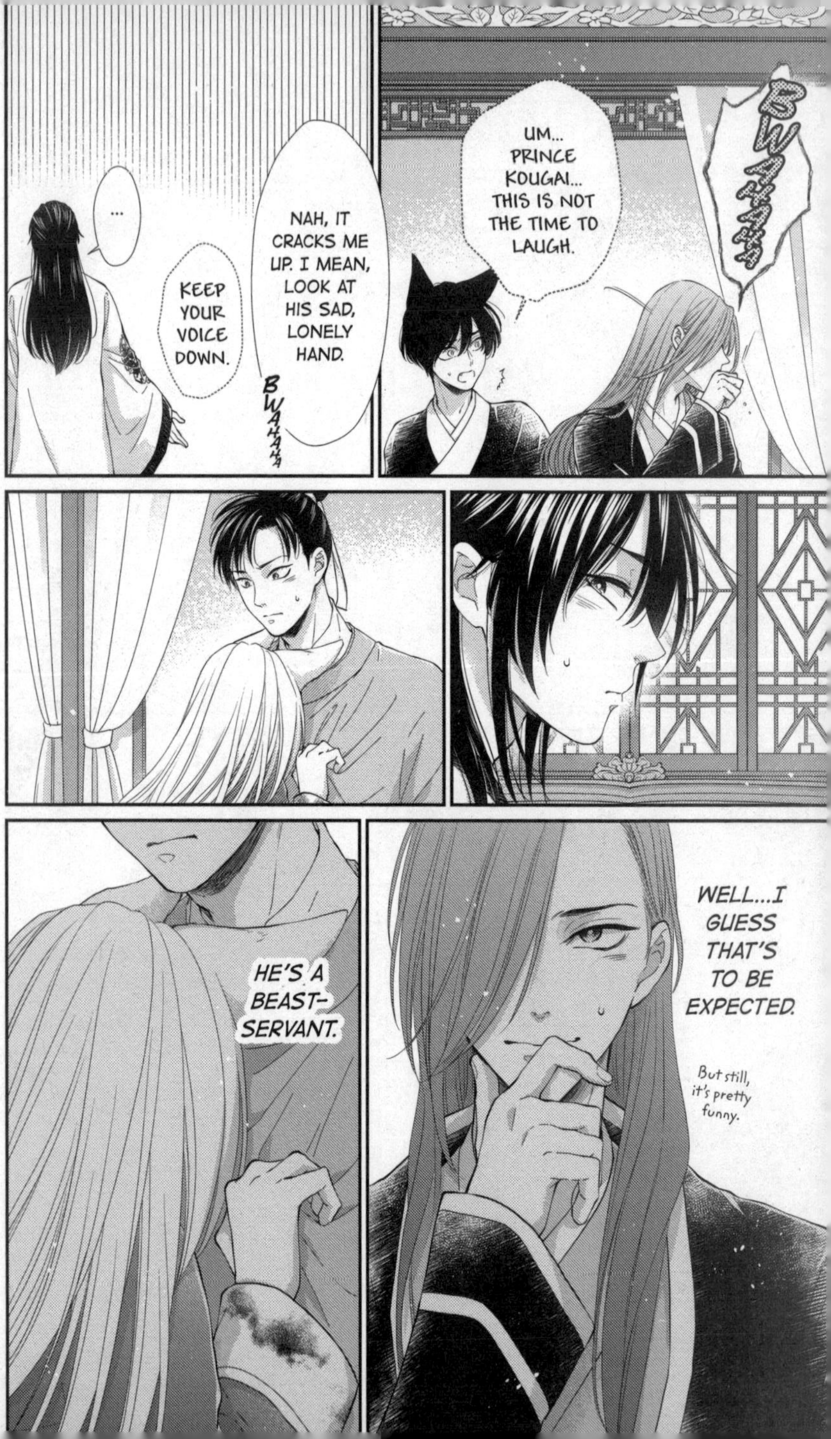
BWAHAHA
UM... PRINCE KOUGAI... THIS IS NOT THE TIME TO LAUGH.
NAH, IT CRACKS ME UP. I MEAN, LOOK AT HIS SAD, LONELY HAND.
BWAHAHAHA
KEEP YOUR VOICE DOWN.
...
WELL...I GUESS THAT'S TO BE EXPECTED.
But still, it's pretty funny.
HE'S A BEAST-SERVANT.

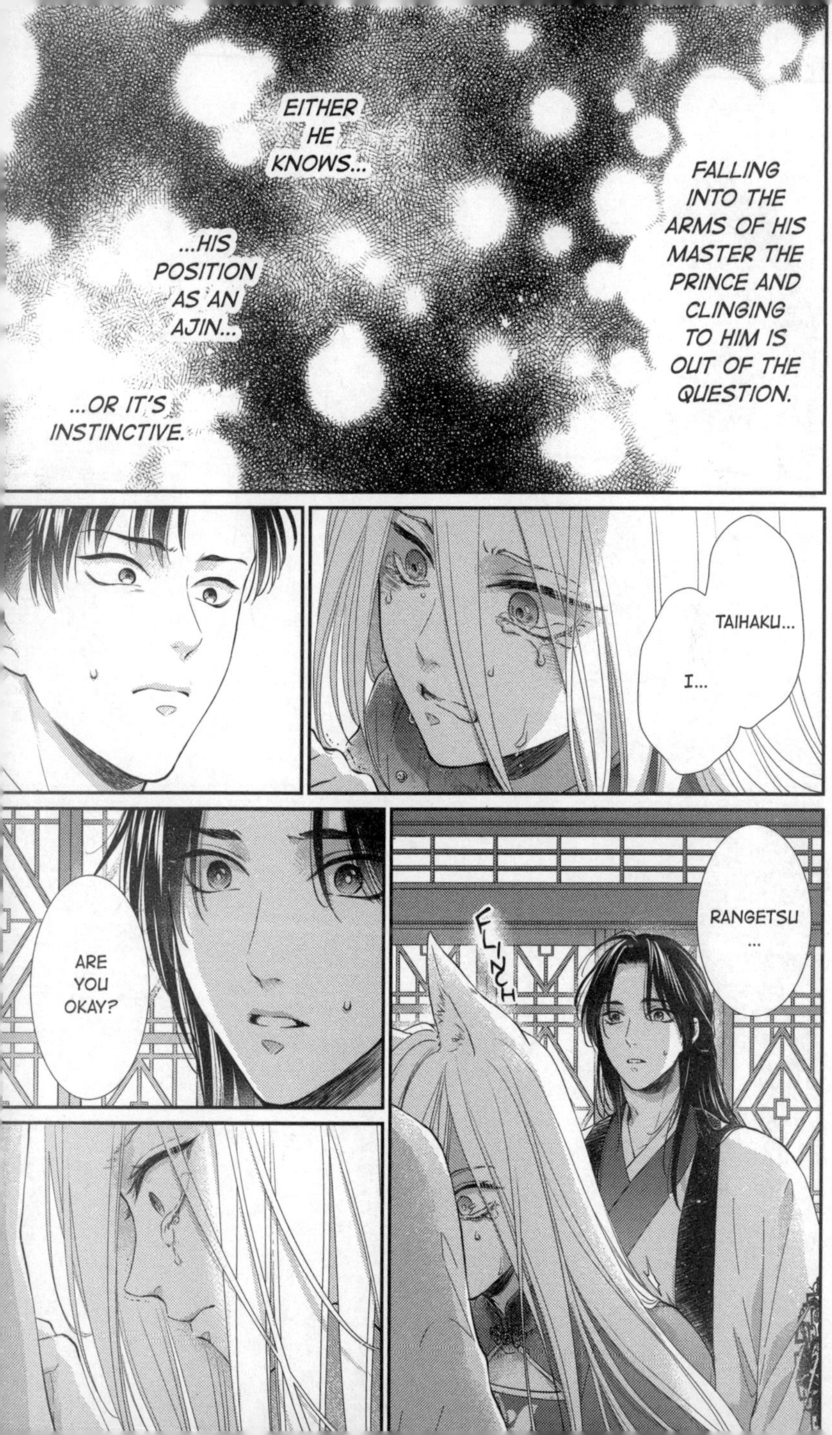
FALLING INTO THE ARMS OF HIS MASTER THE PRINCE AND CLINGING TO HIM IS OUT OF THE QUESTION.
EITHER HE KNOWS...
...HIS POSITION AS AN AJIN...
...OR IT'S INSTINCTIVE.
TAIHAKU...
I...
RANGETSU ...
FLINCH
ARE YOU OKAY?

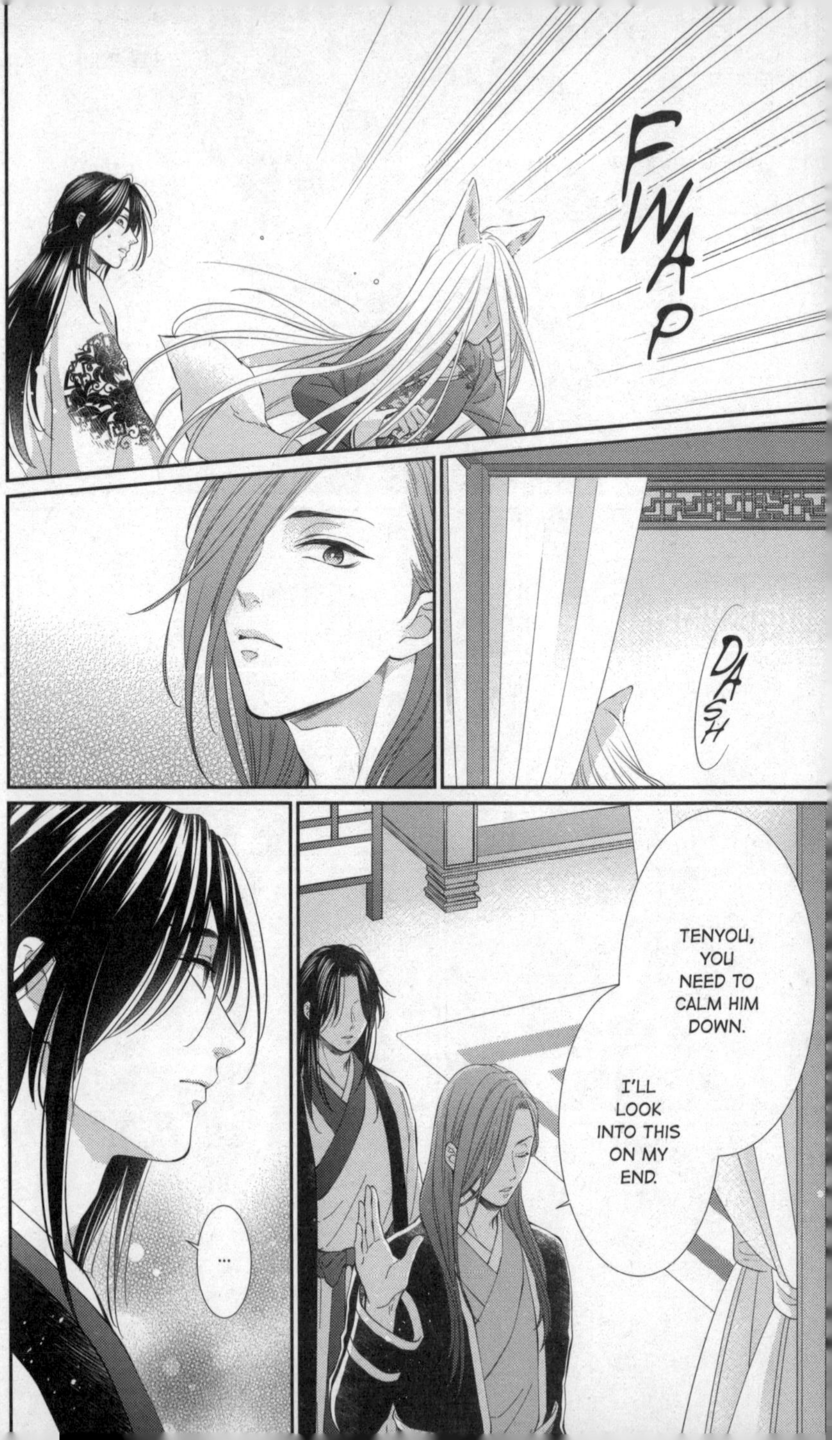
FWAP
DASH
TENYOU, YOU NEED TO CALM HIM DOWN.
I'LL LOOK INTO THIS ON MY END.
...

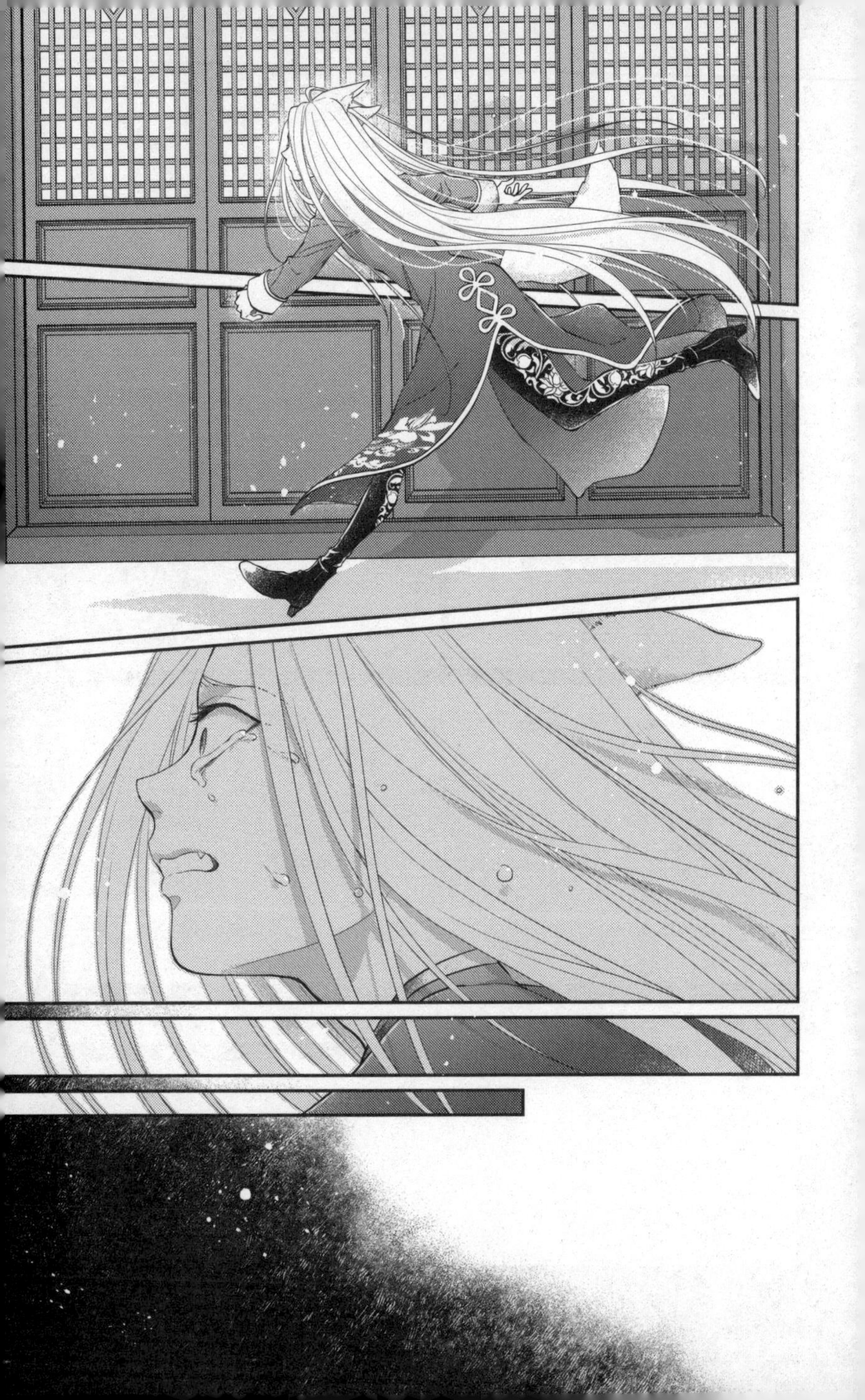

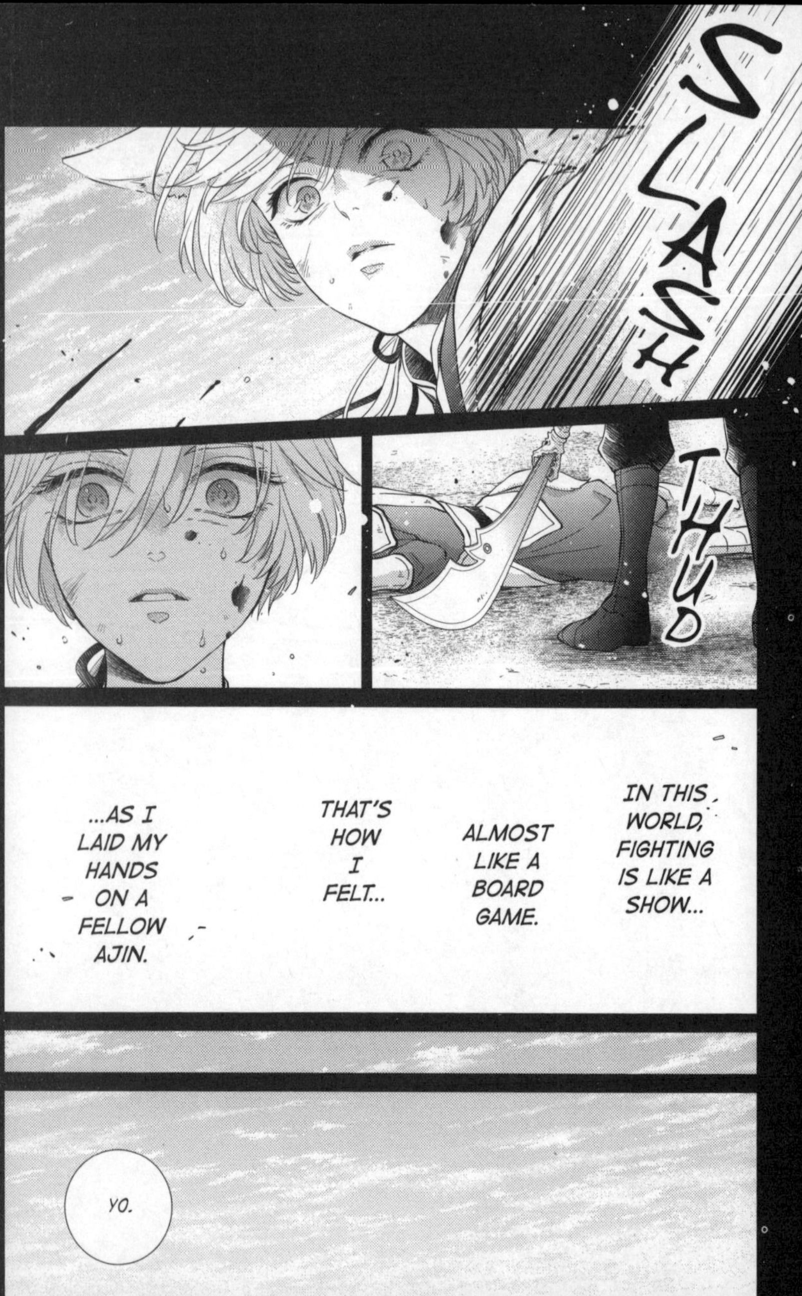
SLASH
THUD
IN THIS WORLD, FIGHTING IS LIKE A SHOW...
ALMOST LIKE A BOARD GAME.
THAT'S HOW I FELT...
...AS I LAID MY HANDS ON A FELLOW AJIN.
YO.

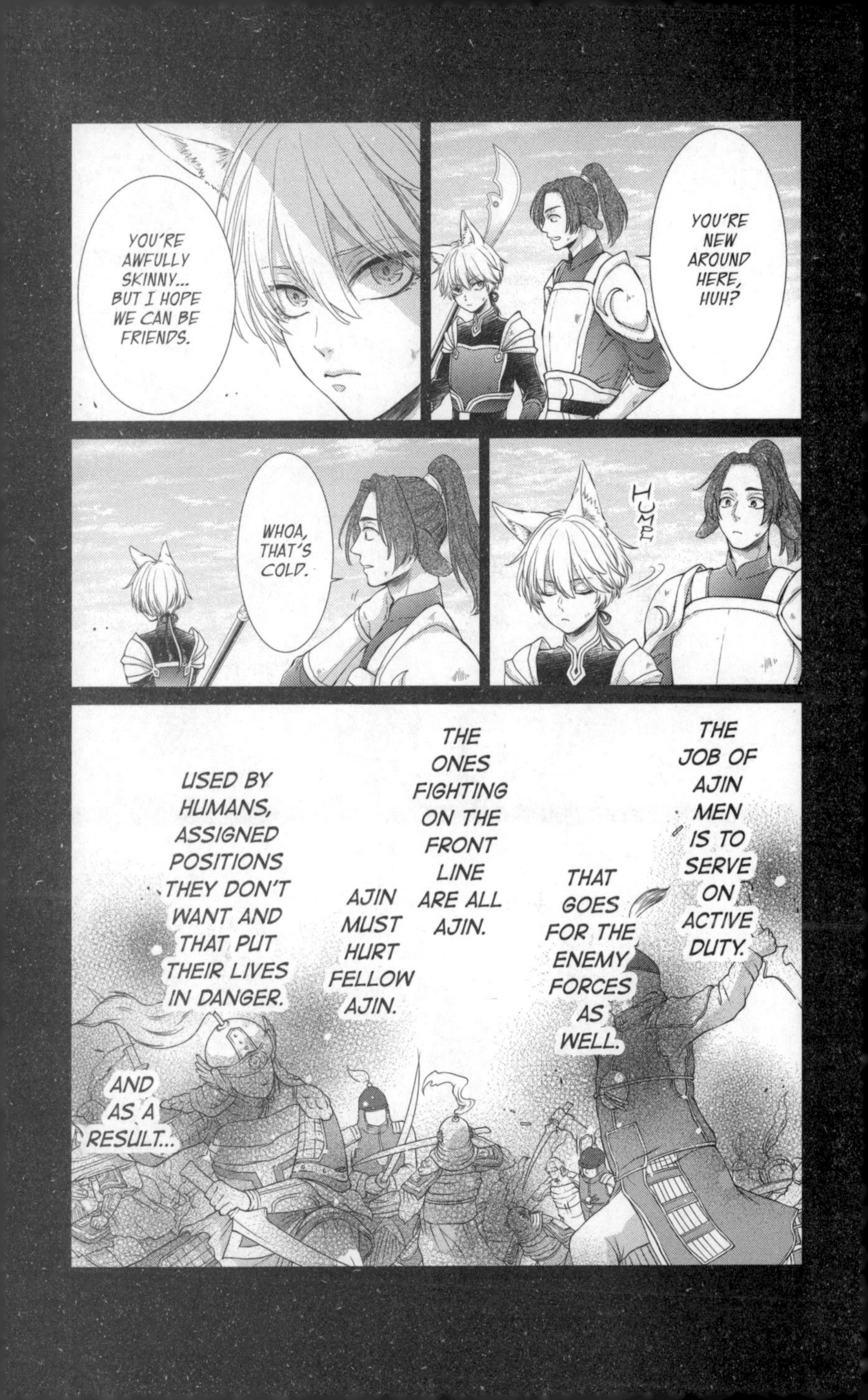
YOU'RE NEW AROUND HERE, HUH?
YOU'RE AWFULLY SKINNY... BUT I HOPE WE CAN BE FRIENDS.
HUMPH
WHOA, THAT'S COLD.
THE JOB OF AJIN MEN IS TO SERVE ON ACTIVE DUTY.
THAT GOES FOR THE ENEMY FORCES AS WELL.
THE ONES FIGHTING ON THE FRONT LINE ARE ALL AJIN.
AJIN MUST HURT FELLOW AJIN.
USED BY HUMANS, ASSIGNED POSITIONS THEY DON'T WANT AND THAT PUT THEIR LIVES IN DANGER.
AND AS A RESULT...

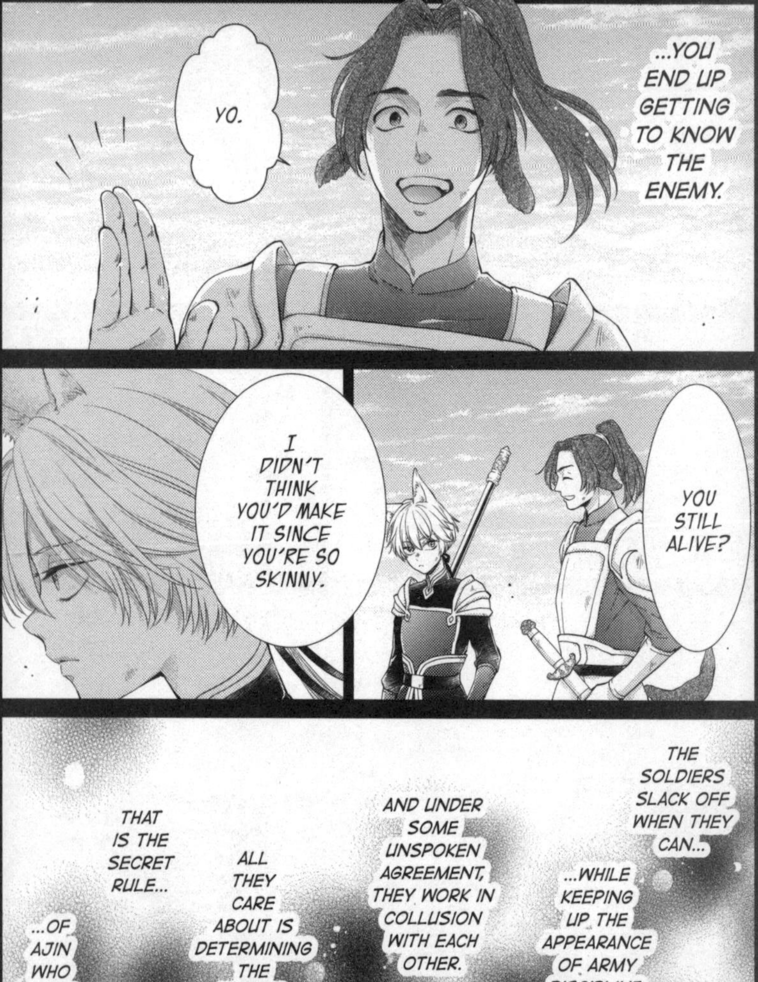
...YOU END UP GETTING TO KNOW THE ENEMY.
YO.
YOU STILL ALIVE?
I DIDN'T THINK YOU'D MAKE IT SINCE YOU'RE SO SKINNY.
THE SOLDIERS SLACK OFF WHEN THEY CAN...
...WHILE KEEPING UP THE APPEARANCE OF ARMY DISCIPLINE.
AND UNDER SOME UNSPOKEN AGREEMENT, THEY WORK IN COLLUSION WITH EACH OTHER.
ALL THEY CARE ABOUT IS DETERMINING THE WINNER.
THAT IS THE SECRET RULE...
...OF AJIN WHO FIGHT ON THE FRONT LINE.

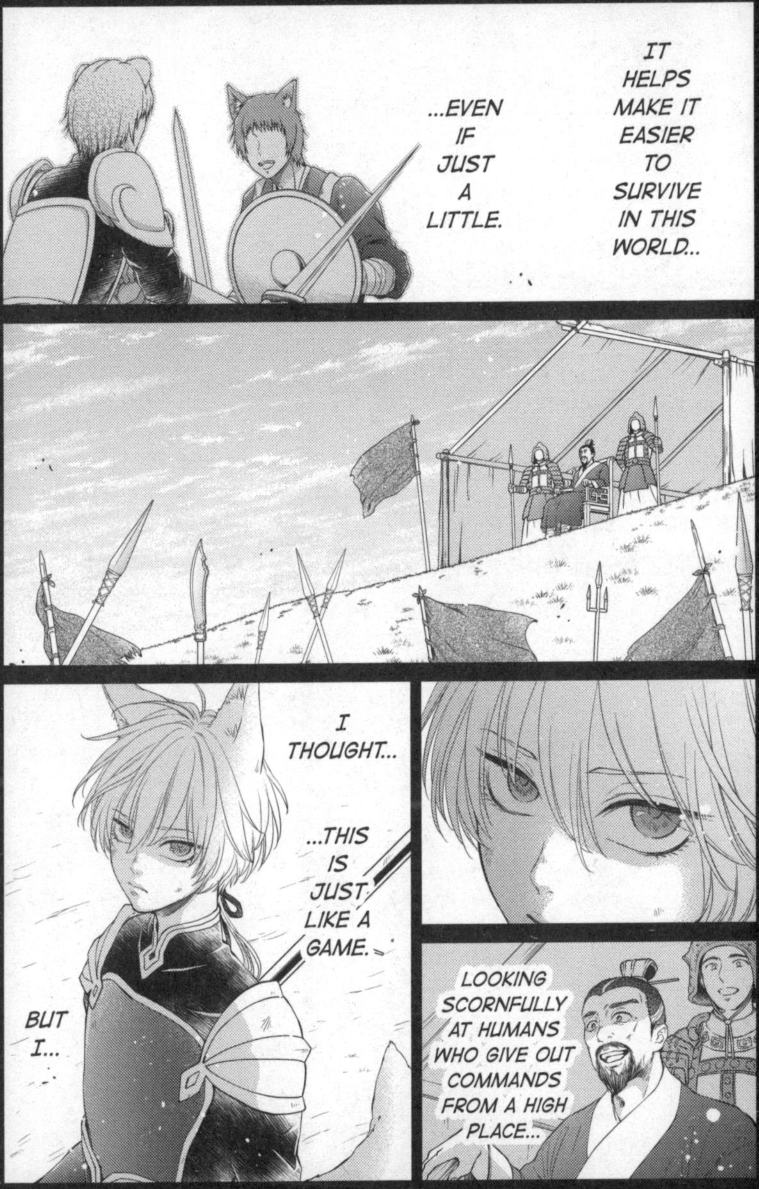
IT HELPS MAKE IT EASIER TO SURVIVE IN THIS WORLD...
...EVEN IF JUST A LITTLE.
LOOKING SCORNFULLY AT HUMANS WHO GIVE OUT COMMANDS FROM A HIGH PLACE...
I THOUGHT...
...THIS IS JUST LIKE A GAME.
BUT I...

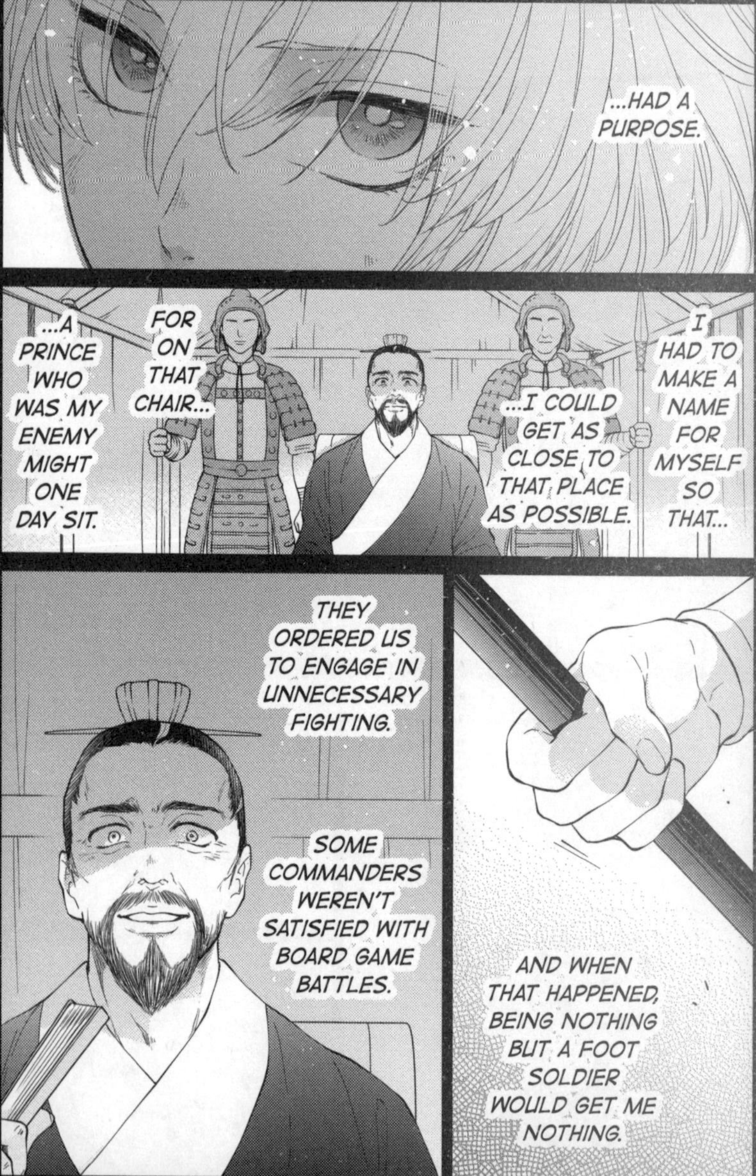
...HAD A PURPOSE.
I HAD TO MAKE A NAME FOR MYSELF SO THAT...
...I COULD GET AS CLOSE TO THAT PLACE AS POSSIBLE.
FOR ON THAT CHAIR...
...A PRINCE WHO WAS MY ENEMY MIGHT ONE DAY SIT.
AND WHEN THAT HAPPENED, BEING NOTHING BUT A FOOT SOLDIER WOULD GET ME NOTHING.
THEY ORDERED US TO ENGAGE IN UNNECESSARY FIGHTING.
SOME COMMANDERS WEREN'T SATISFIED WITH BOARD GAME BATTLES.

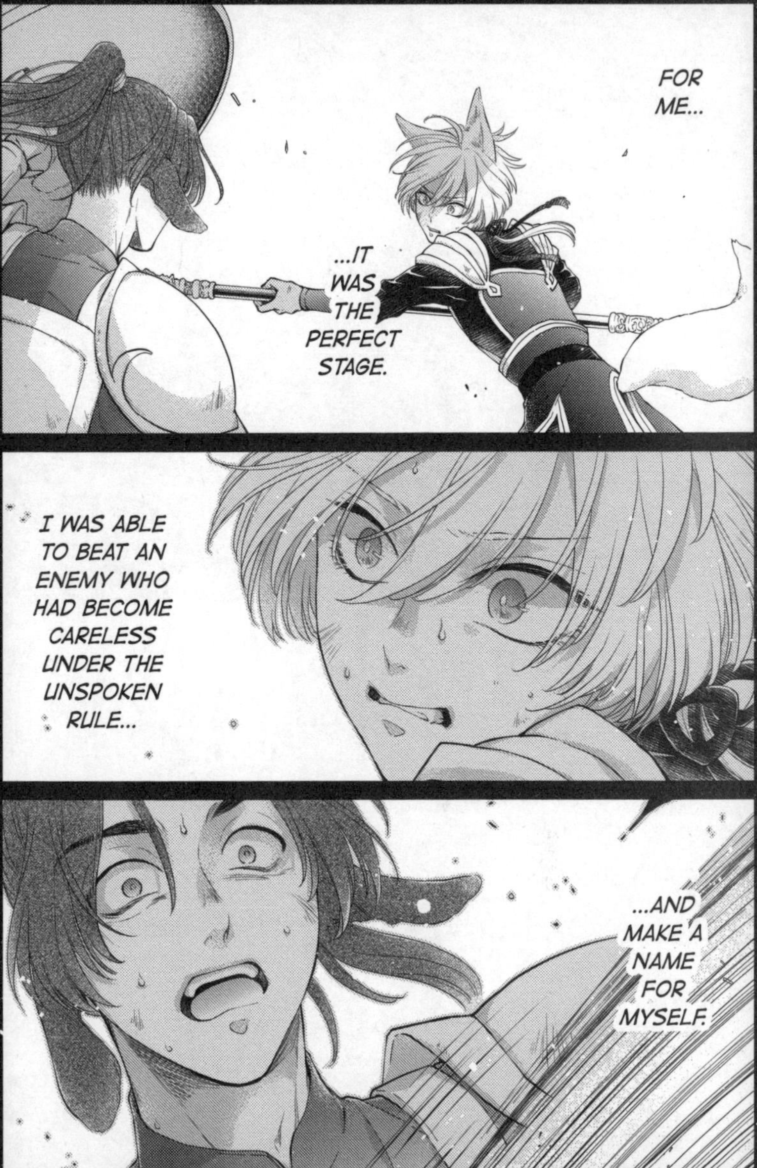
FOR ME...
...IT WAS THE PERFECT STAGE.
I WAS ABLE TO BEAT AN ENEMY WHO HAD BECOME CARELESS UNDER THE UNSPOKEN RULE...
...AND MAKE A NAME FOR MYSELF.

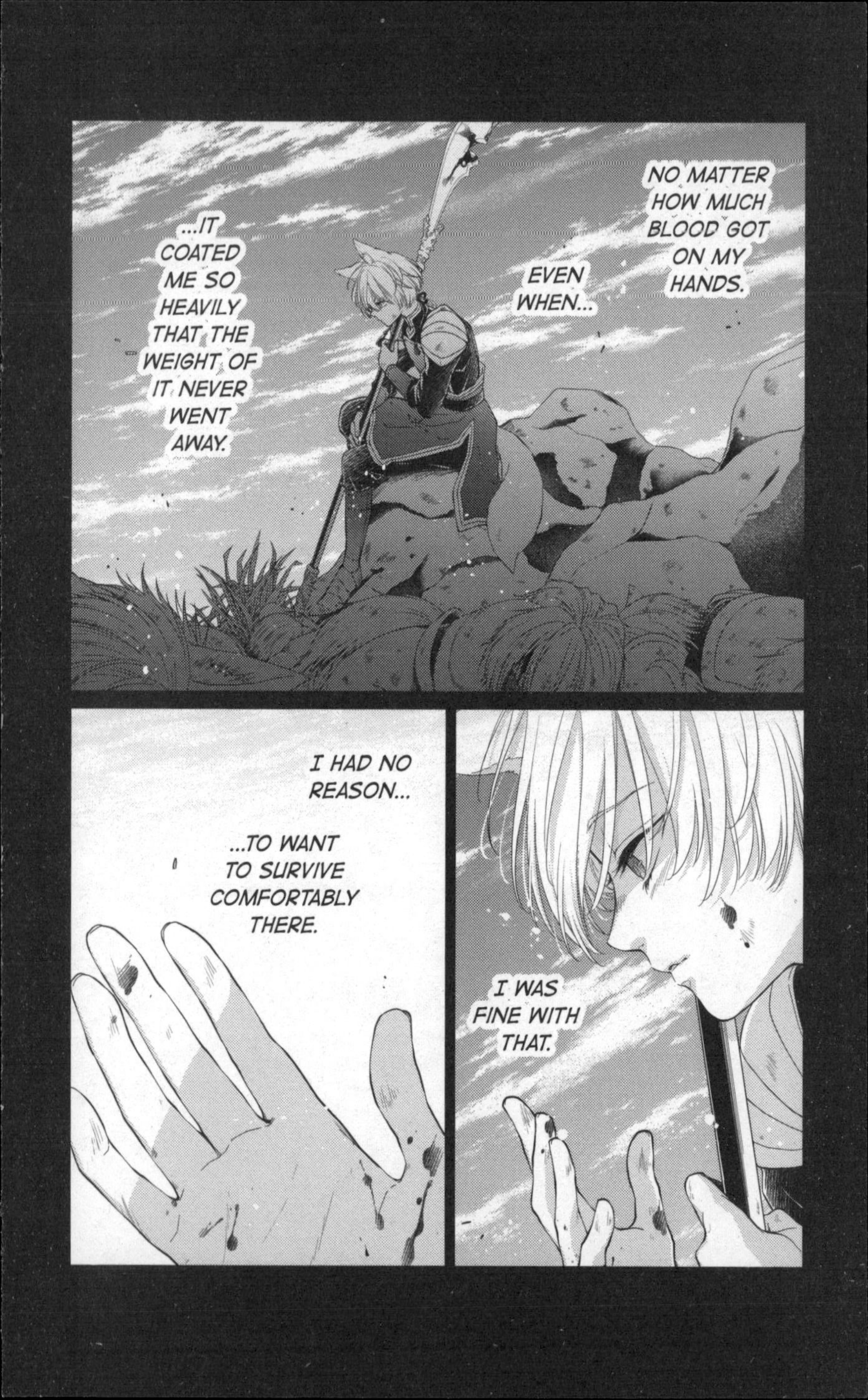
NO MATTER HOW MUCH BLOOD GOT ON MY HANDS.
EVEN WHEN...
...IT COATED ME SO HEAVILY THAT THE WEIGHT OF IT NEVER WENT AWAY.
I WAS FINE WITH THAT.
I HAD NO REASON...
...TO WANT TO SURVIVE COMFORTABLY THERE.

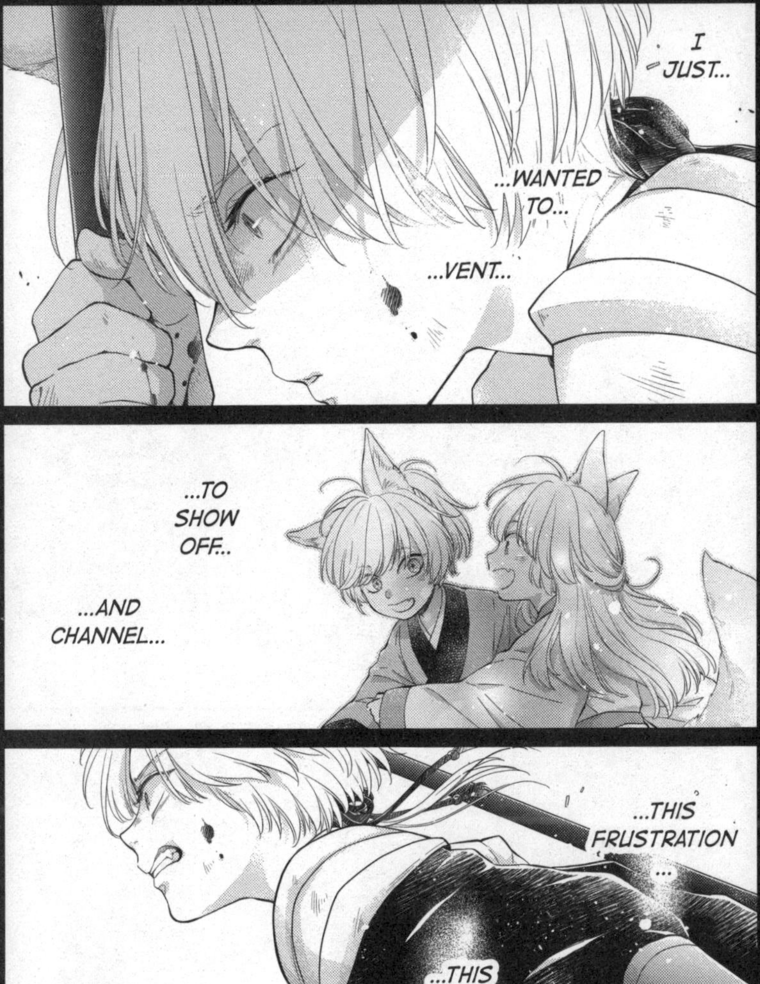
I JUST...
...WANTED TO...
...VENT...
...TO SHOW OFF...
...AND CHANNEL...
...THIS FRUSTRATION ...
...THIS LONELI-NESS...
...AND THIS ANGER.

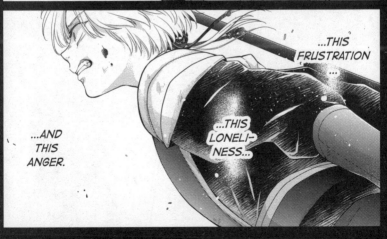

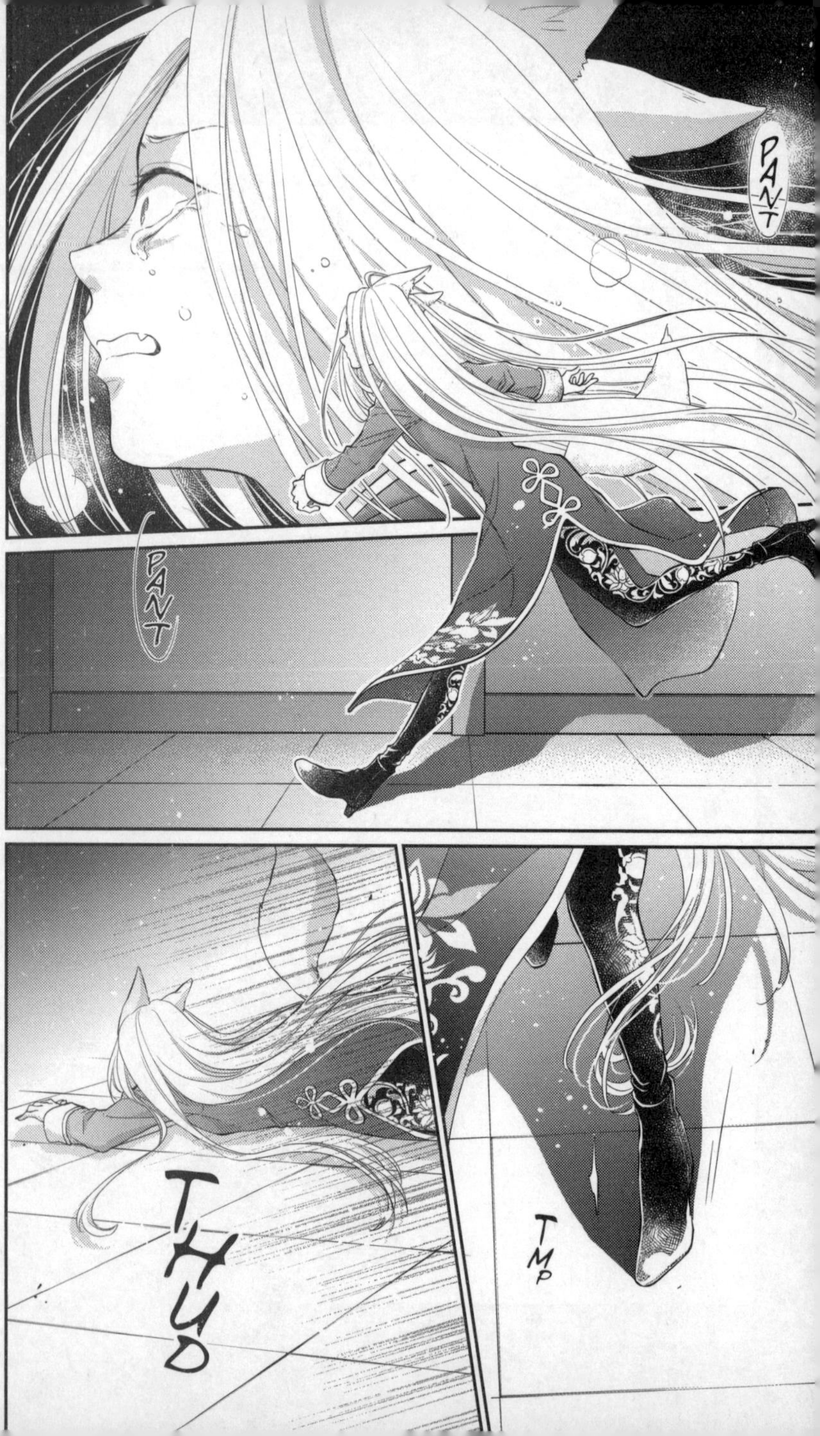
PANT
PANT
TMP
THUD

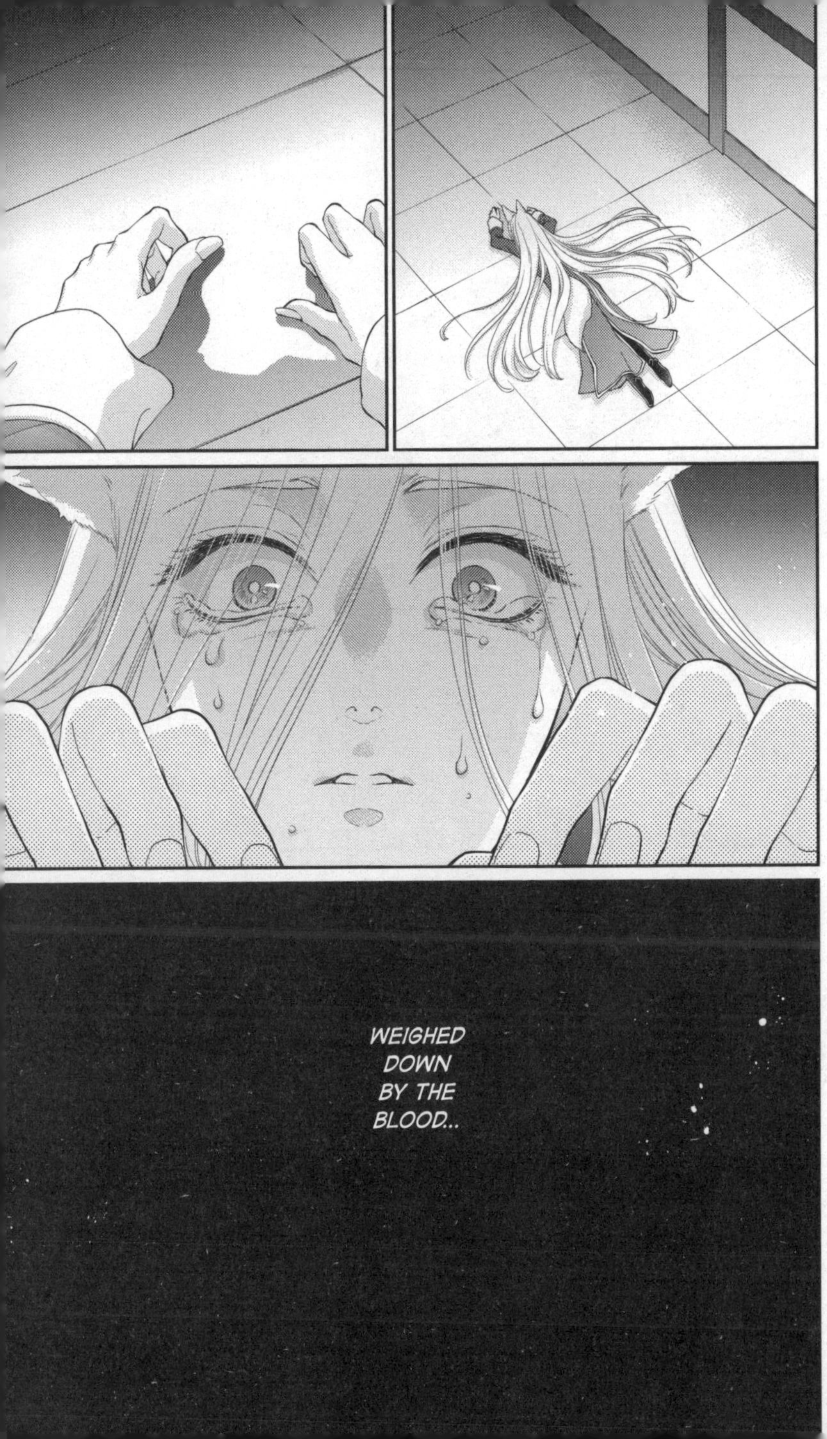
WEIGHED DOWN BY THE BLOOD...

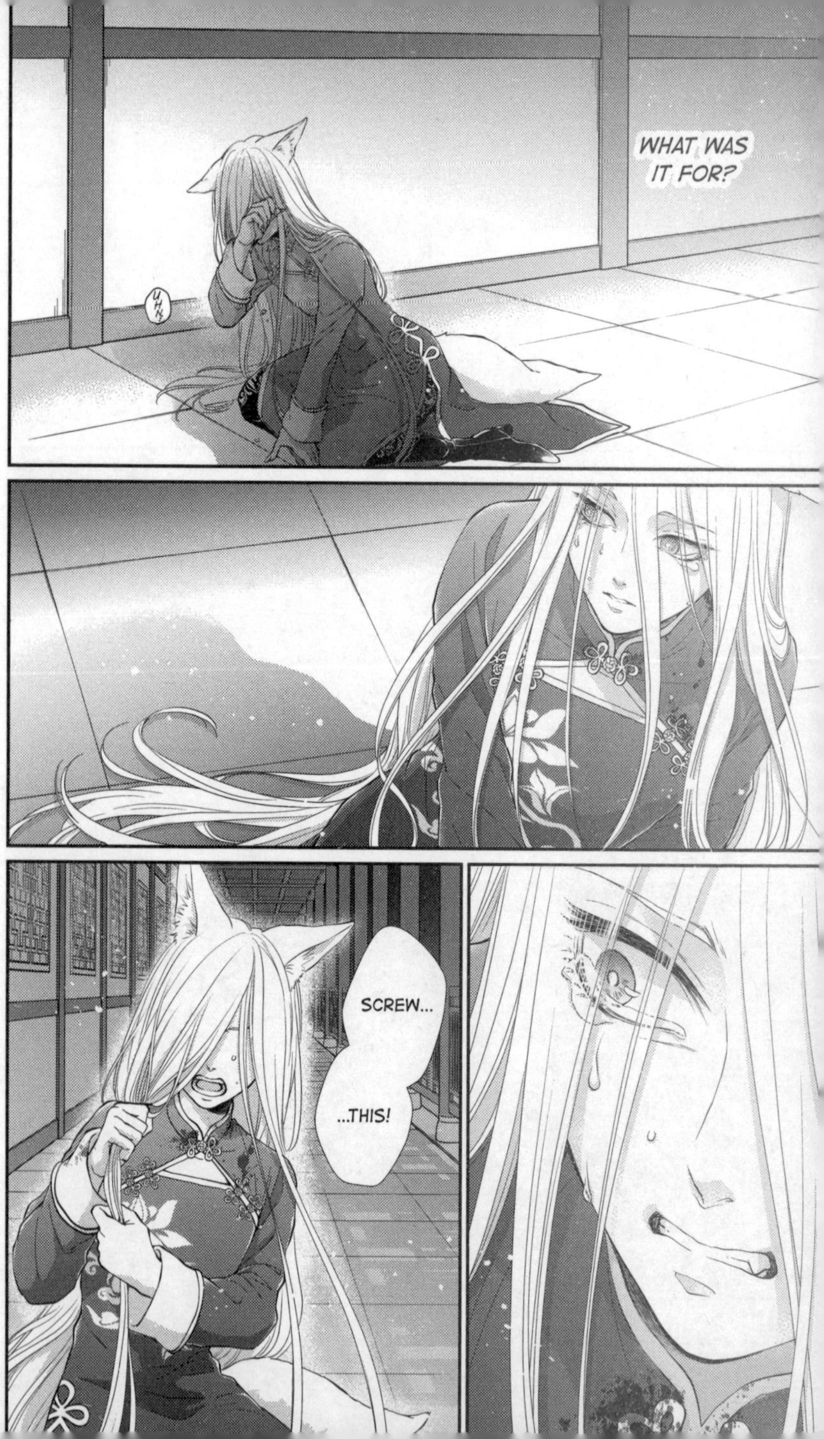
WHAT WAS IT FOR?
UHN
SCREW...
...THIS!

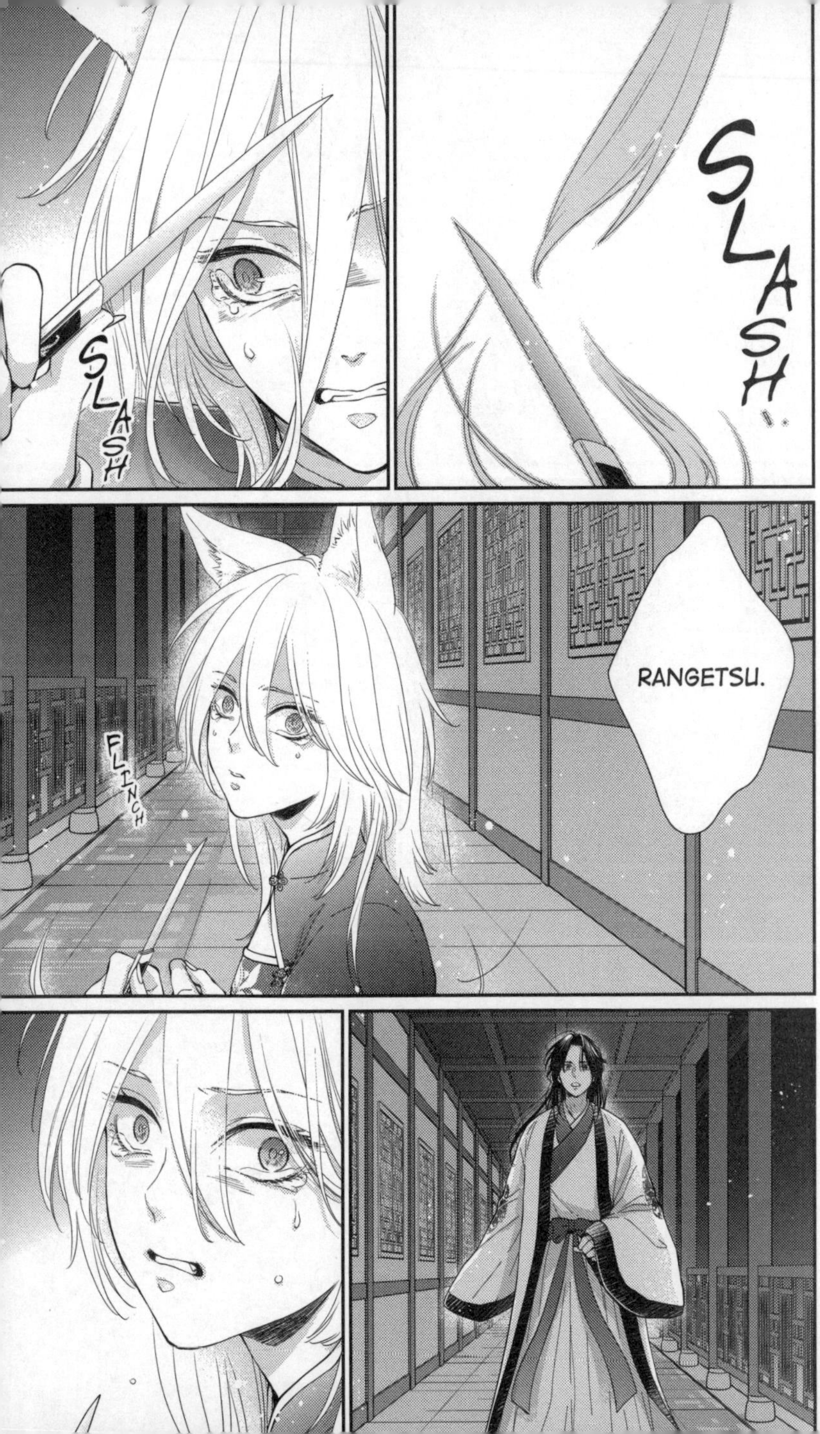
SLASH
SLASH
RANGETSU.
FLINCH

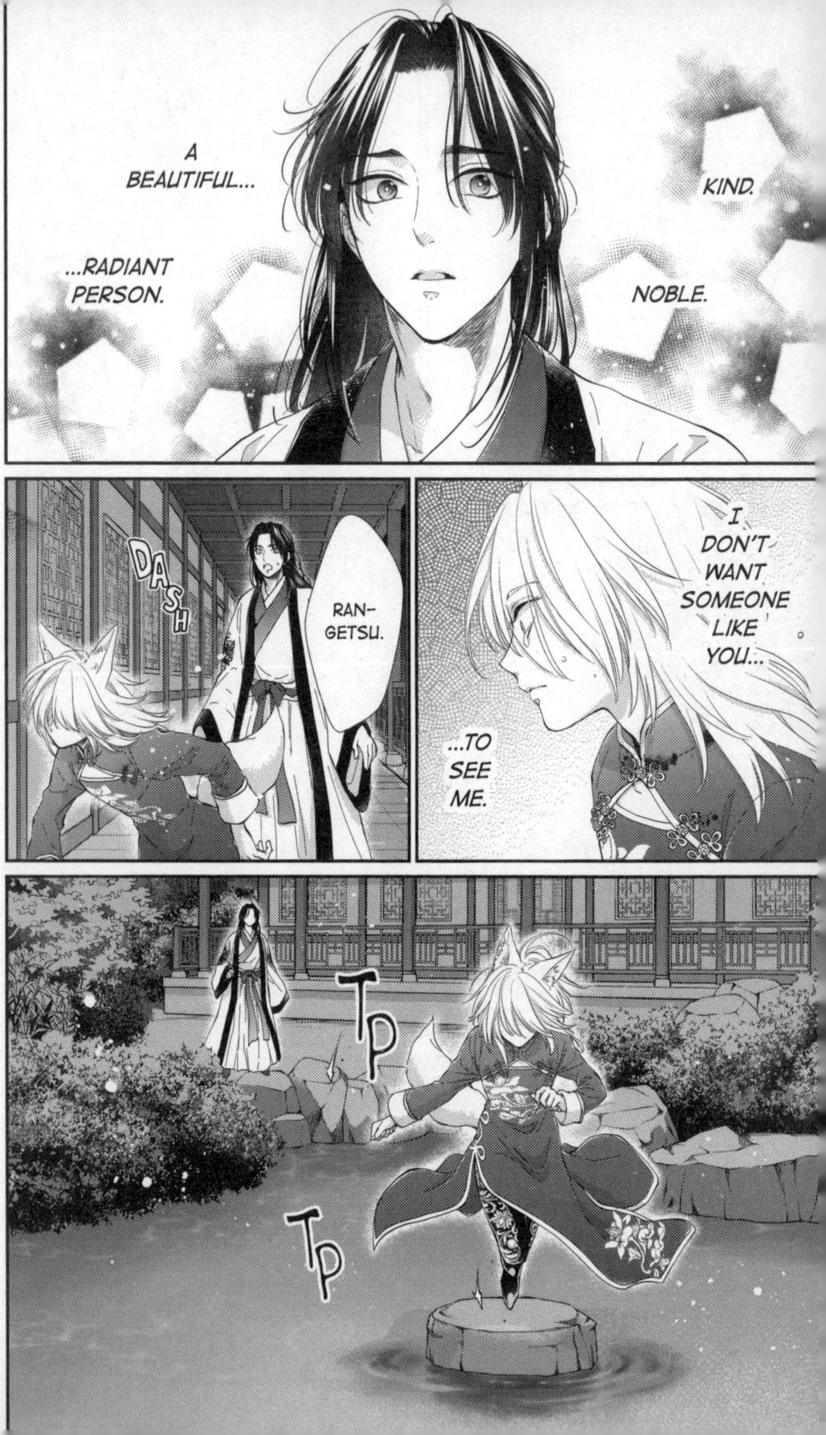
KIND.
NOBLE.
A BEAUTIFUL...
...RADIANT PERSON.
I DON'T WANT SOMEONE LIKE YOU...
...TO SEE ME.
RAN-GETSU.
DASH
TP
TP

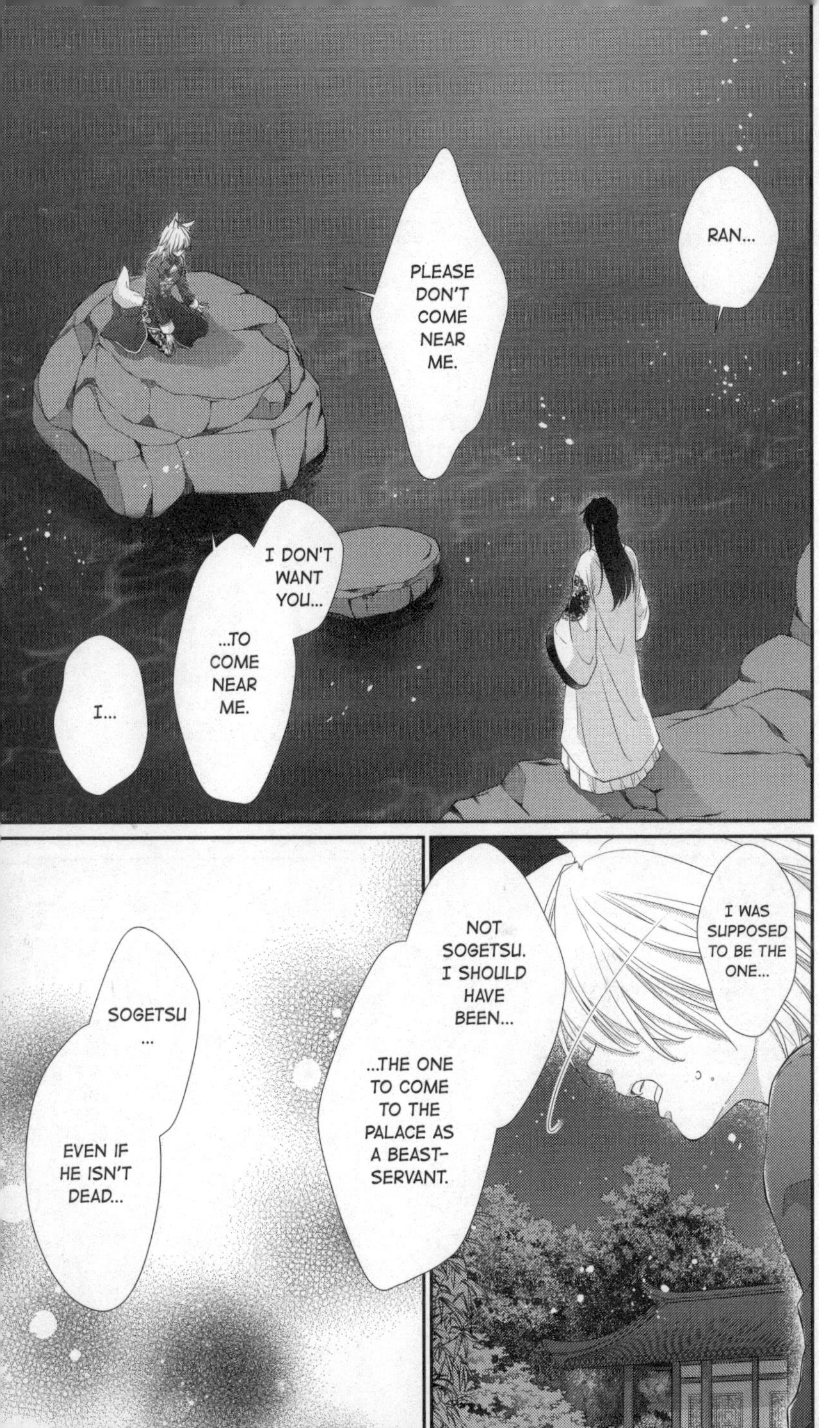
RAN...
PLEASE DON'T COME NEAR ME.
I DON'T WANT YOU...
...TO COME NEAR ME.
I...
I WAS SUPPOSED TO BE THE ONE...
NOT SOGETSU. I SHOULD HAVE BEEN...
...THE ONE TO COME TO THE PALACE AS A BEAST-SERVANT.
SOGETSU...
EVEN IF HE ISN'T DEAD...

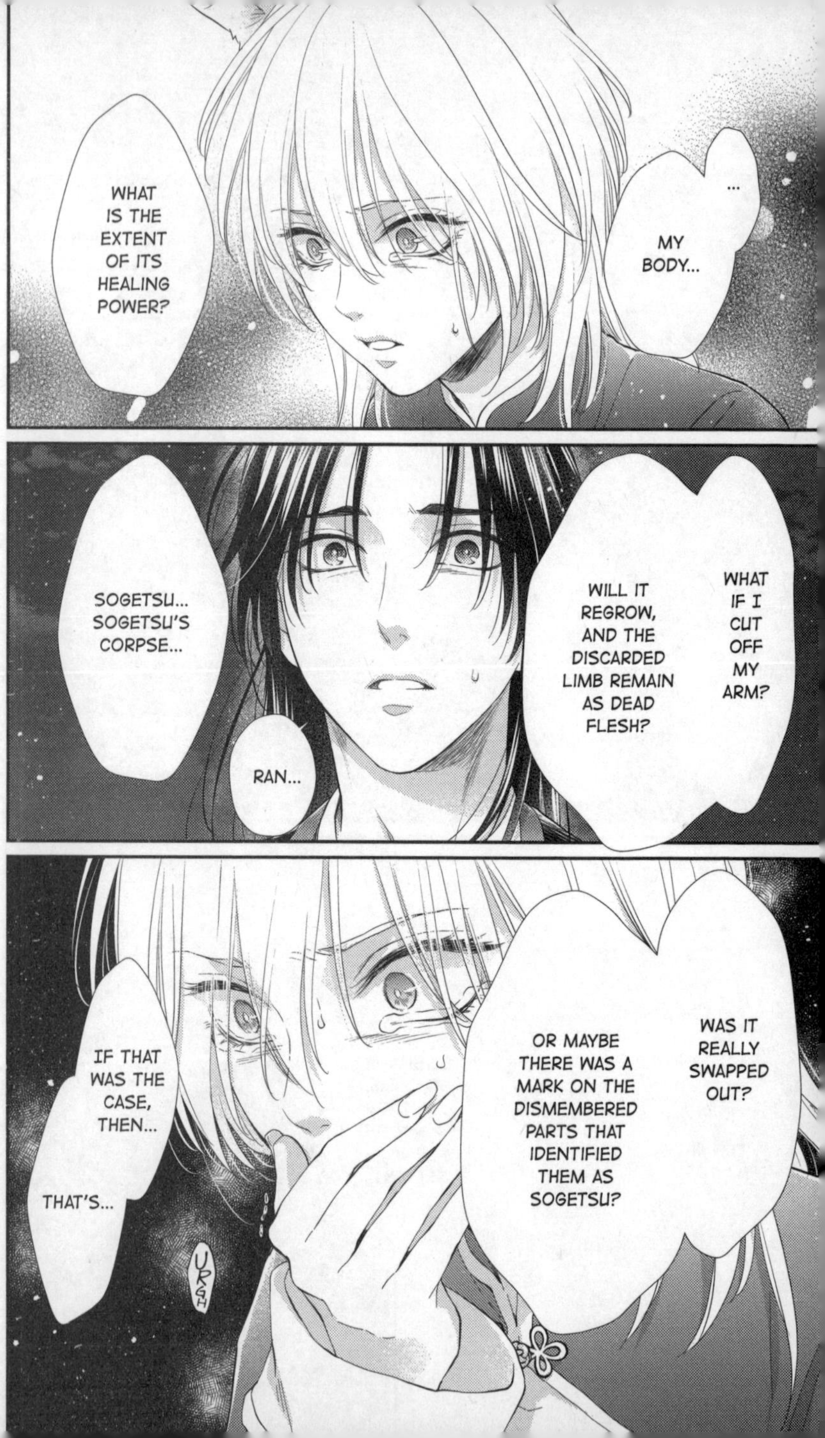
...
MY BODY...
WHAT IS THE EXTENT OF ITS HEALING POWER?
WHAT IF I CUT OFF MY ARM?
WILL IT REGROW, AND THE DISCARDED LIMB REMAIN AS DEAD FLESH?
SOGETSU... SOGETSU'S CORPSE...
RAN...
WAS IT REALLY SWAPPED OUT?
OR MAYBE THERE WAS A MARK ON THE DISMEMBERED PARTS THAT IDENTIFIED THEM AS SOGETSU?
IF THAT WAS THE CASE, THEN...
THAT'S...
URGH

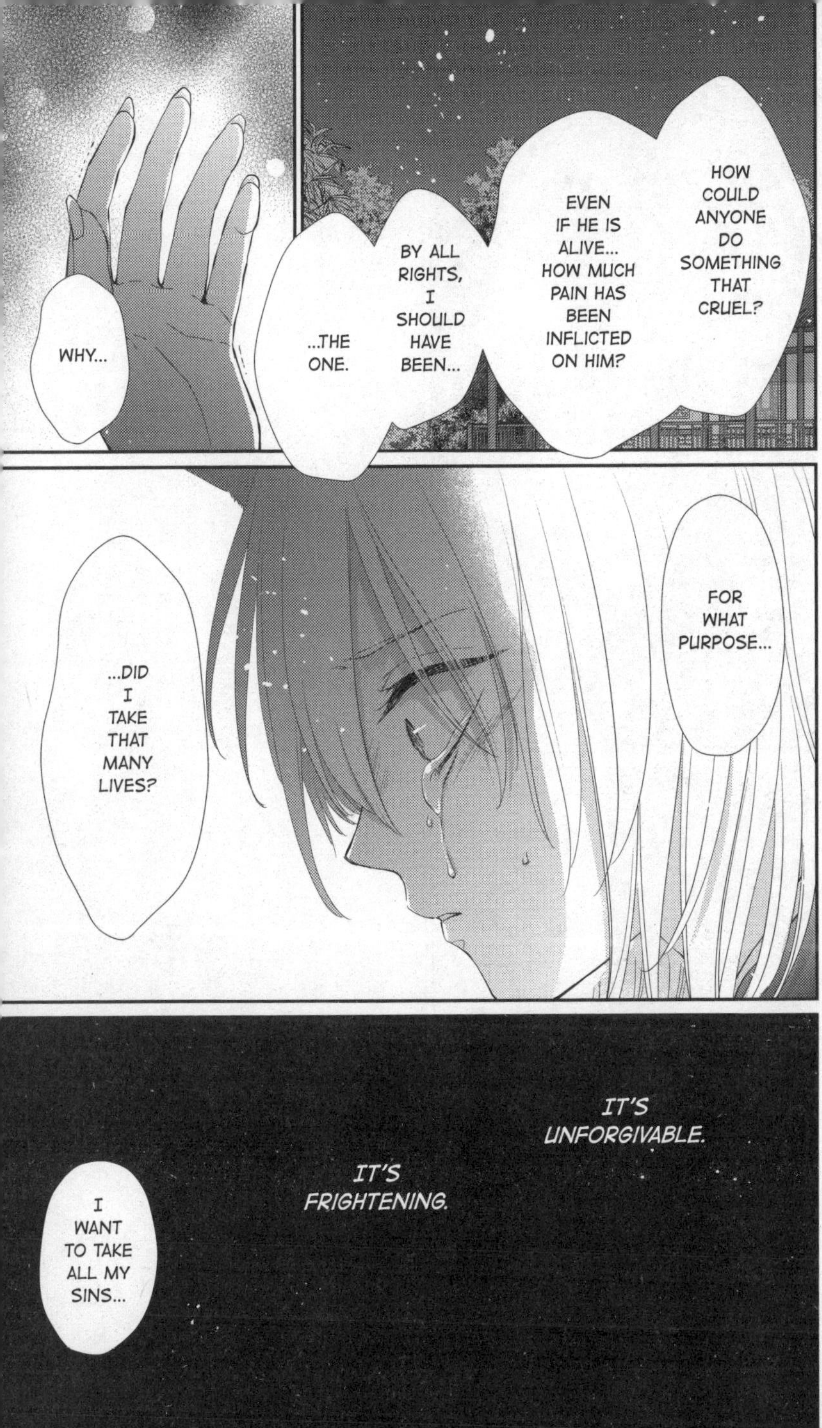
HOW COULD ANYONE DO SOMETHING THAT CRUEL?
EVEN IF HE IS ALIVE... HOW MUCH PAIN HAS BEEN INFLICTED ON HIM?
BY ALL RIGHTS, I SHOULD HAVE BEEN...
...THE ONE.
WHY...
FOR WHAT PURPOSE...
...DID I TAKE THAT MANY LIVES?
IT'S UNFORGIVABLE.
IT'S FRIGHTENING.
I WANT TO TAKE ALL MY SINS...

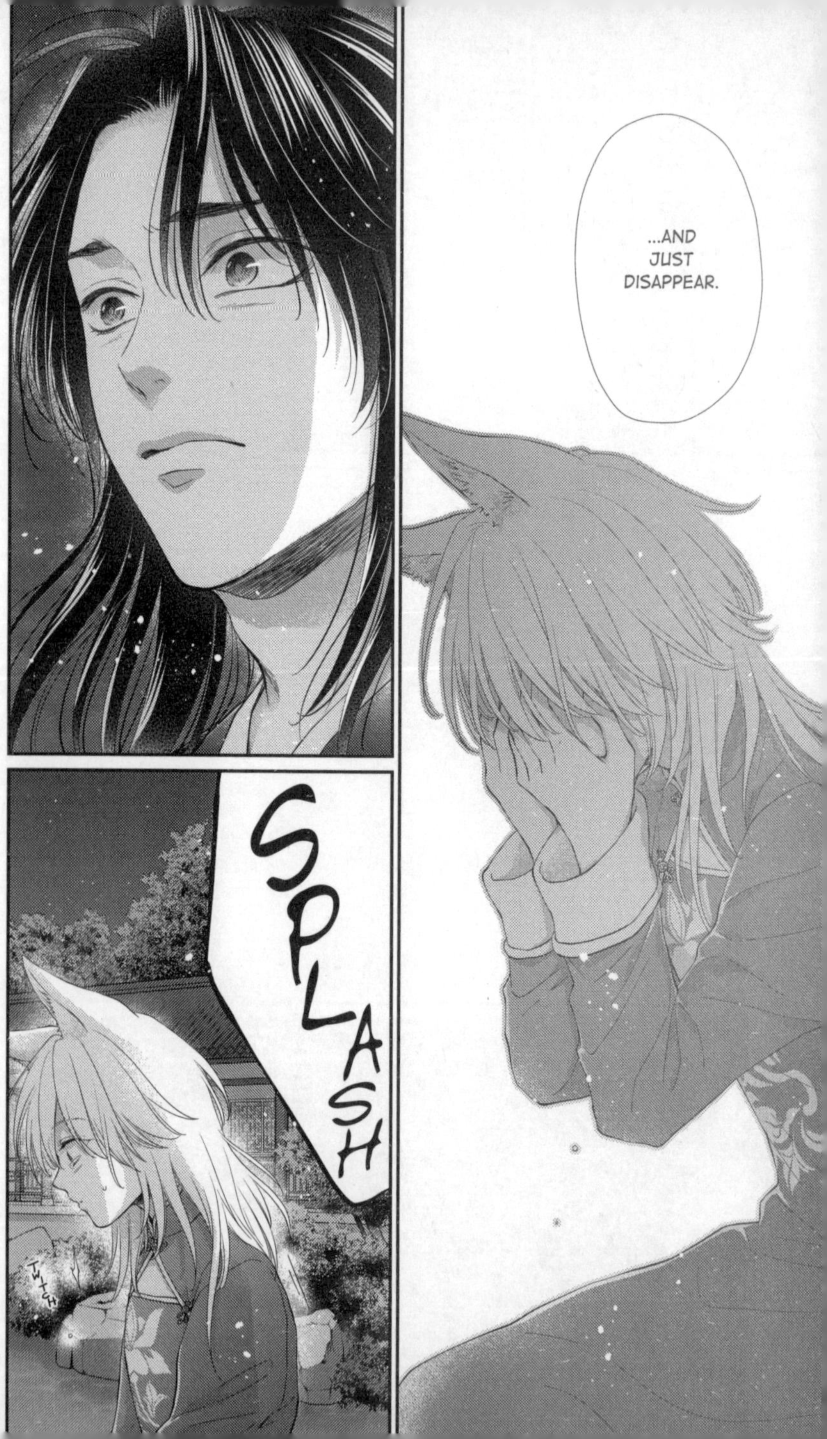
...AND JUST DISAPPEAR.
SPLASH
TWITCH

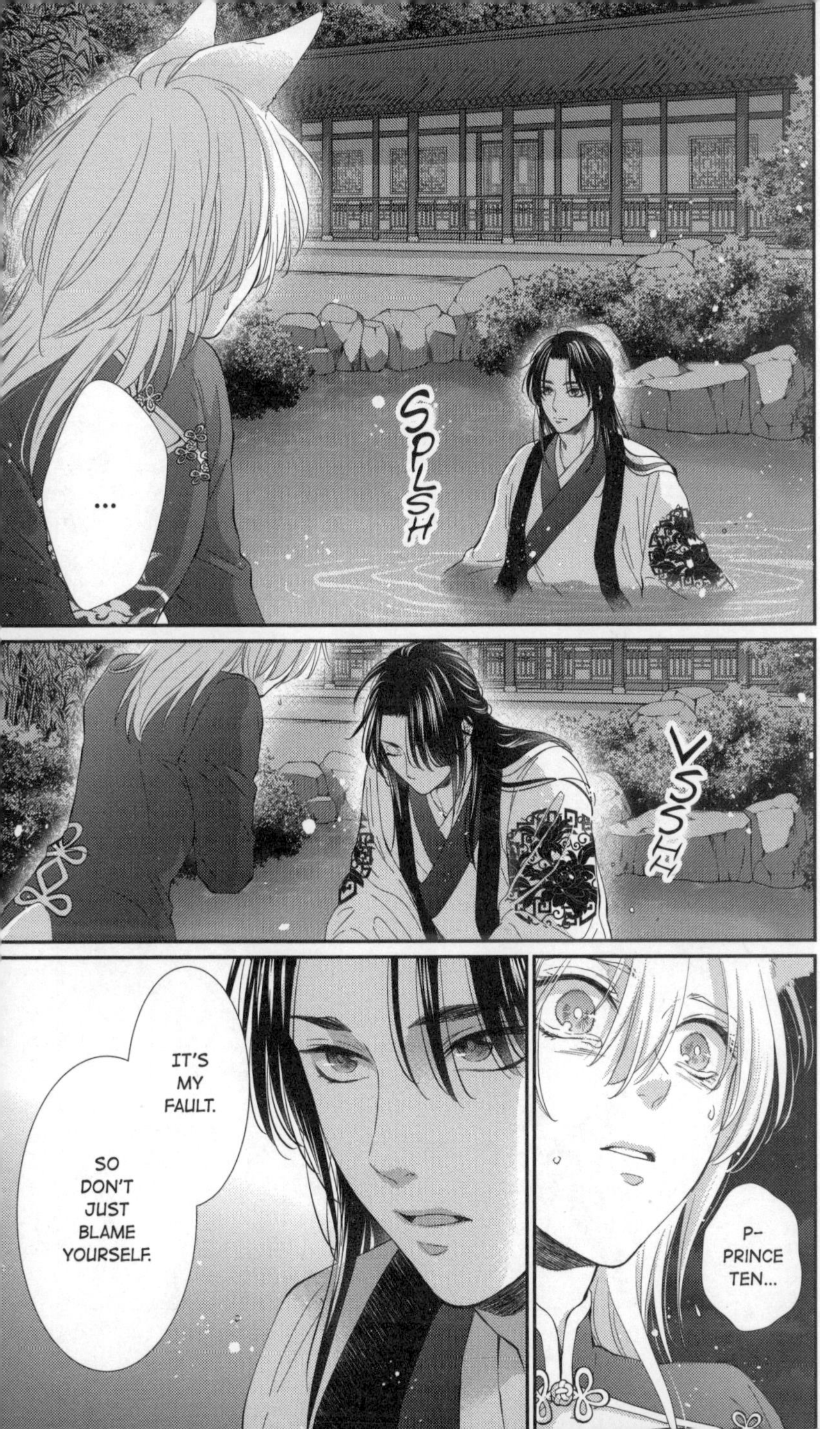
SPLSH
...
VSSH
P-PRINCE TEN...
IT'S MY FAULT.
SO DON'T JUST BLAME YOURSELF.

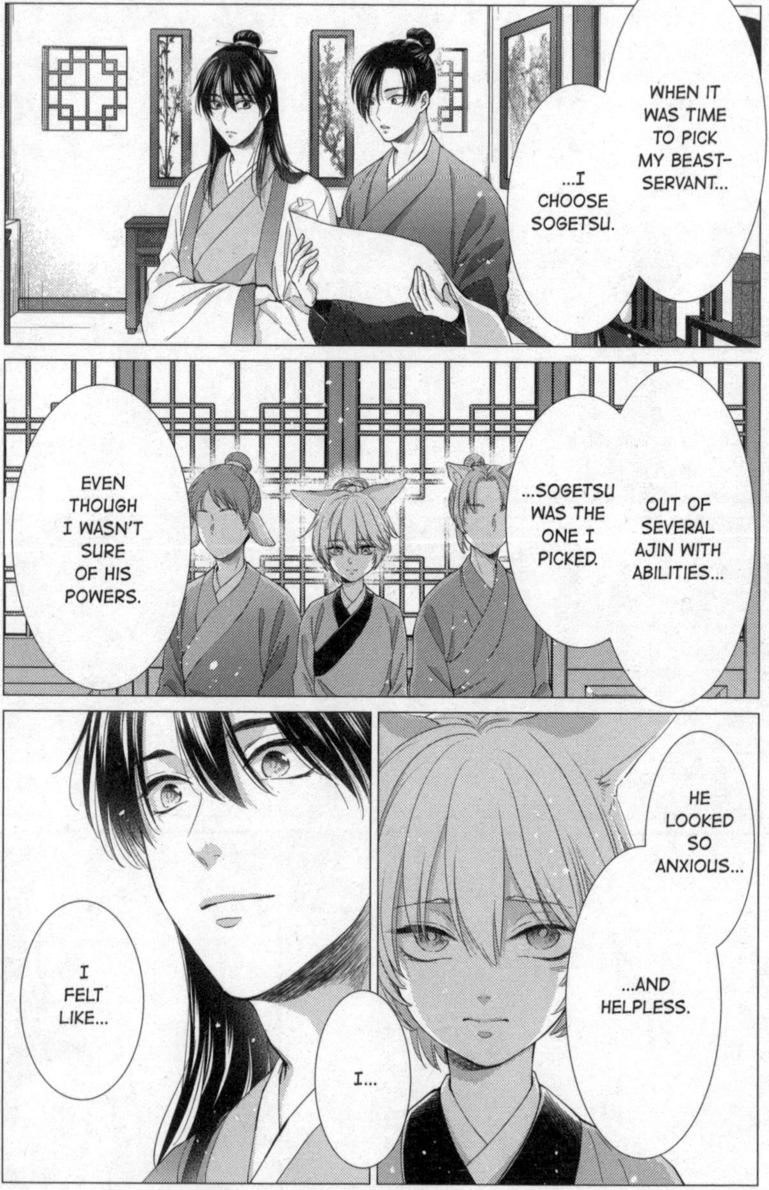
WHEN IT WAS TIME TO PICK MY BEAST-SERVANT...
...I CHOOSE SOGETSU.
OUT OF SEVERAL AJIN WITH ABILITIES...
...SOGETSU WAS THE ONE I PICKED.
EVEN THOUGH I WASN'T SURE OF HIS POWERS.
HE LOOKED SO ANXIOUS...
...AND HELPLESS.
I...
I FELT LIKE...

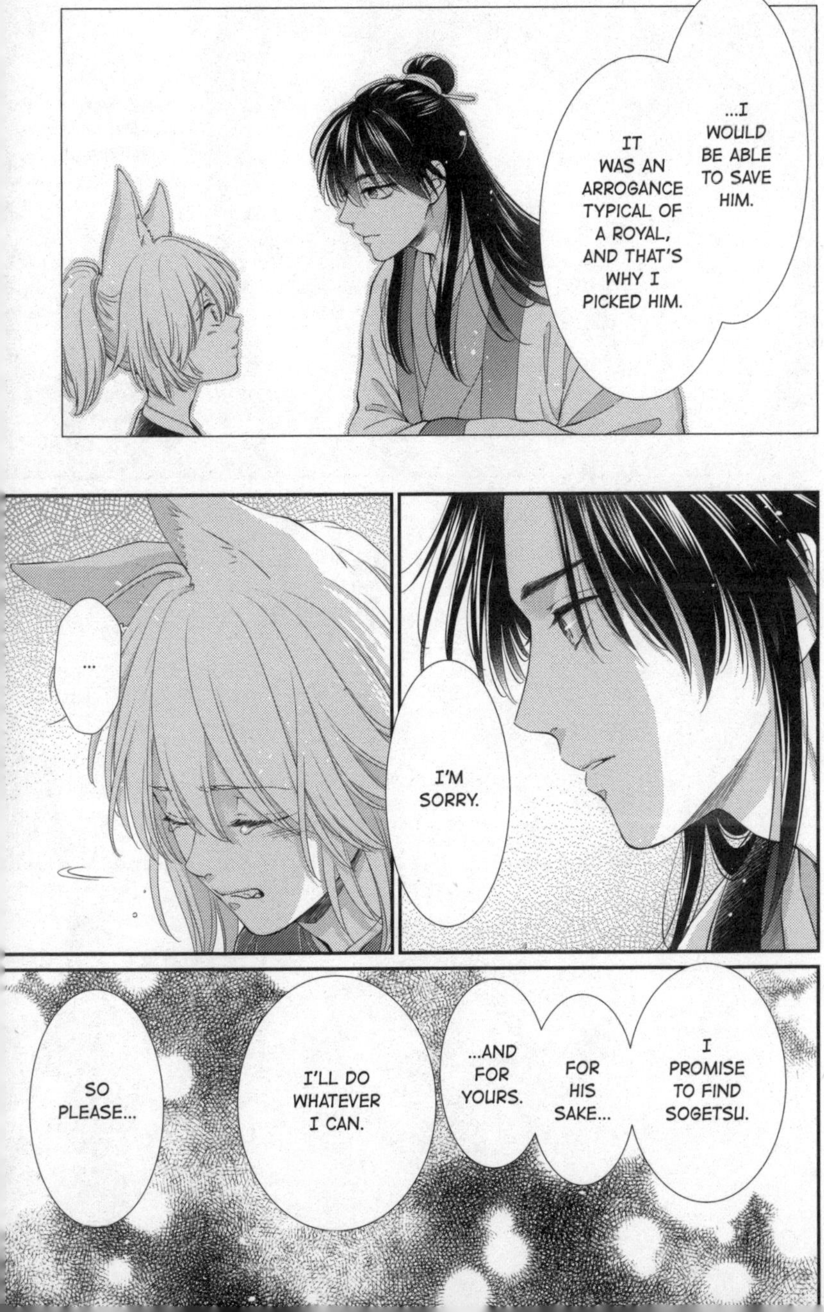
...I WOULD BE ABLE TO SAVE HIM.
IT WAS AN ARROGANCE TYPICAL OF A ROYAL, AND THAT'S WHY I PICKED HIM.
I'M SORRY.
...
I PROMISE TO FIND SOGETSU.
FOR HIS SAKE...
...AND FOR YOURS.
I'LL DO WHATEVER I CAN.
SO PLEASE...

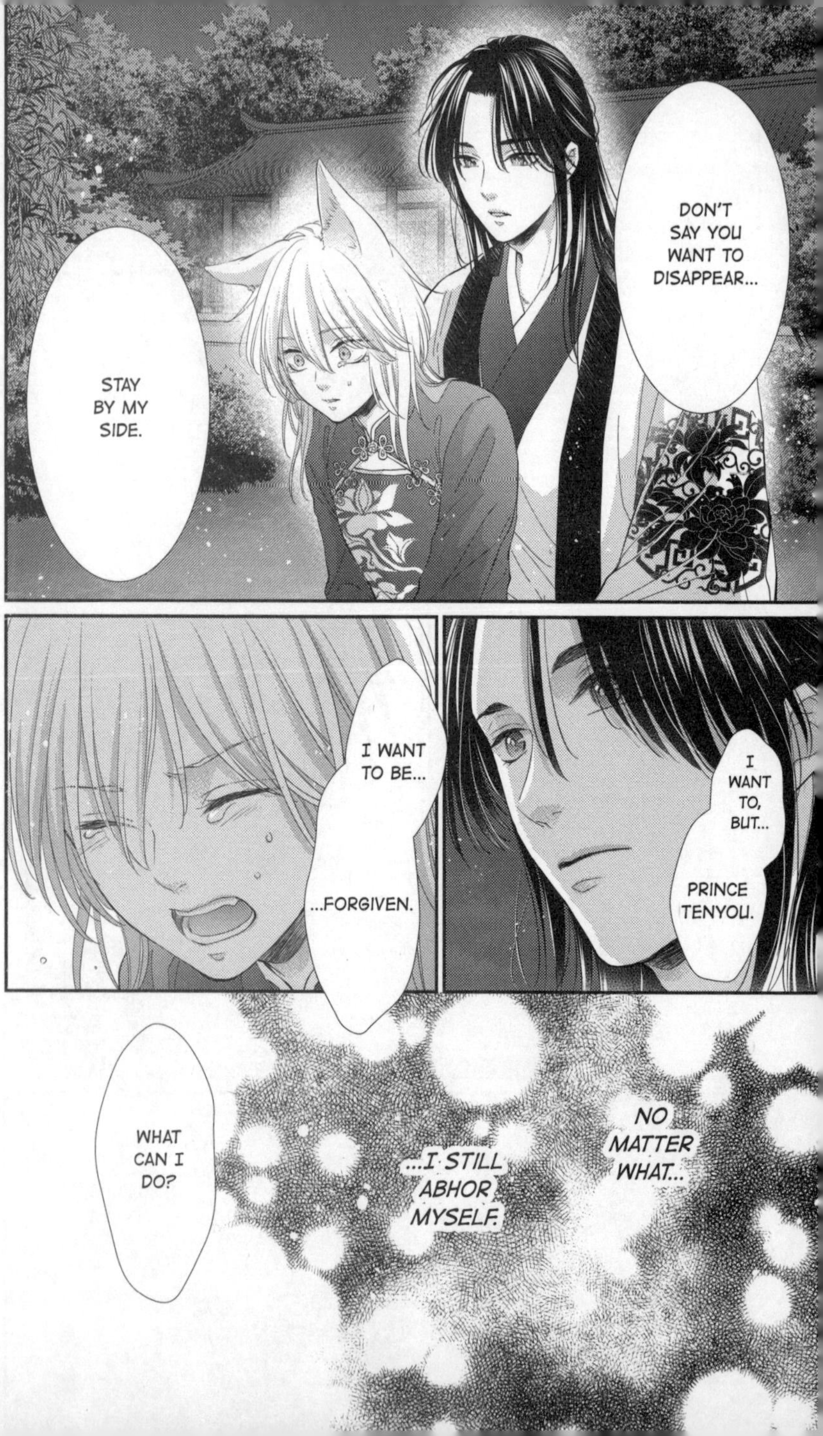
DON'T SAY YOU WANT TO DISAPPEAR...
STAY BY MY SIDE.
I WANT TO, BUT...
PRINCE TENYOU.
I WANT TO BE...
...FORGIVEN.
NO MATTER WHAT...
...I STILL ABHOR MYSELF.
WHAT CAN I DO?

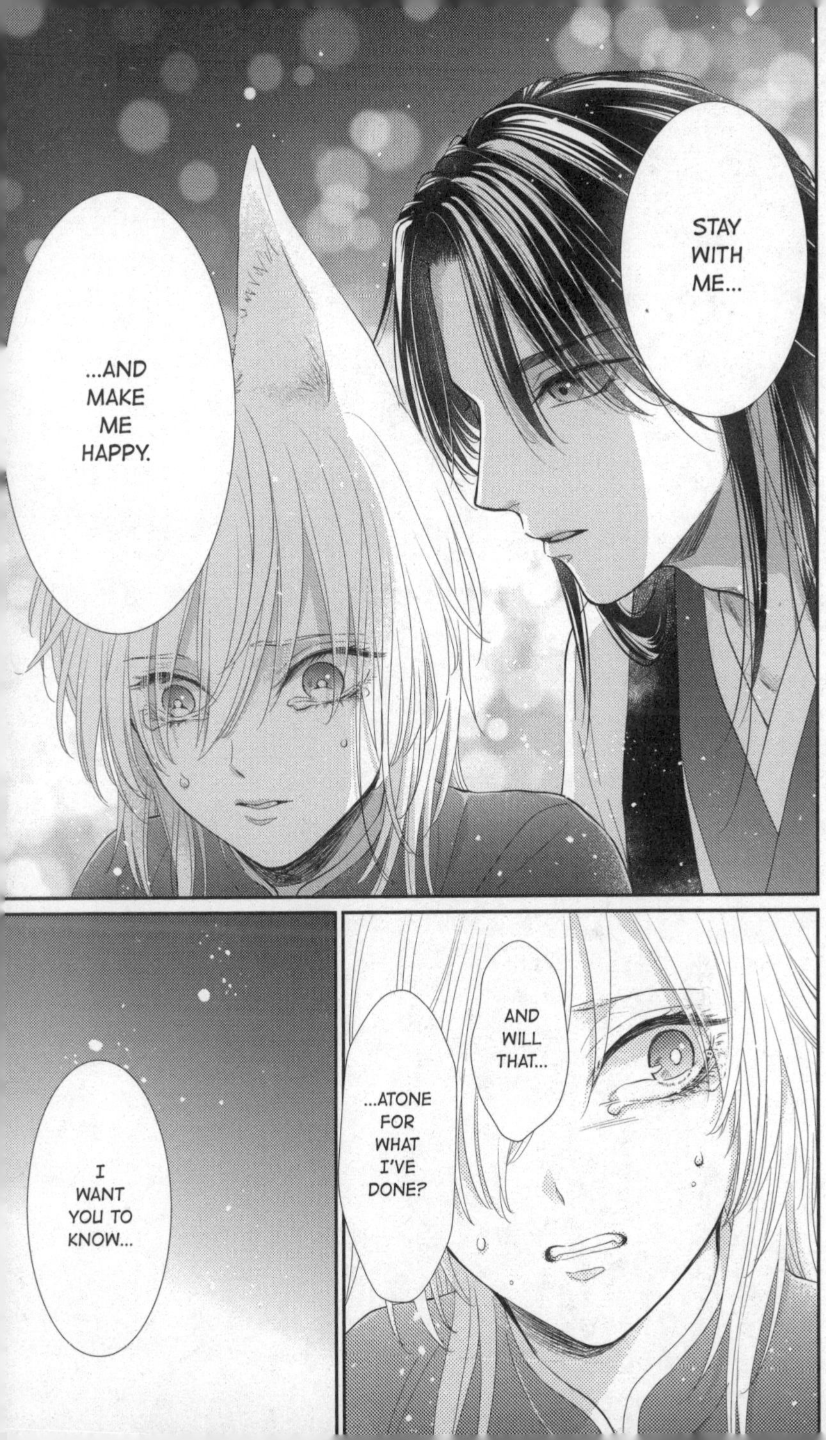
STAY WITH ME...
...AND MAKE ME HAPPY.
AND WILL THAT...
...ATONE FOR WHAT I'VE DONE?
I WANT YOU TO KNOW...

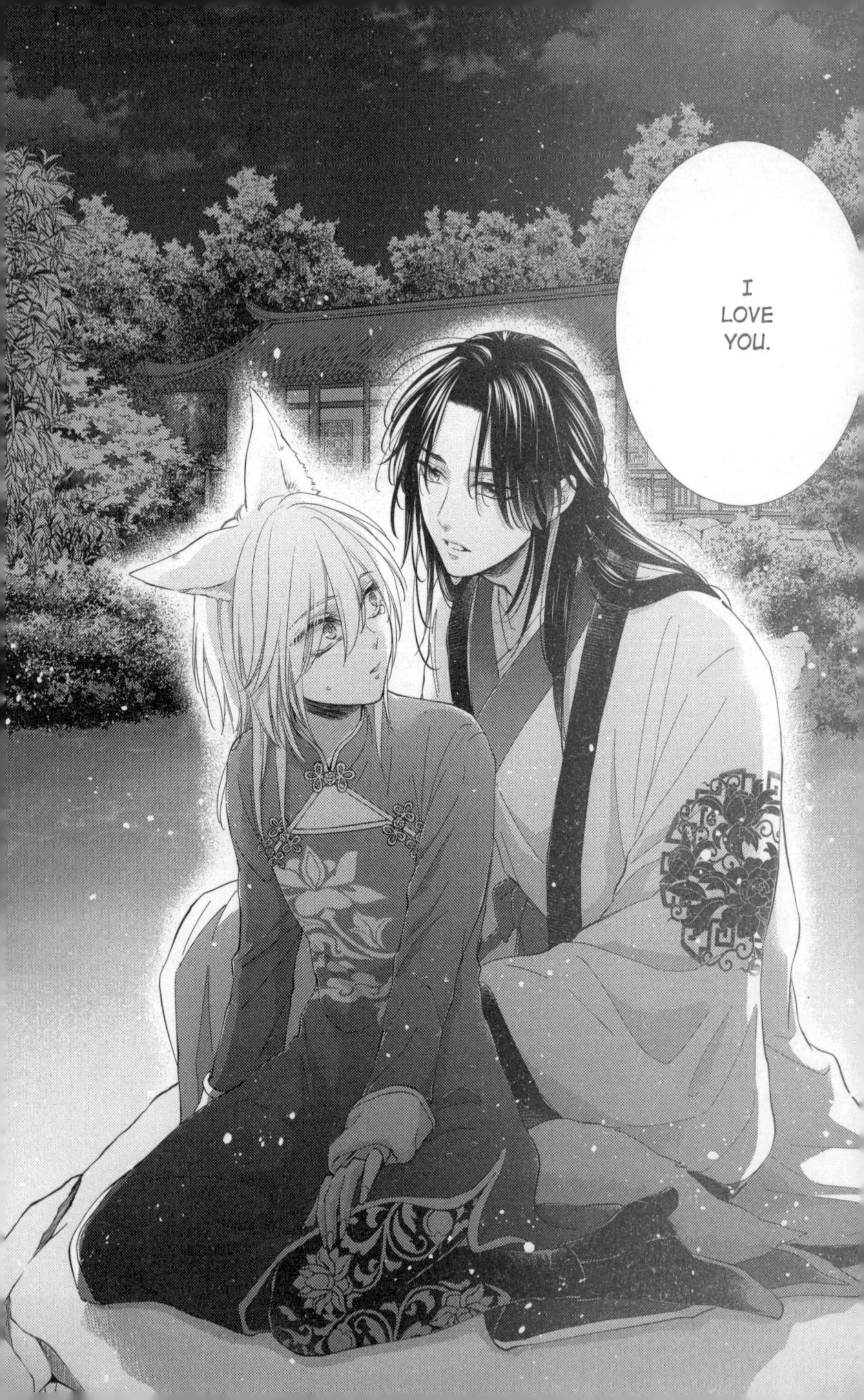
I LOVE YOU.

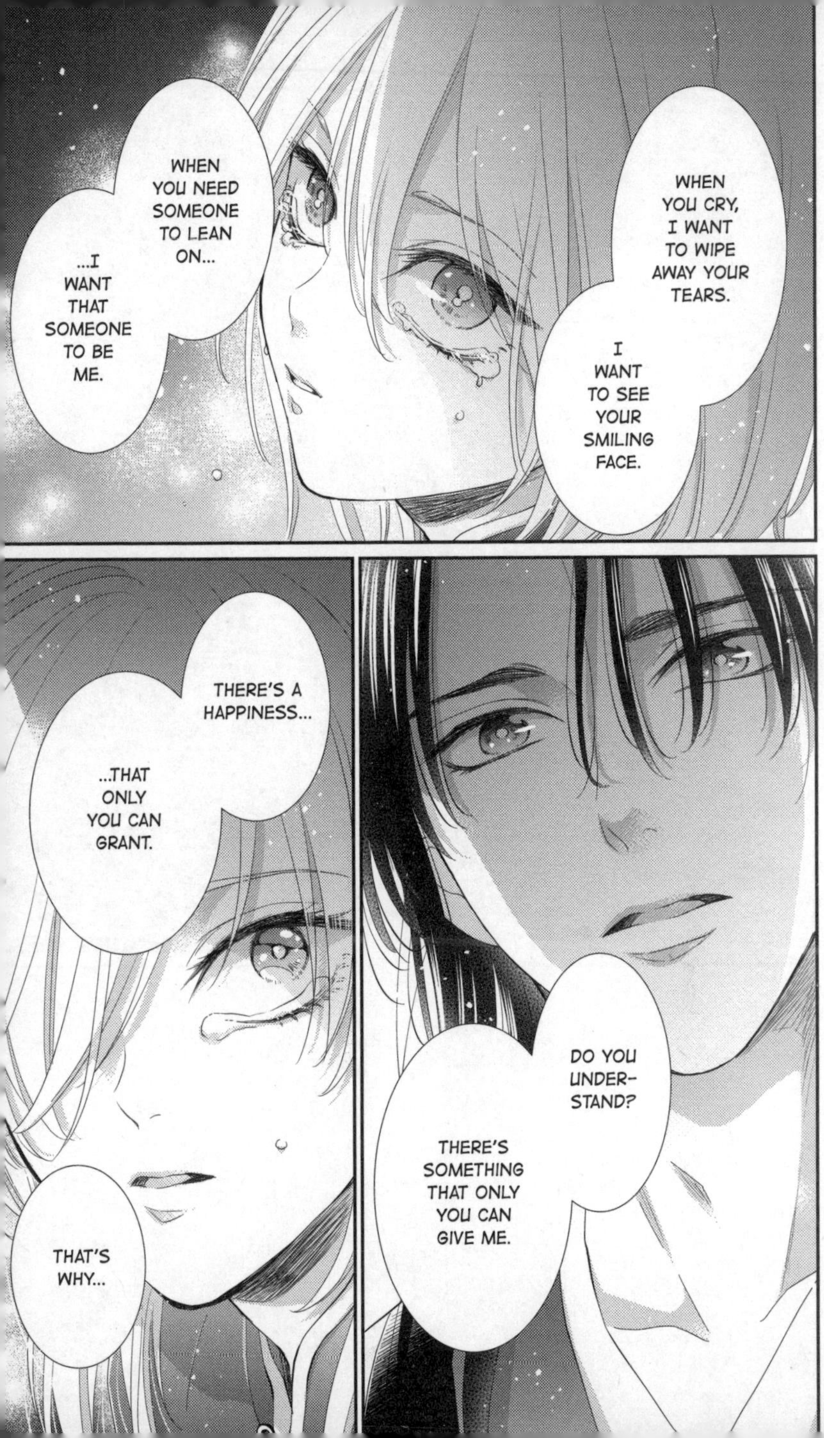
WHEN YOU CRY, I WANT TO WIPE AWAY YOUR TEARS.
I WANT TO SEE YOUR SMILING FACE.
WHEN YOU NEED SOMEONE TO LEAN ON...
...I WANT THAT SOMEONE TO BE ME.
DO YOU UNDER-STAND?
THERE'S SOMETHING THAT ONLY YOU CAN GIVE ME.
THERE'S A HAPPINESS...
...THAT ONLY YOU CAN GRANT.
THAT'S WHY...

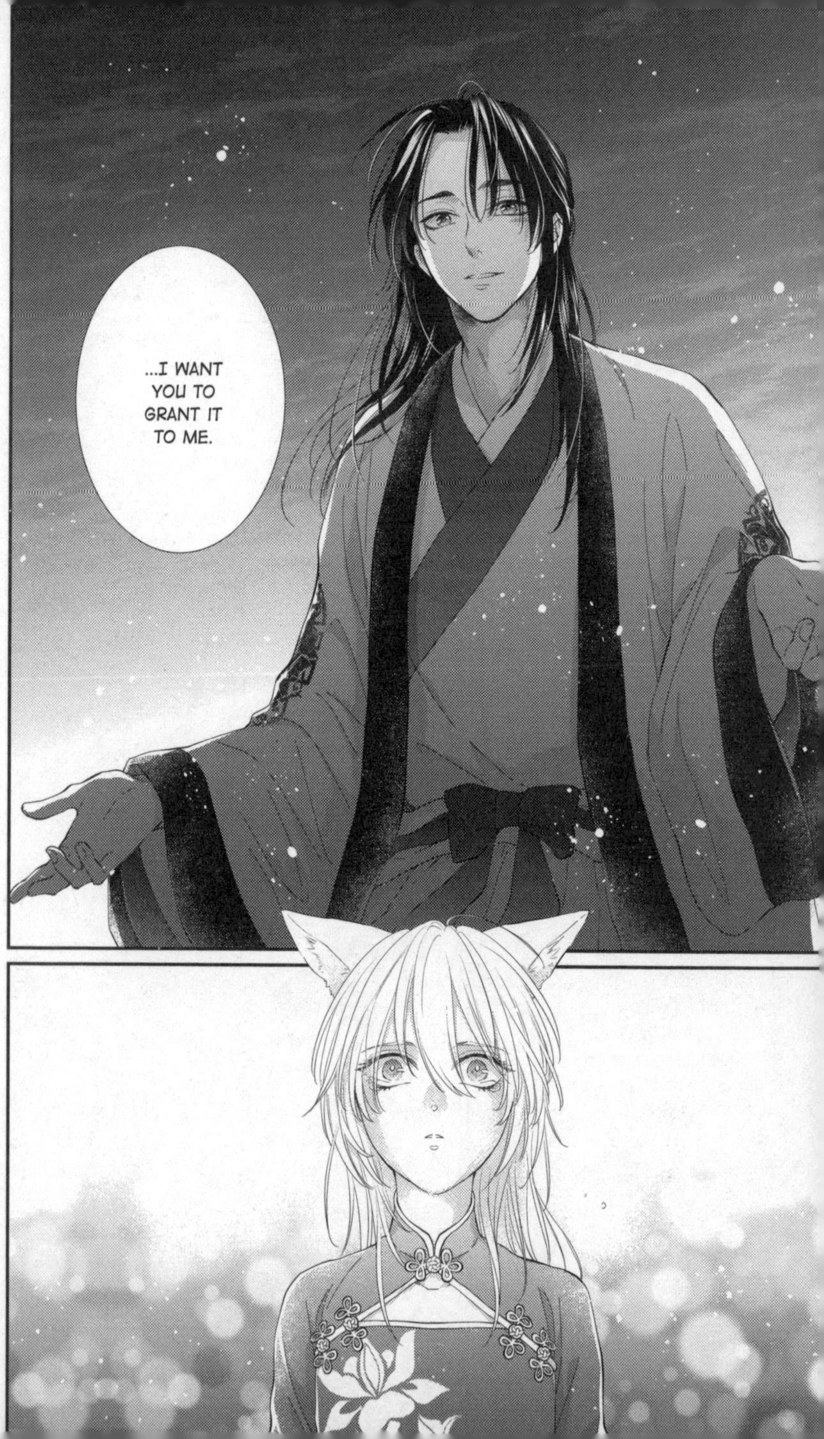
...I WANT YOU TO GRANT IT TO ME.

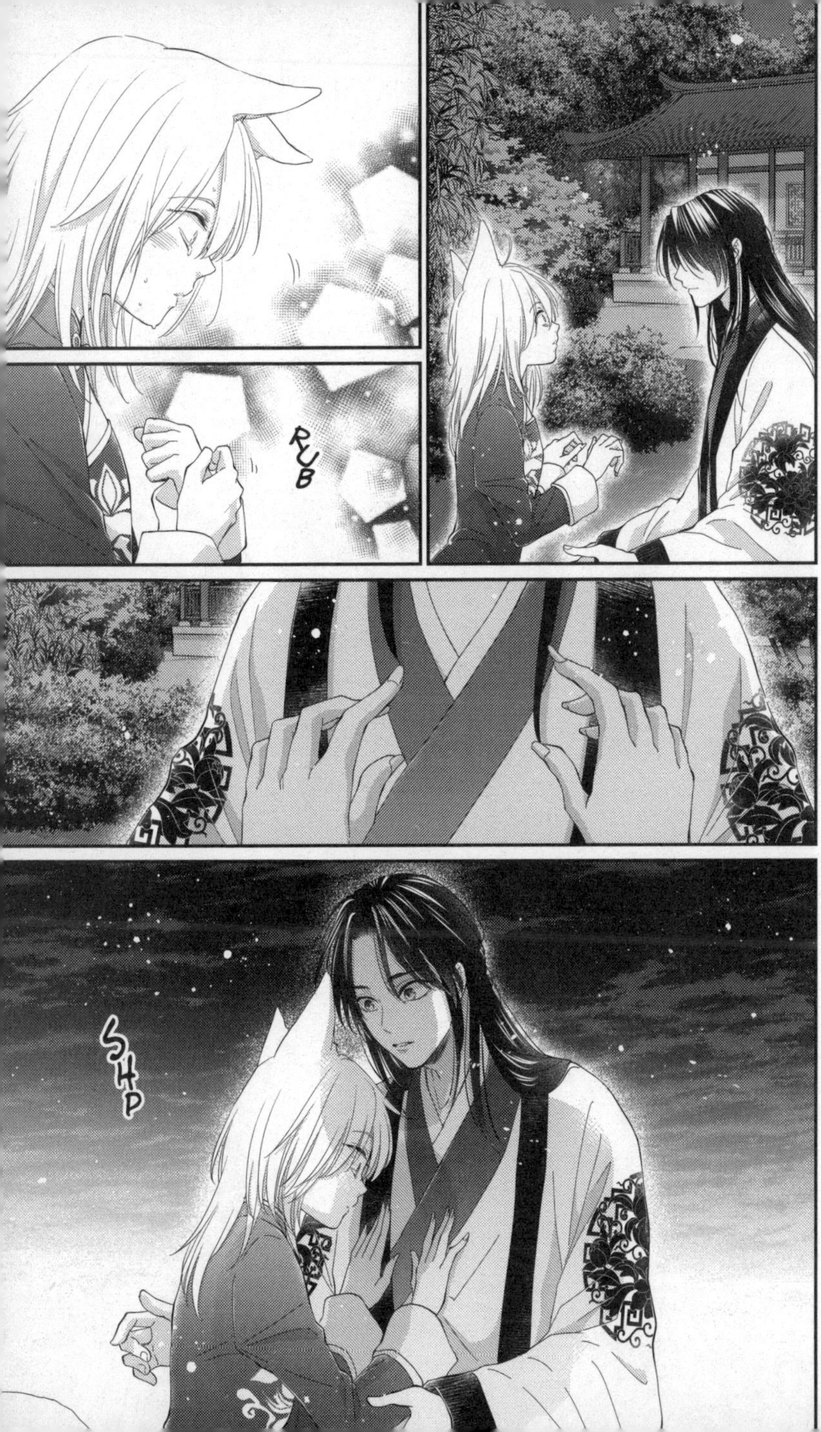
RUB
SHP

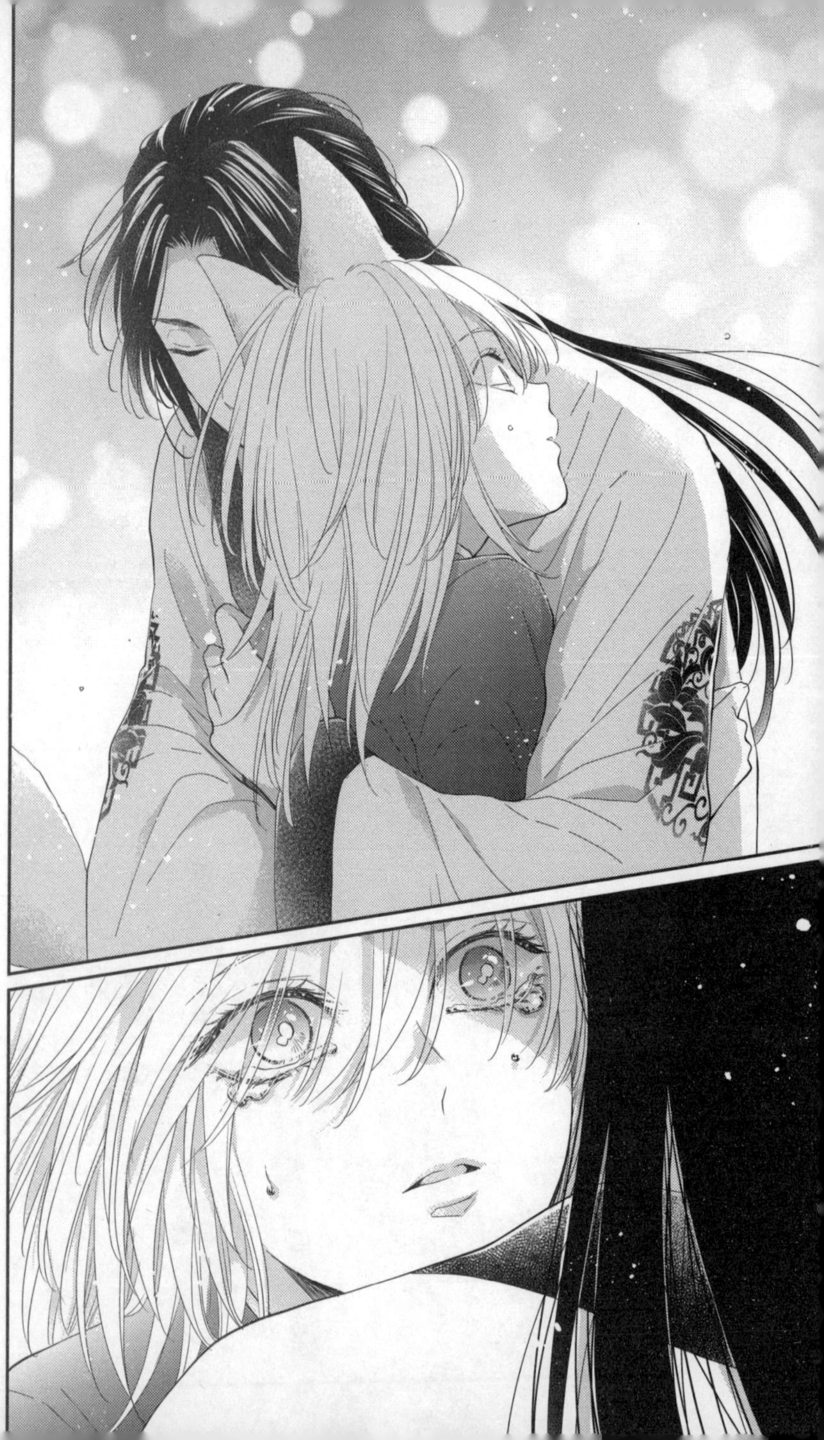

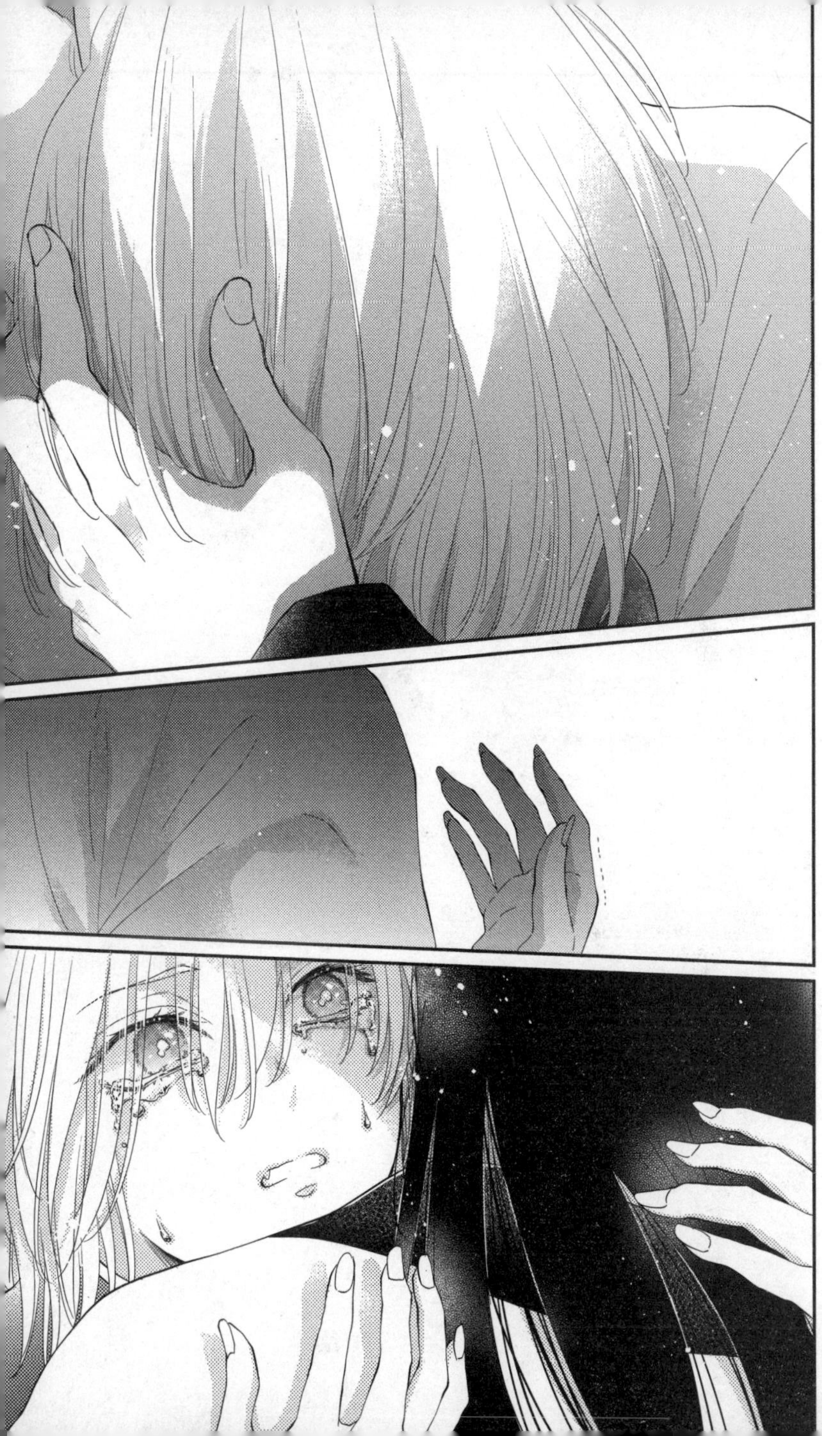

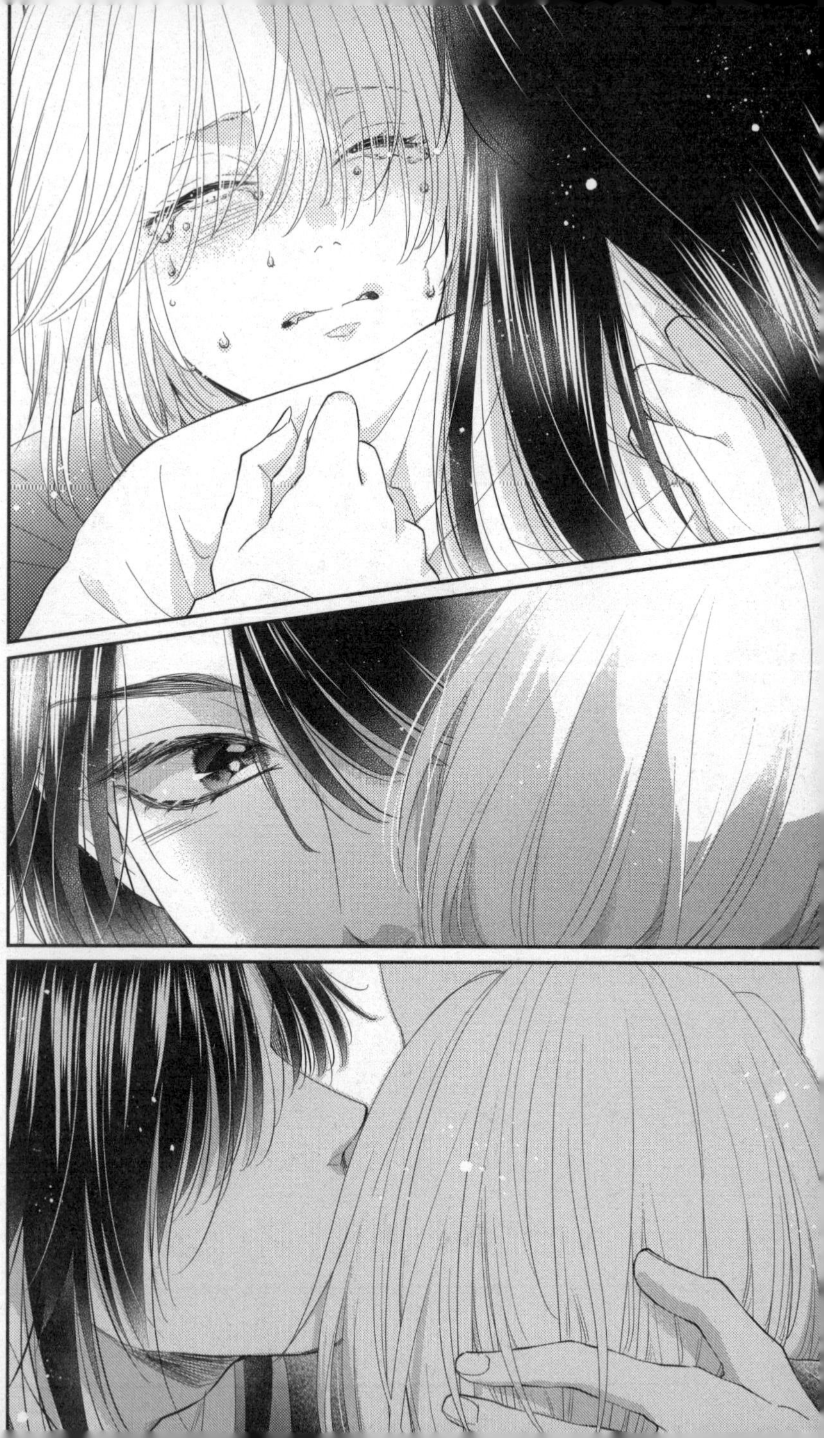

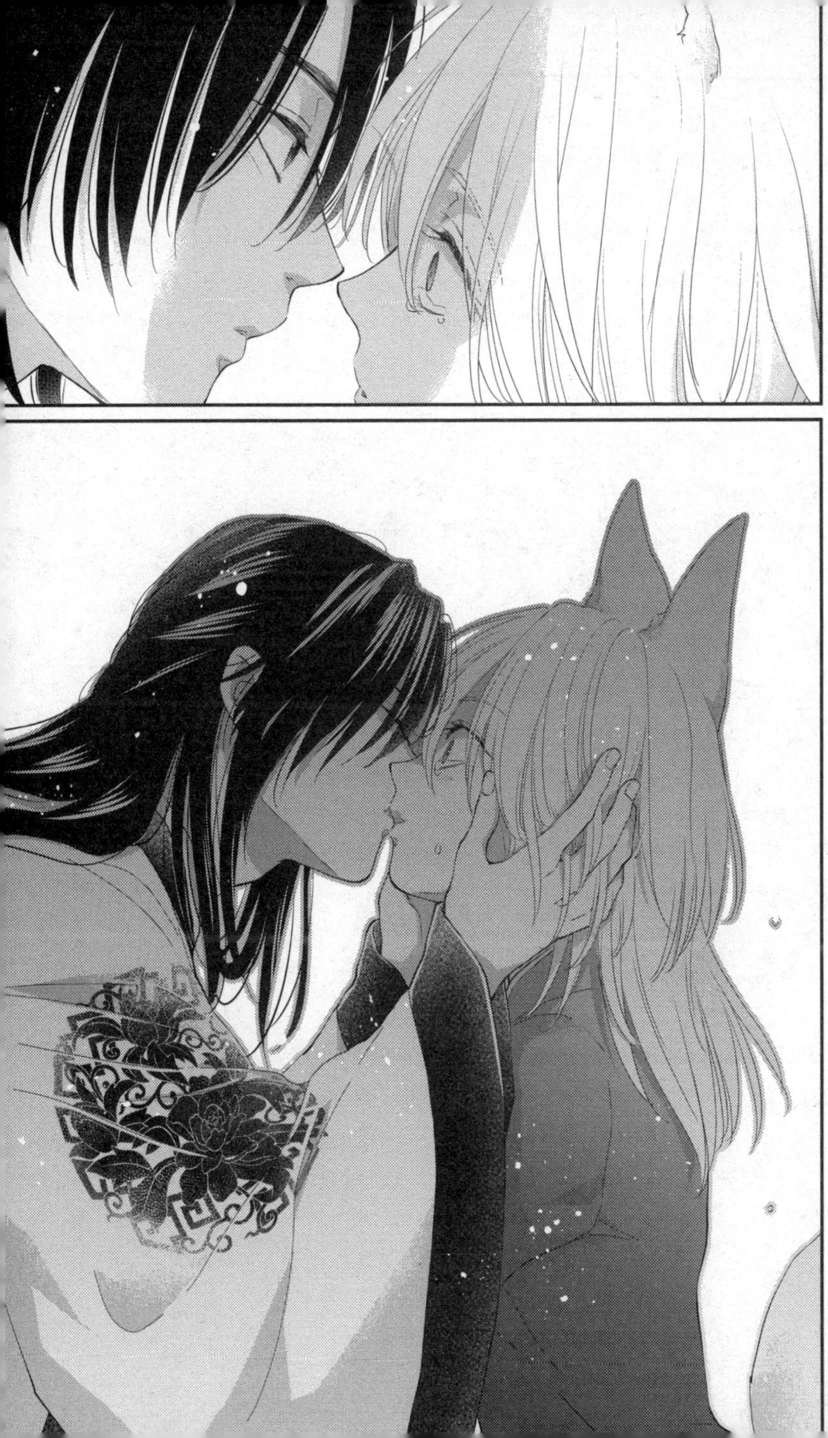

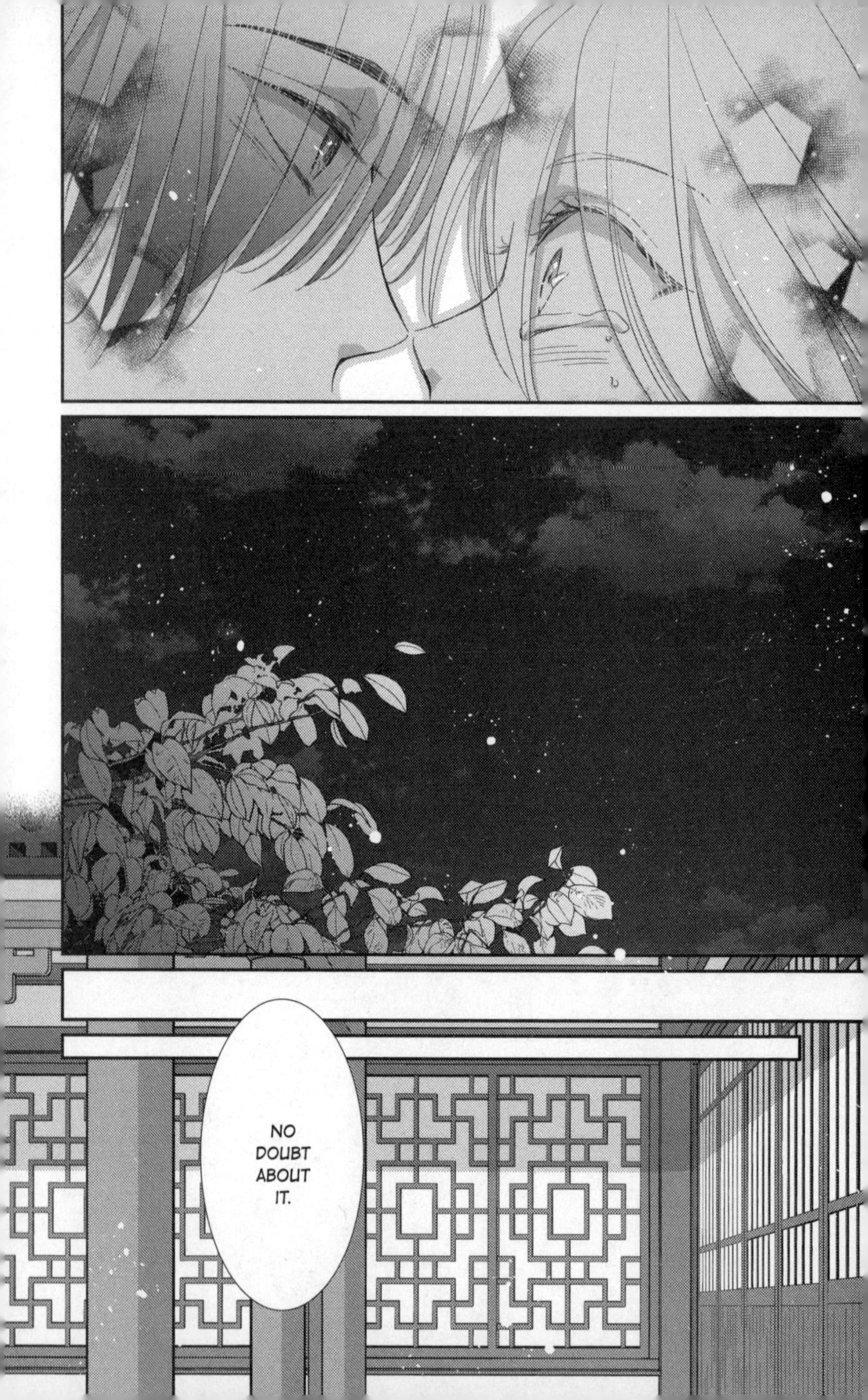
NO DOUBT ABOUT IT.

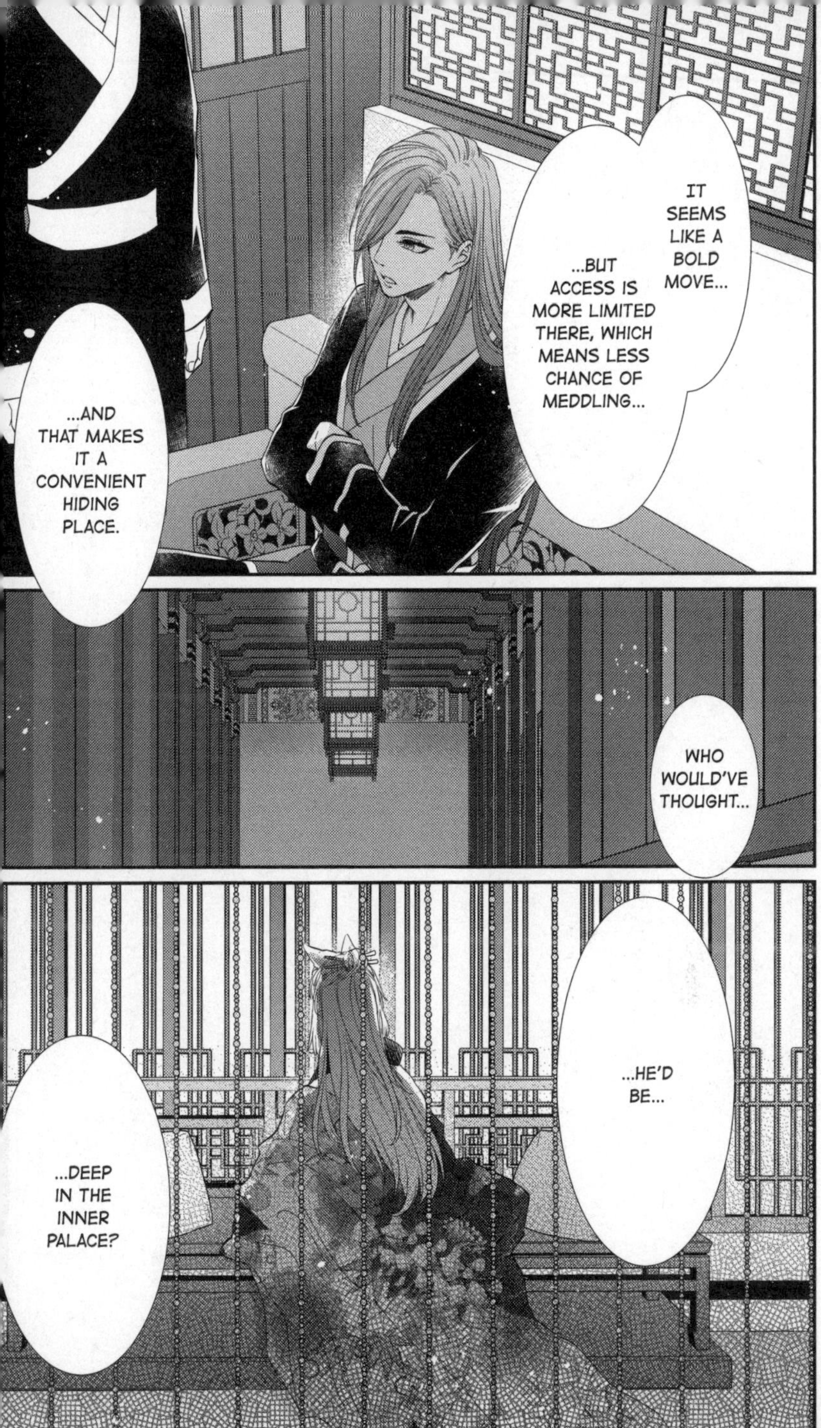
IT SEEMS LIKE A BOLD MOVE...
...BUT ACCESS IS MORE LIMITED THERE, WHICH MEANS LESS CHANCE OF MEDDLING...
...AND THAT MAKES IT A CONVENIENT HIDING PLACE.
WHO WOULD'VE THOUGHT...
...HE'D BE...
...DEEP IN THE INNER PALACE?

THE
KING'S
Beast

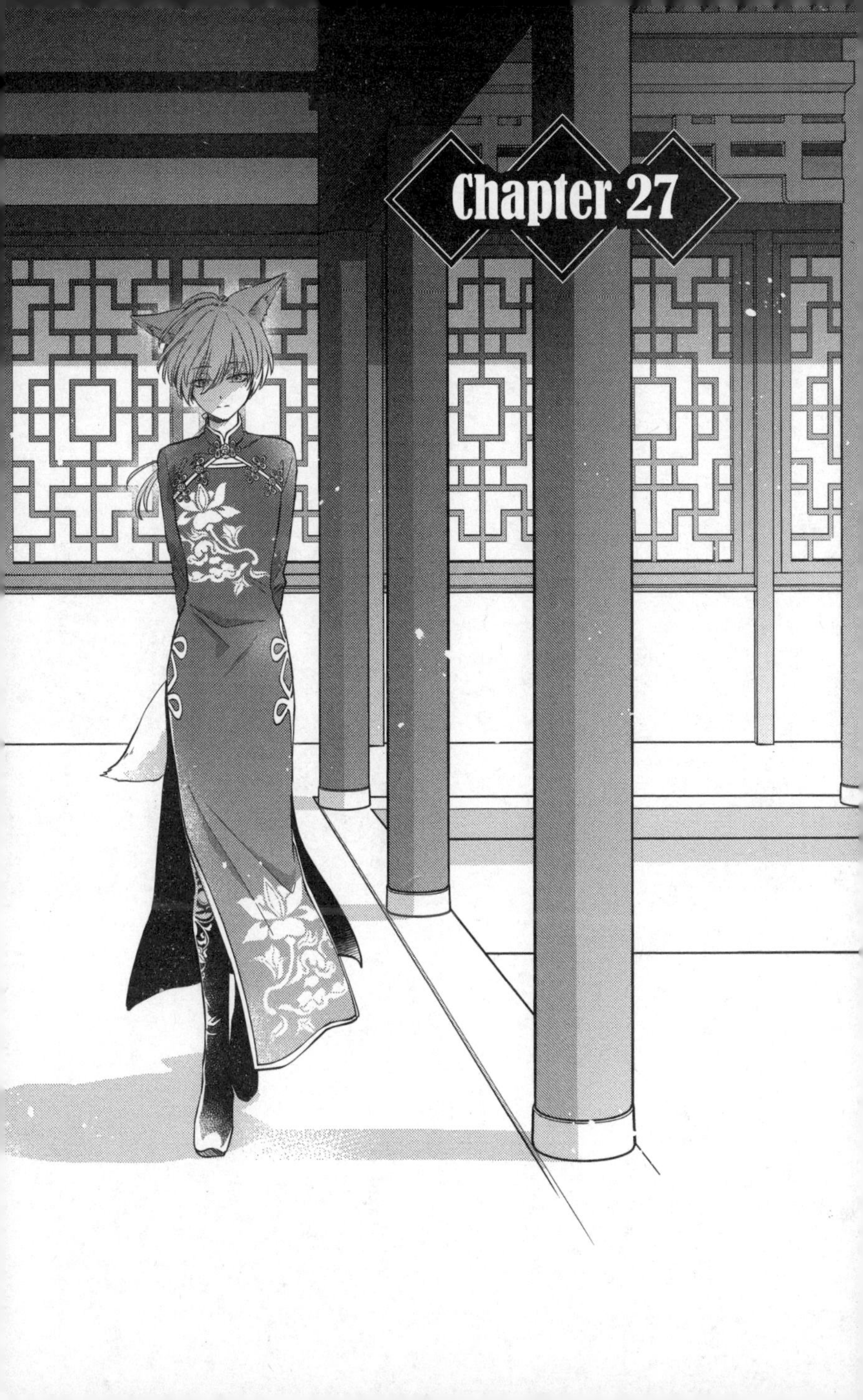
Chapter 27

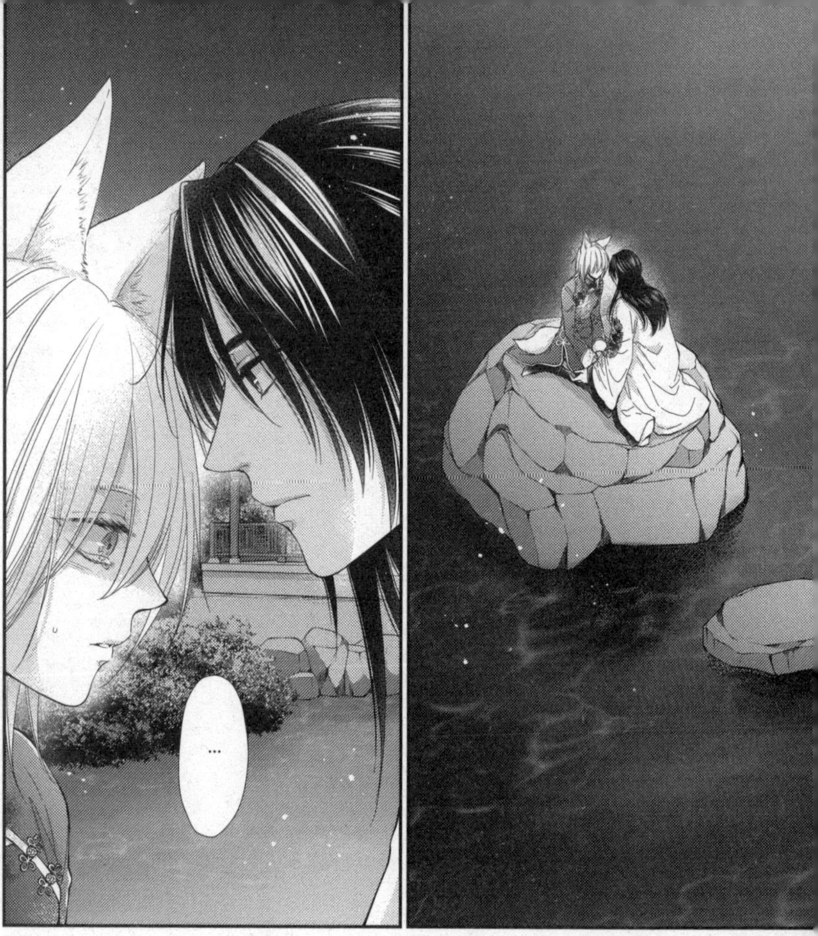
...

THE KING'S Beast

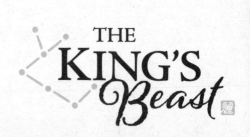

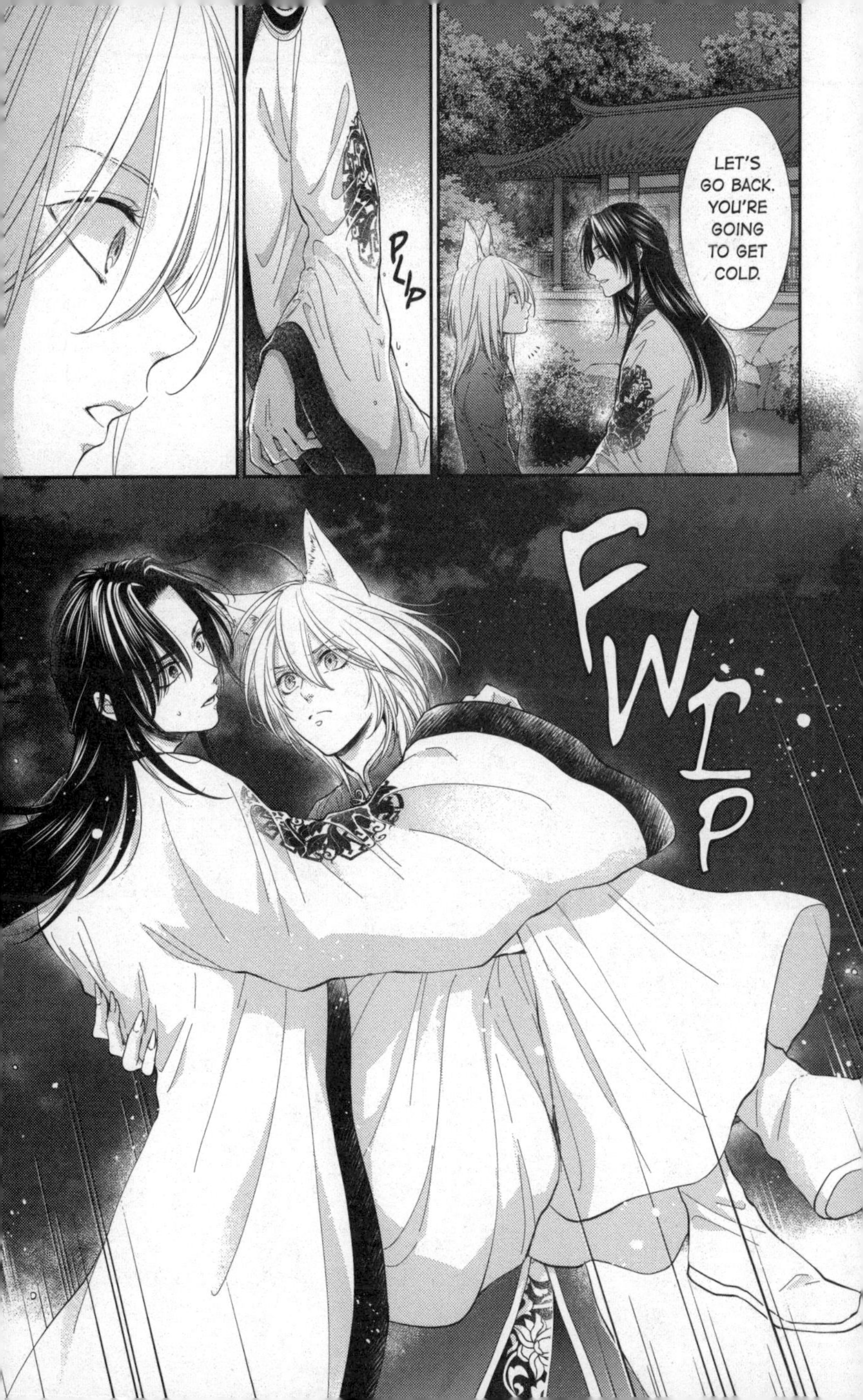
LET'S GO BACK. YOU'RE GOING TO GET COLD.
PLIP
FWIP

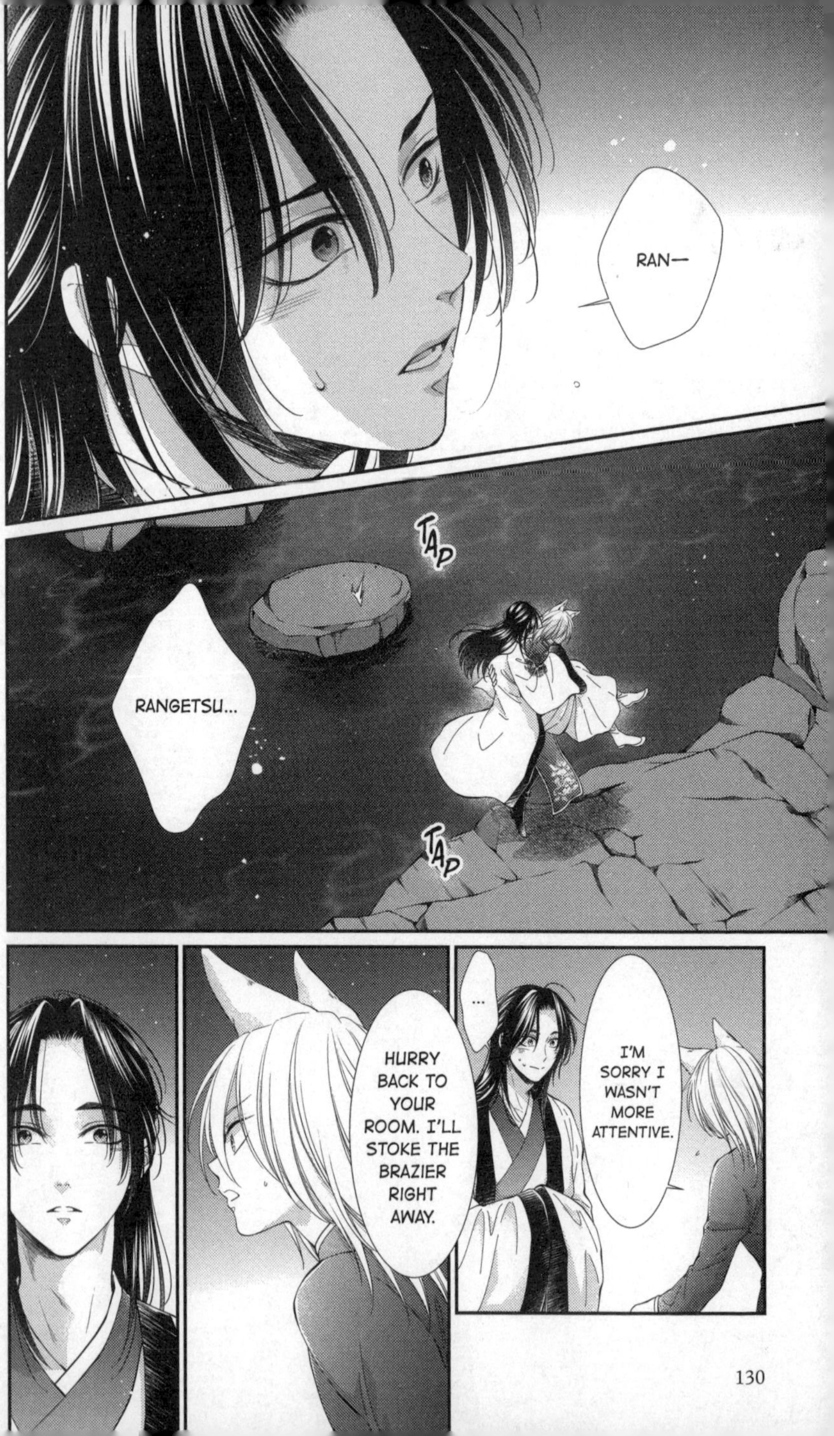
RAN—
TAP
RANGETSU...
TAP
I'M SORRY I WASN'T MORE ATTENTIVE.
...
HURRY BACK TO YOUR ROOM. I'LL STOKE THE BRAZIER RIGHT AWAY.

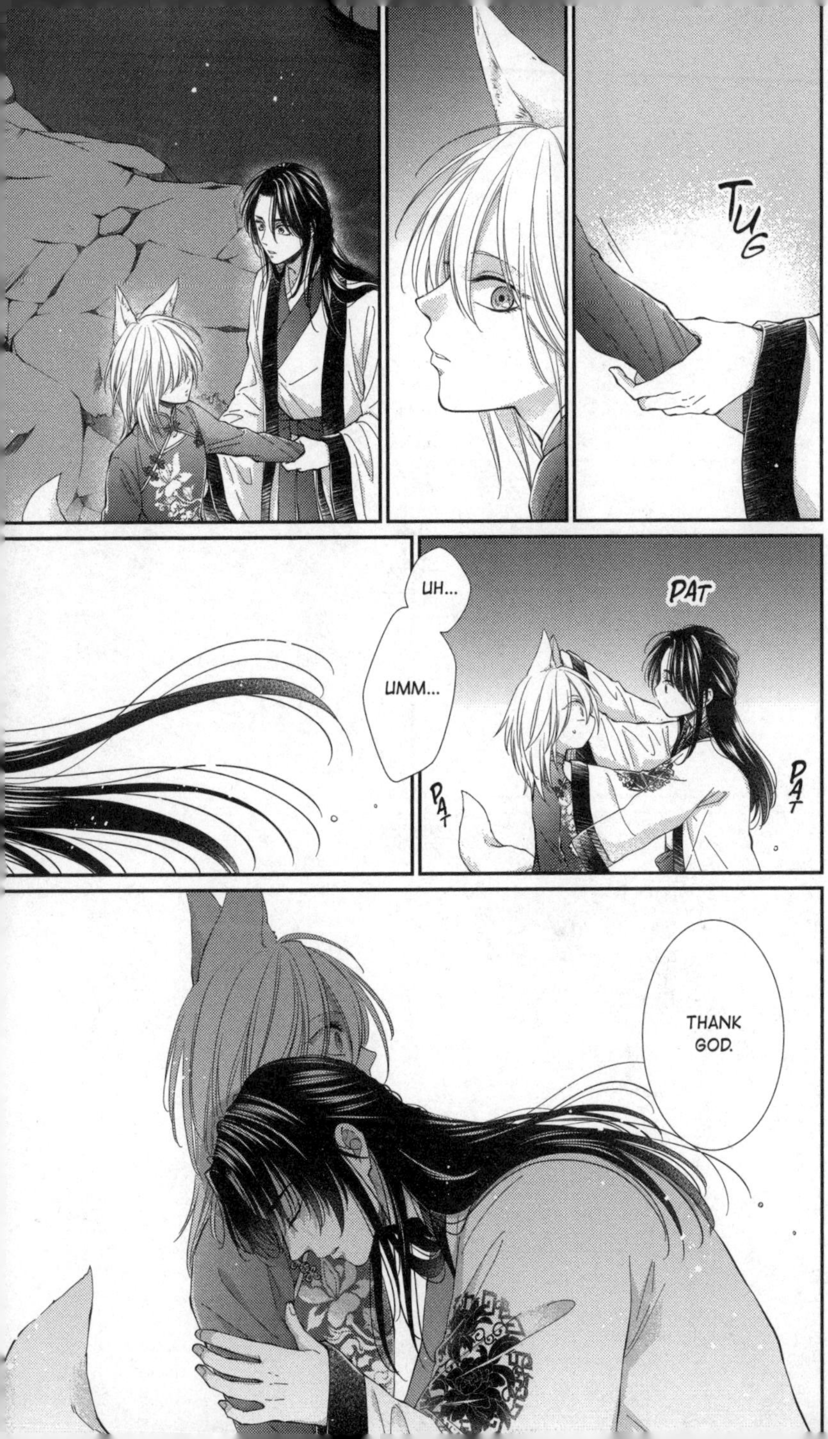
TUG
PAT
UH...
UMM...
PAT
PAT
THANK GOD.

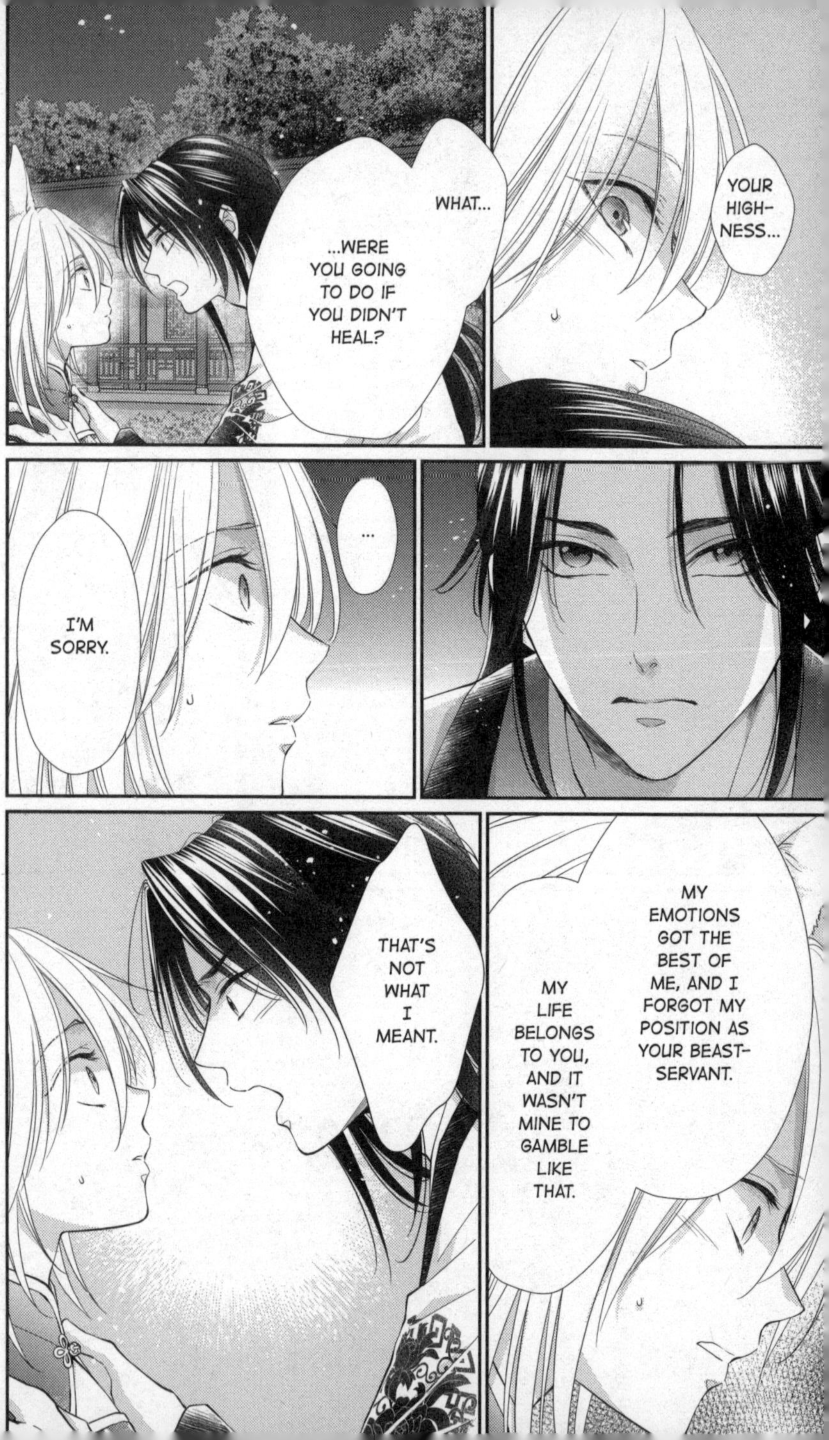
YOUR HIGH-NESS...
WHAT...
...WERE YOU GOING TO DO IF YOU DIDN'T HEAL?
...
I'M SORRY.
MY EMOTIONS GOT THE BEST OF ME, AND I FORGOT MY POSITION AS YOUR BEAST-SERVANT.
MY LIFE BELONGS TO YOU, AND IT WASN'T MINE TO GAMBLE LIKE THAT.
THAT'S NOT WHAT I MEANT.

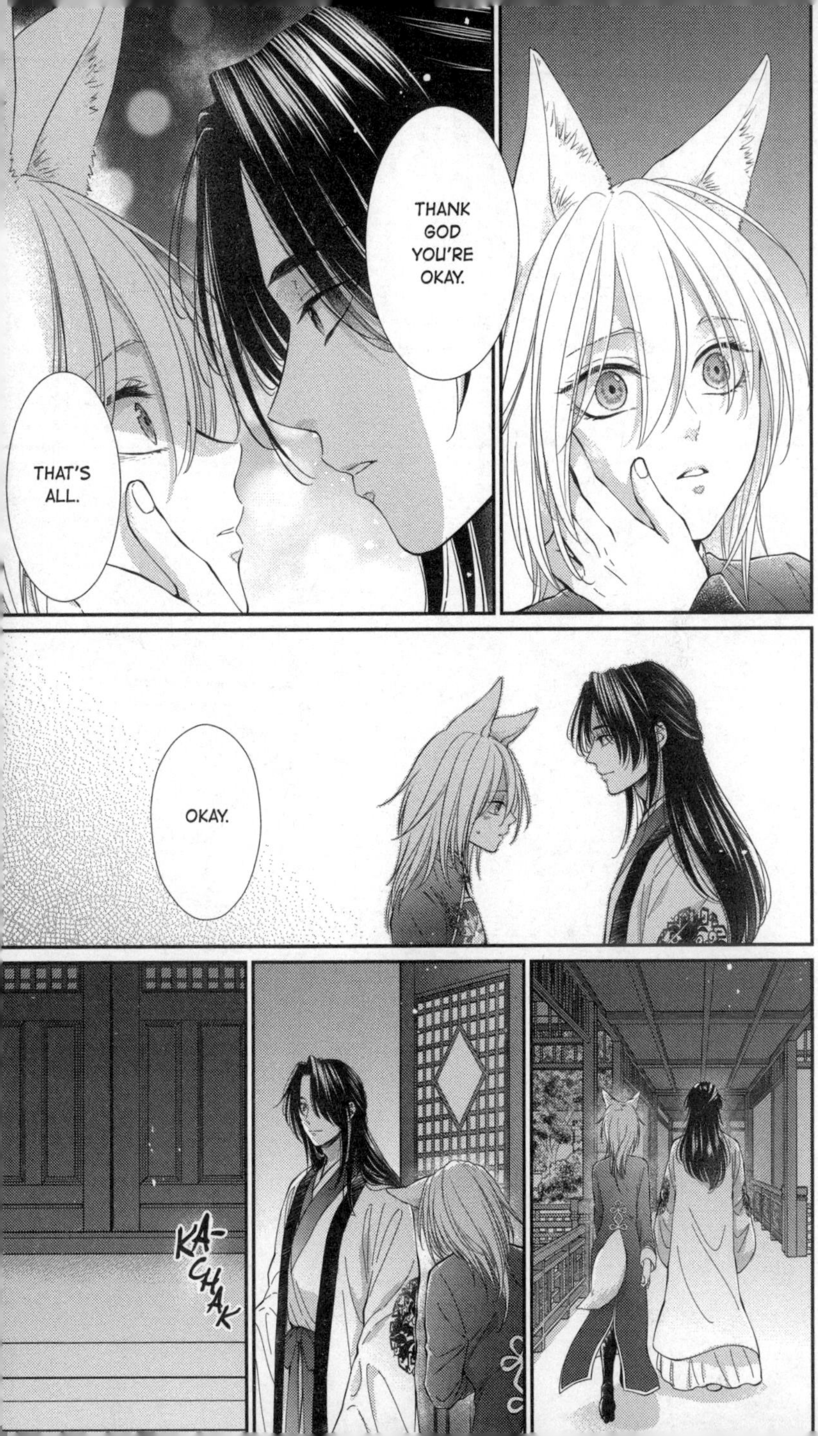
THANK GOD YOU'RE OKAY.
THAT'S ALL.
OKAY.
KA-CHAK

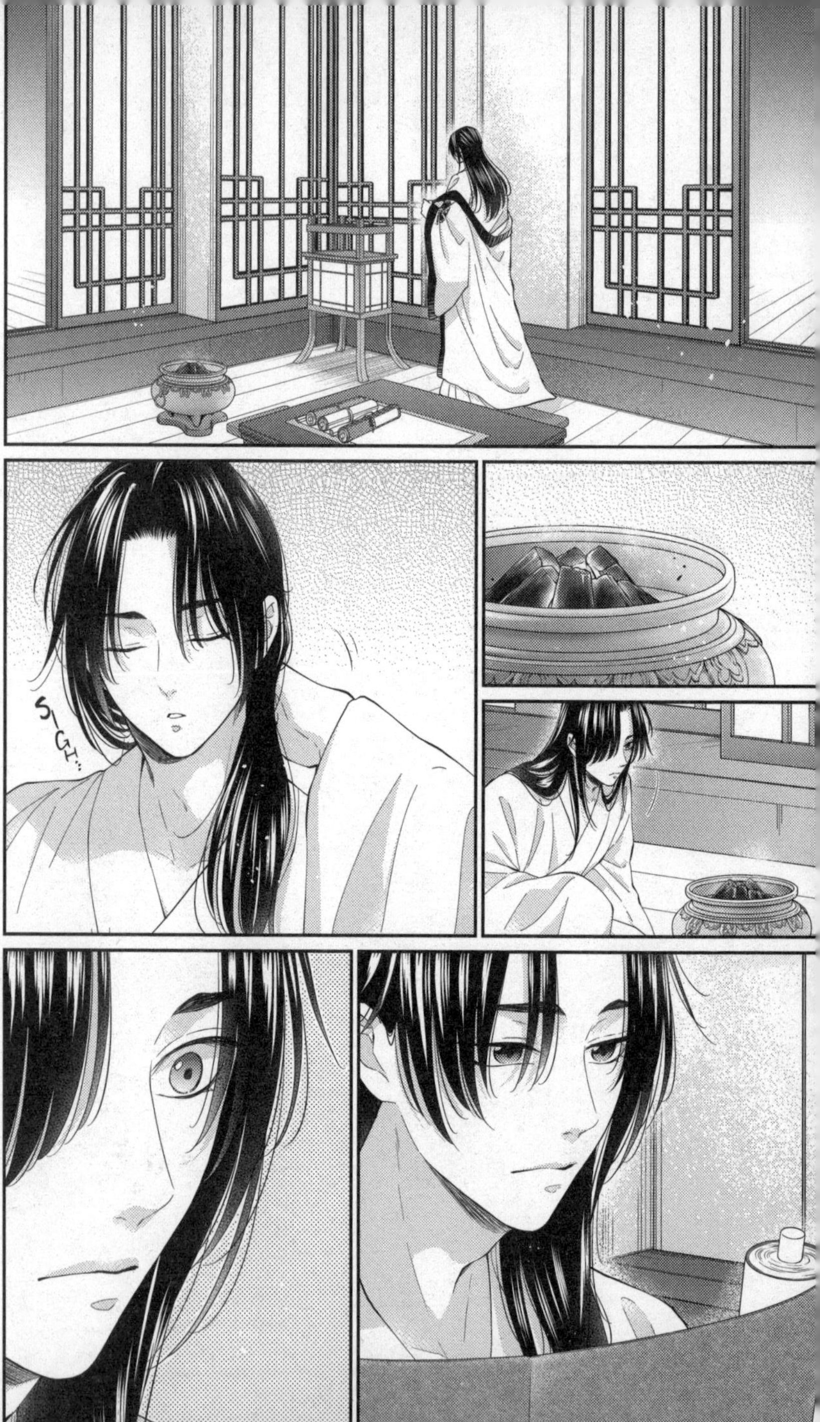
SIGH...

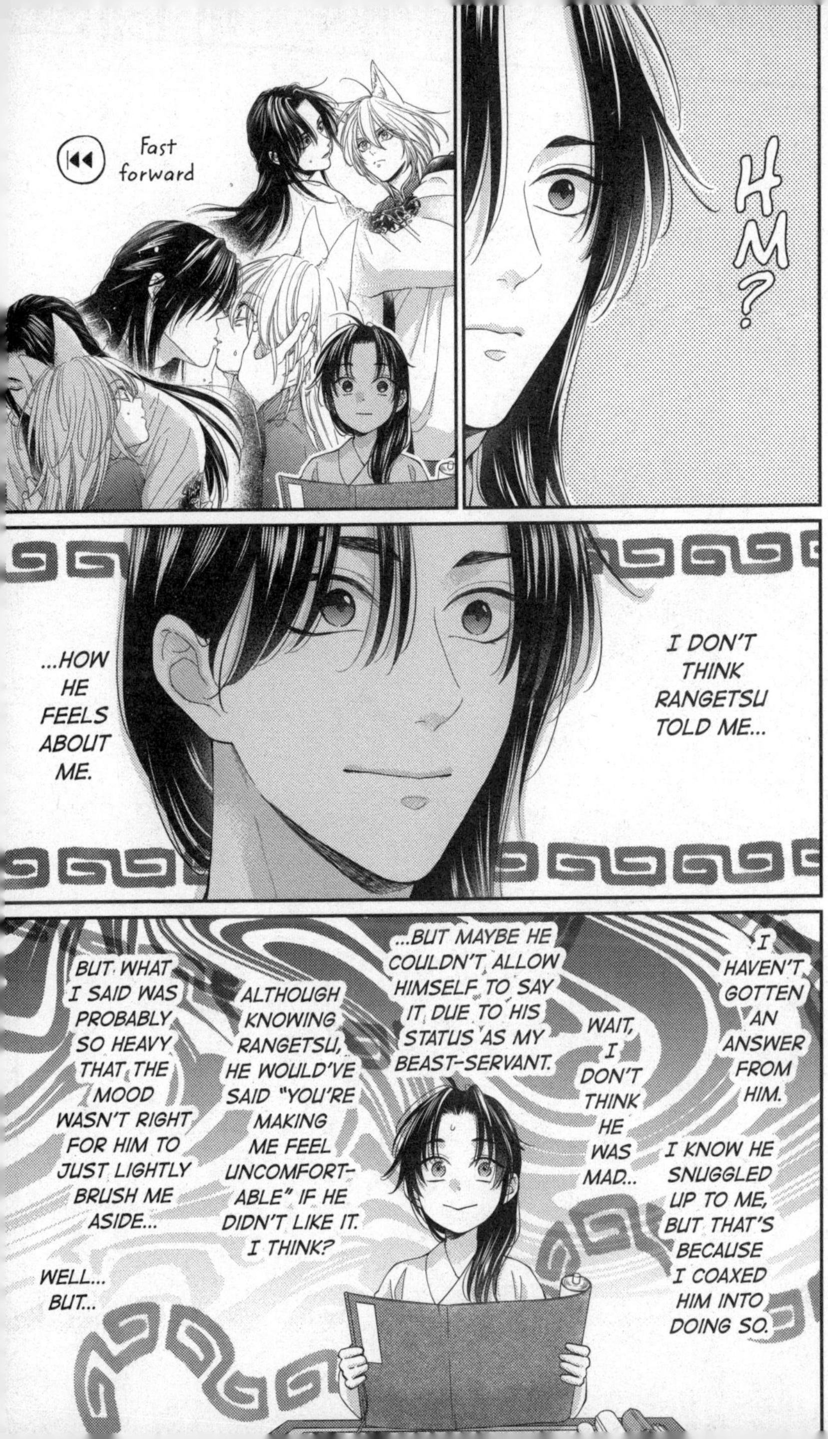
HM?
Fast forward
I DON'T THINK RANGETSU TOLD ME...
...HOW HE FEELS ABOUT ME.
I HAVEN'T GOTTEN AN ANSWER FROM HIM.
I KNOW HE SNUGGLED UP TO ME, BUT THAT'S BECAUSE I COAXED HIM INTO DOING SO.
WAIT, I DON'T THINK HE WAS MAD...
...BUT MAYBE HE COULDN'T ALLOW HIMSELF TO SAY IT DUE TO HIS STATUS AS MY BEAST-SERVANT.
ALTHOUGH KNOWING RANGETSU, HE WOULD'VE SAID "YOU'RE MAKING ME FEEL UNCOMFORT-ABLE" IF HE DIDN'T LIKE IT. I THINK?
BUT WHAT I SAID WAS PROBABLY SO HEAVY THAT THE MOOD WASN'T RIGHT FOR HIM TO JUST LIGHTLY BRUSH ME ASIDE...
WELL... BUT...

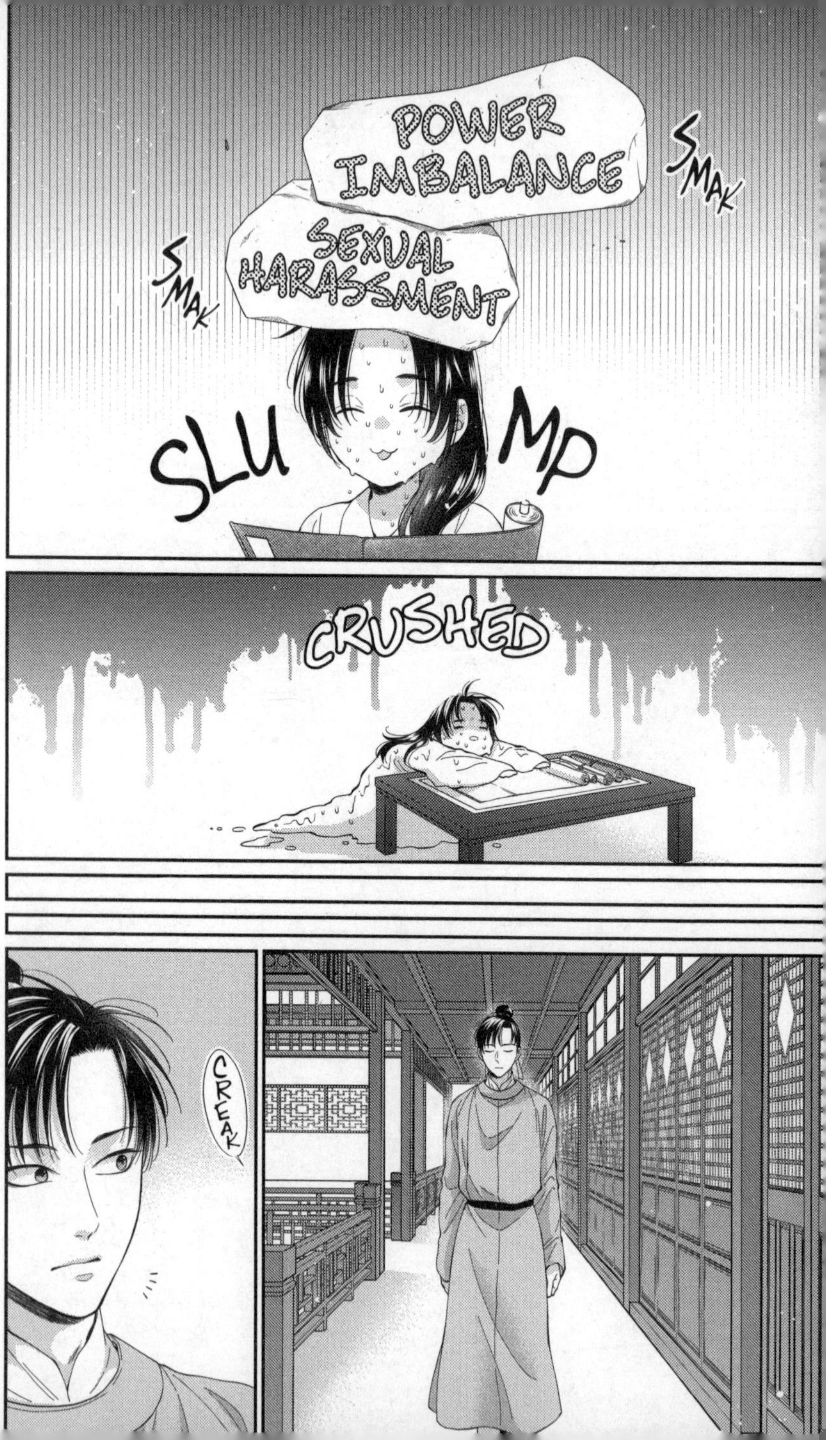
POWER IMBALANCE
SMAK
SEXUAL HARASSMENT
SMAK
SLUMP
CRUSHED
CREAK

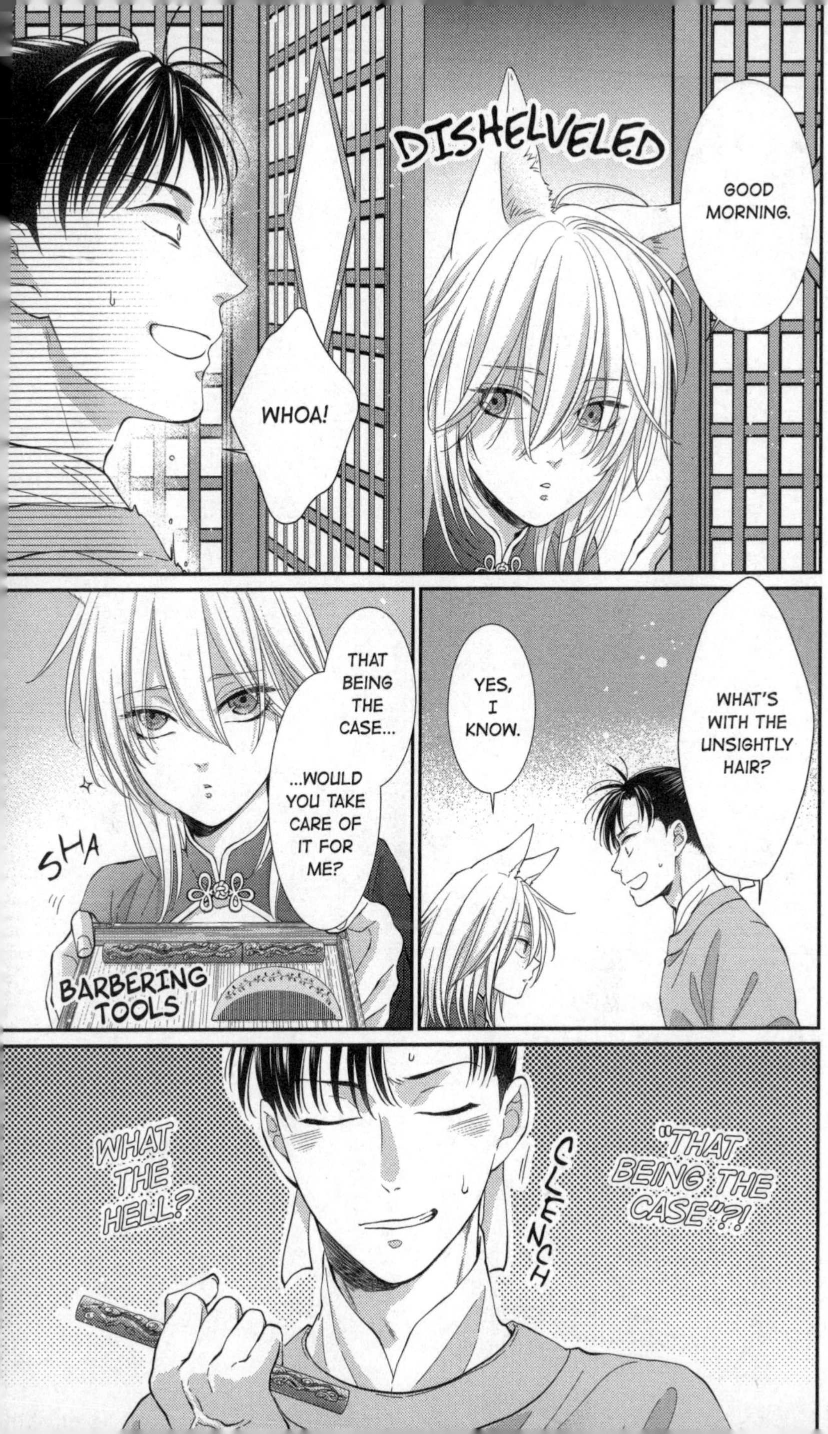
GOOD MORNING.
DISHELVELED
WHOA!
WHAT'S WITH THE UNSIGHTLY HAIR?
YES, I KNOW.
THAT BEING THE CASE...
...WOULD YOU TAKE CARE OF IT FOR ME?
SHA
BARBERING TOOLS
"THAT BEING THE CASE"?!
CLENCH
WHAT THE HELL?

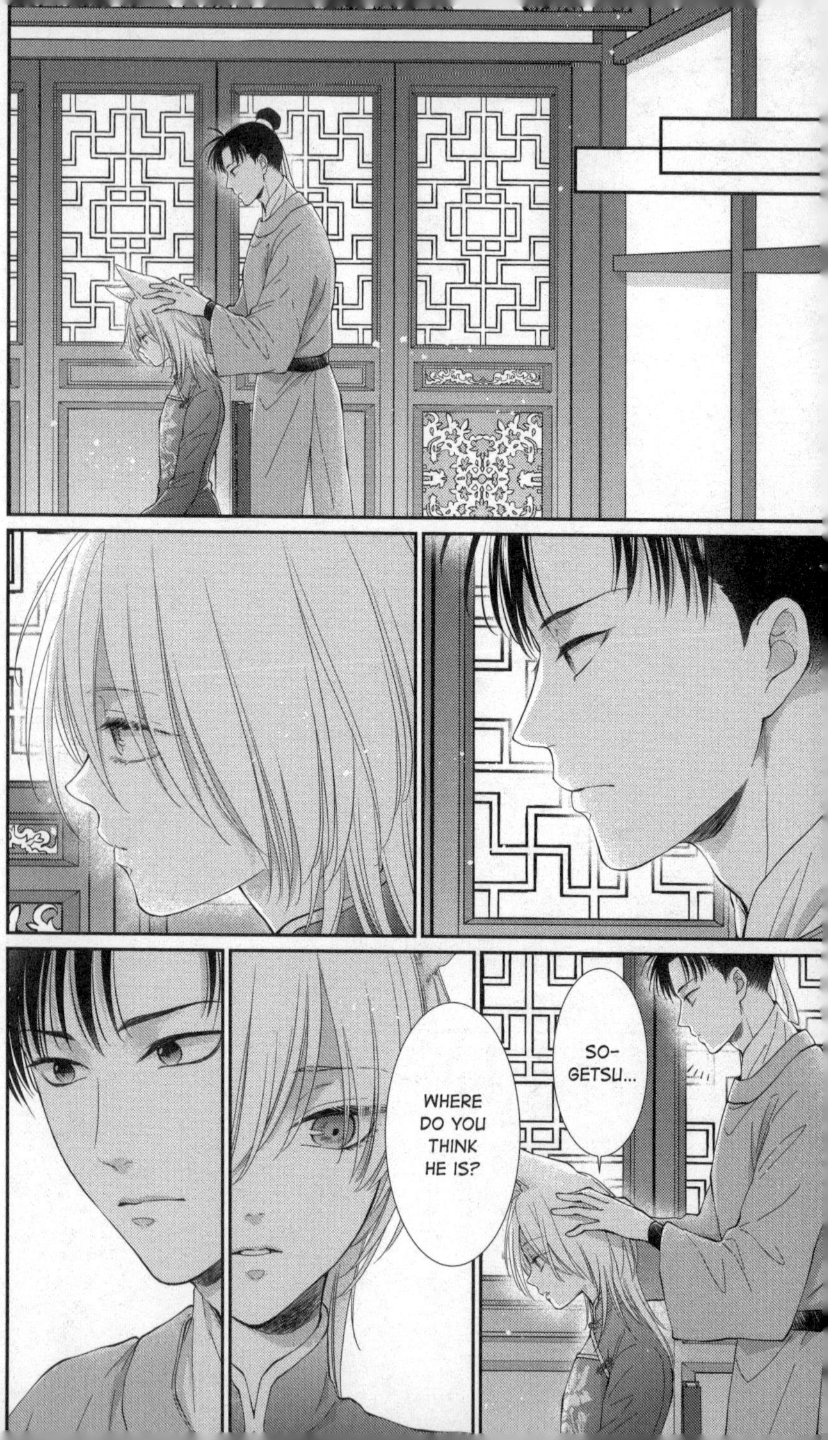
SO-GETSU...
WHERE DO YOU THINK HE IS?

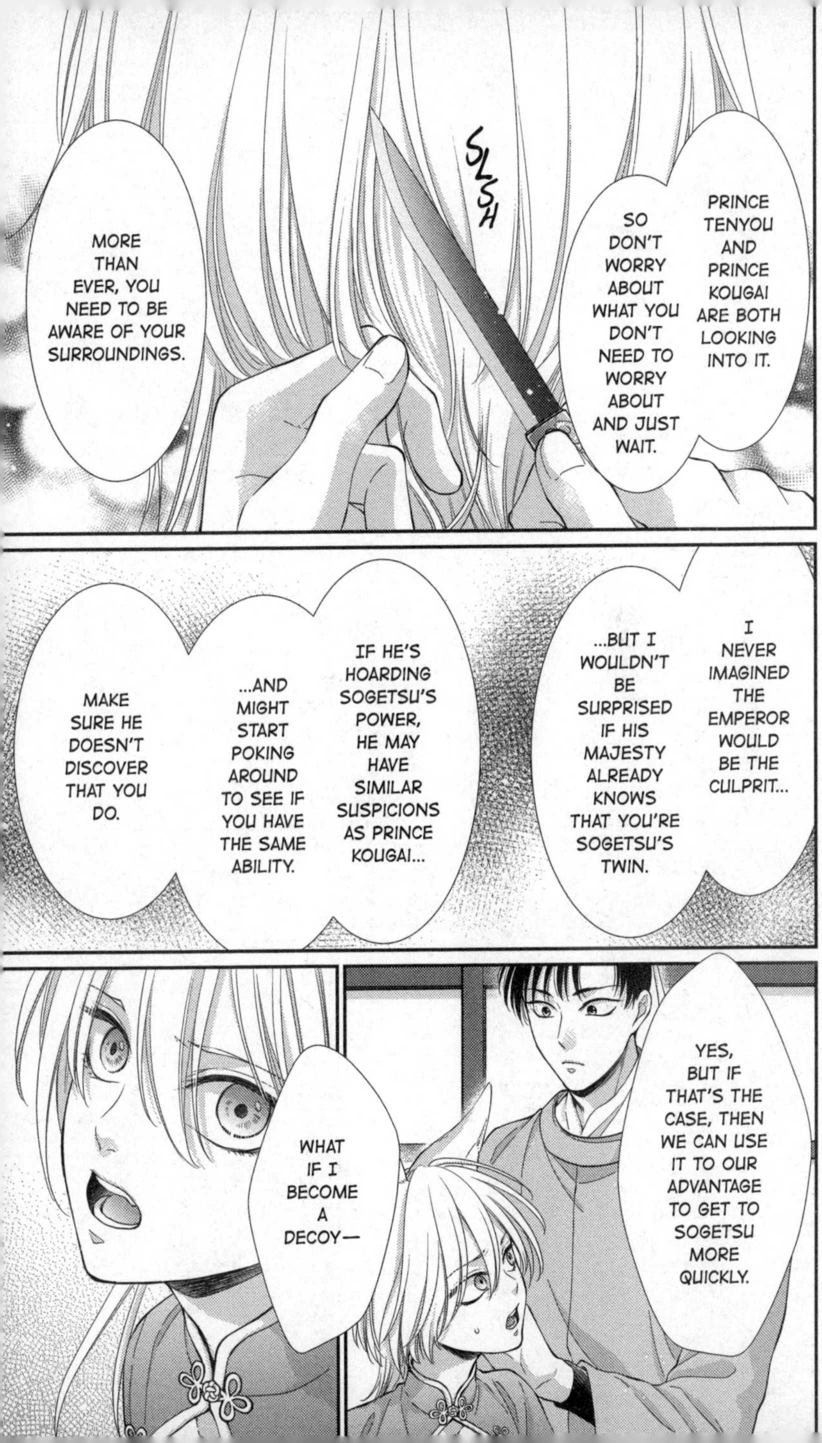
PRINCE TENYOU AND PRINCE KOUGAI ARE BOTH LOOKING INTO IT.
SO DON'T WORRY ABOUT WHAT YOU DON'T NEED TO WORRY ABOUT AND JUST WAIT.
SLSH
MORE THAN EVER, YOU NEED TO BE AWARE OF YOUR SURROUNDINGS.
I NEVER IMAGINED THE EMPEROR WOULD BE THE CULPRIT...
...BUT I WOULDN'T BE SURPRISED IF HIS MAJESTY ALREADY KNOWS THAT YOU'RE SOGETSU'S TWIN.
IF HE'S HOARDING SOGETSU'S POWER, HE MAY HAVE SIMILAR SUSPICIONS AS PRINCE KOUGAI...
...AND MIGHT START POKING AROUND TO SEE IF YOU HAVE THE SAME ABILITY.
MAKE SURE HE DOESN'T DISCOVER THAT YOU DO.
YES, BUT IF THAT'S THE CASE, THEN WE CAN USE IT TO OUR ADVANTAGE TO GET TO SOGETSU MORE QUICKLY.
WHAT IF I BECOME A DECOY—

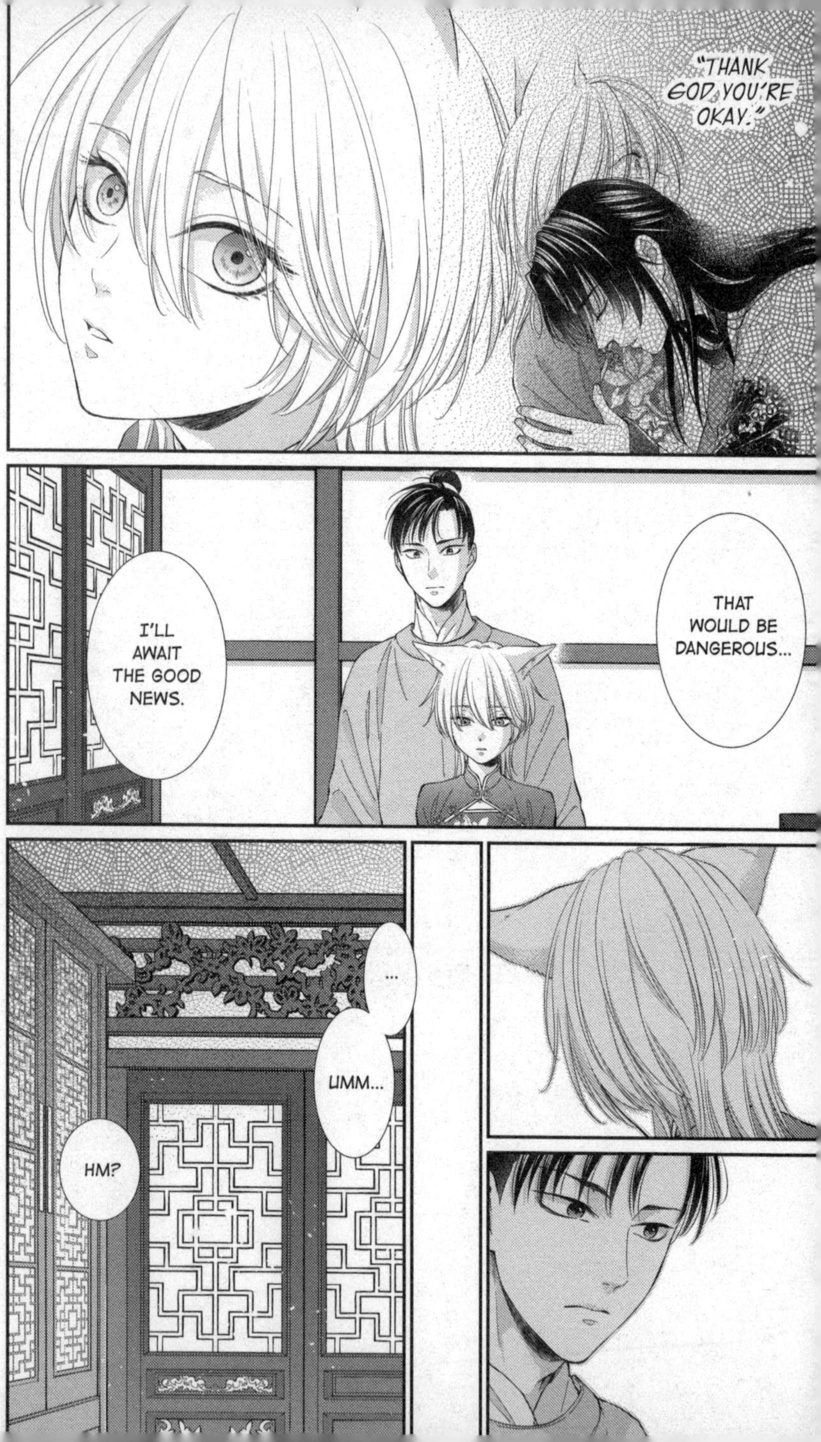
"THANK GOD YOU'RE OKAY."
THAT WOULD BE DANGEROUS...
I'LL AWAIT THE GOOD NEWS.
...
UMM...
HM?

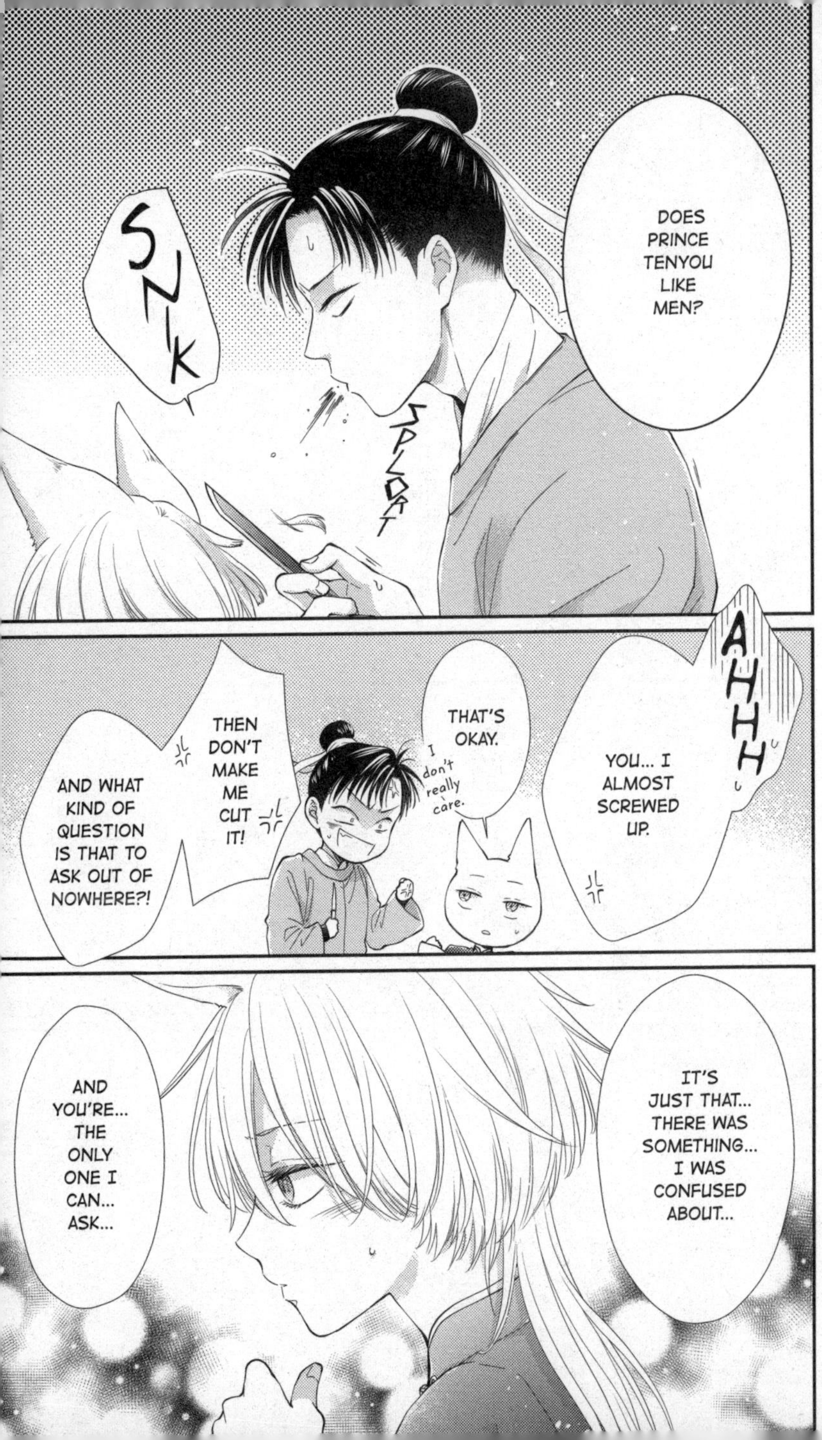
DOES PRINCE TENYOU LIKE MEN?
SNIK
SPLORT
AHHH
YOU... I ALMOST SCREWED UP.
THAT'S OKAY.
I don't really care.
THEN DON'T MAKE ME CUT IT!
AND WHAT KIND OF QUESTION IS THAT TO ASK OUT OF NOWHERE?!
IT'S JUST THAT... THERE WAS SOMETHING... I WAS CONFUSED ABOUT...
AND YOU'RE... THE ONLY ONE I CAN... ASK...

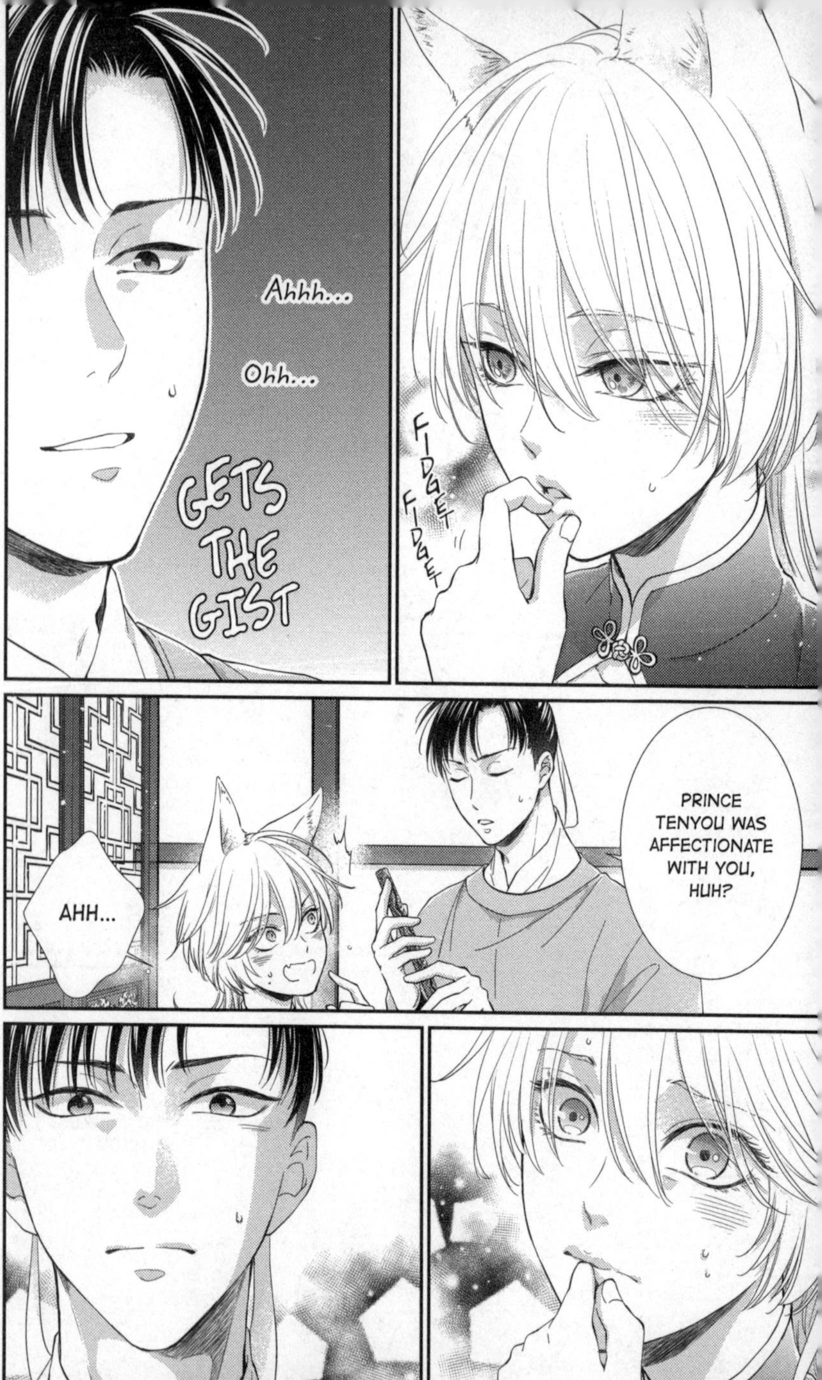
FIDGET FIDGET
Ahhh...
Ohh...
GETS THE GIST
PRINCE TENYOU WAS AFFECTIONATE WITH YOU, HUH?
AHH...

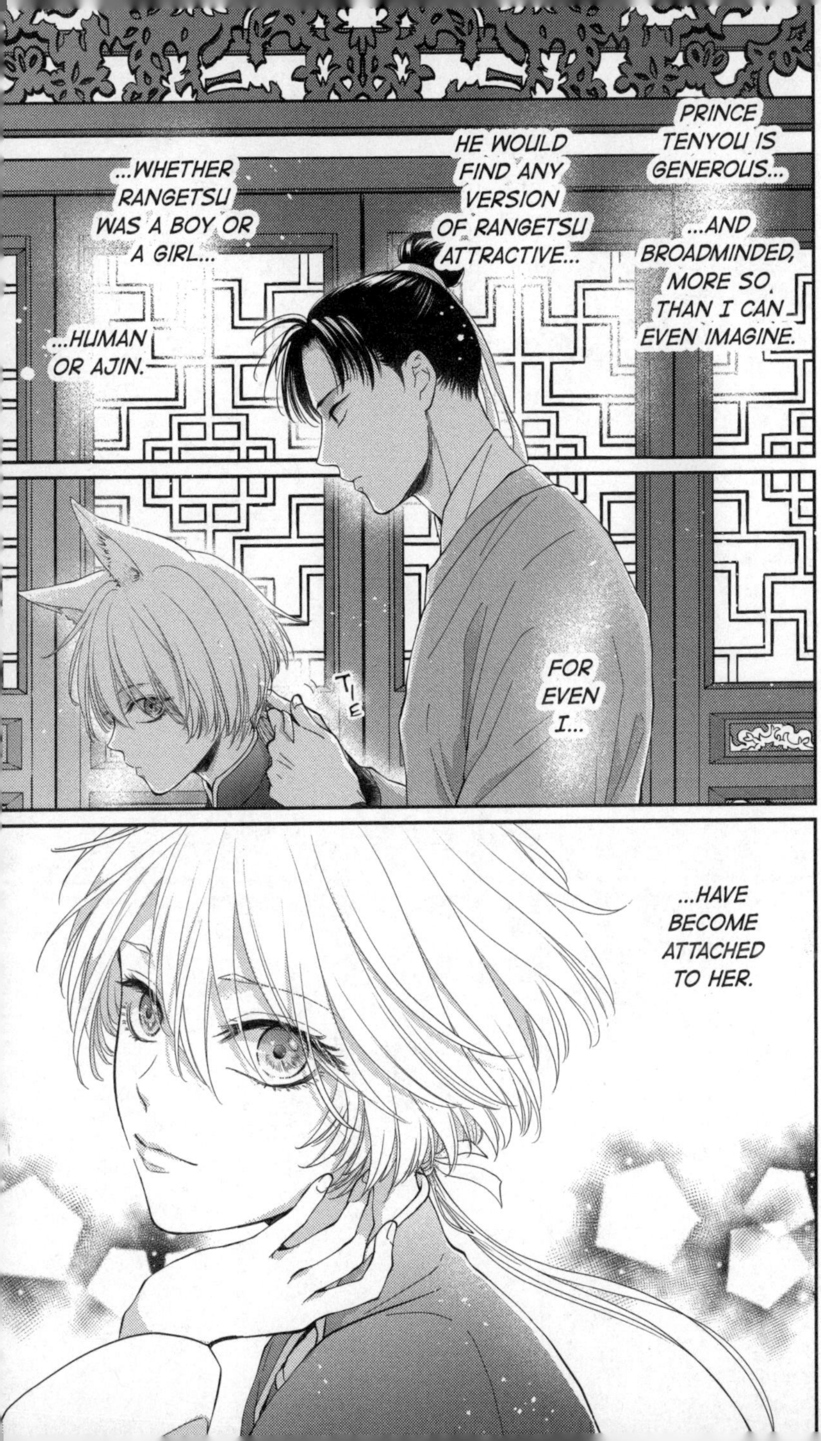
PRINCE TENYOU IS GENEROUS...
...AND BROADMINDED, MORE SO THAN I CAN EVEN IMAGINE.
HE WOULD FIND ANY VERSION OF RANGETSU ATTRACTIVE...
...WHETHER RANGETSU WAS A BOY OR A GIRL...
...HUMAN OR AJIN.
FOR EVEN I...
TIE
...HAVE BECOME ATTACHED TO HER.

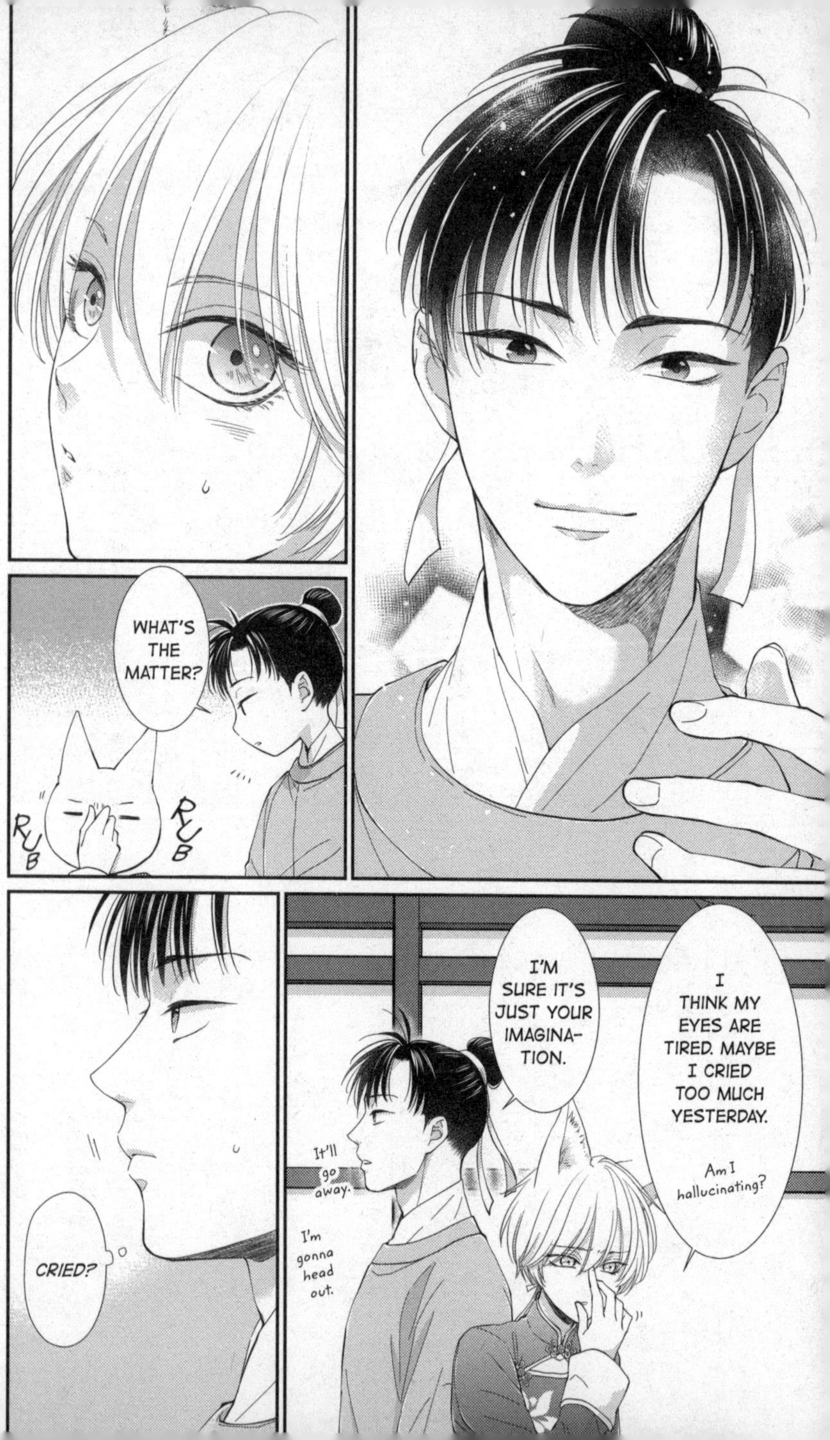
WHAT'S THE MATTER?
RUB RUB
I THINK MY EYES ARE TIRED. MAYBE I CRIED TOO MUCH YESTERDAY.
Am I hallucinating?
I'M SURE IT'S JUST YOUR IMAGINATION.
It'll go away.
I'm gonna head out.
CRIED?

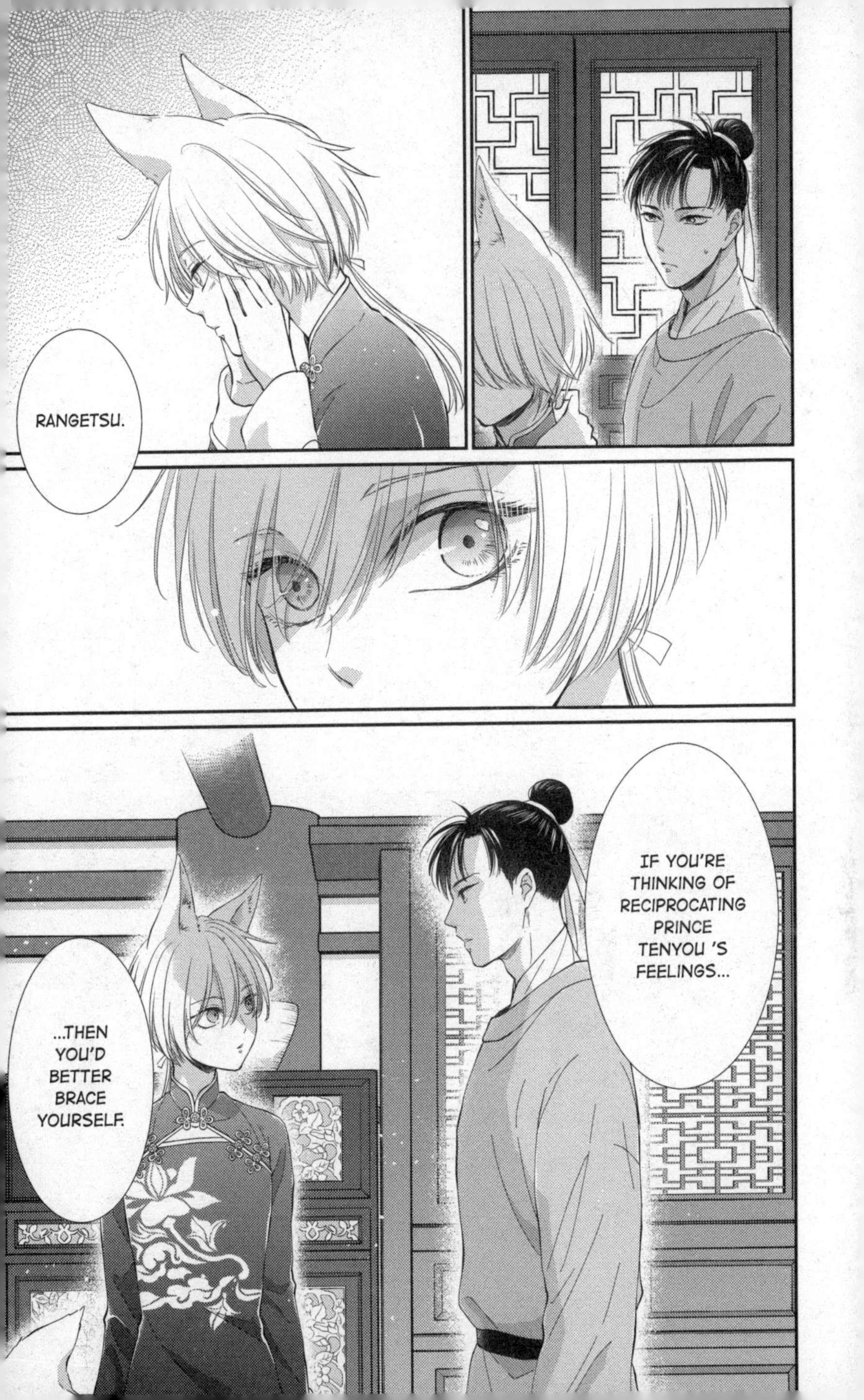
RANGETSU.
IF YOU'RE THINKING OF RECIPROCATING PRINCE TENYOU 'S FEELINGS...
...THEN YOU'D BETTER BRACE YOURSELF.

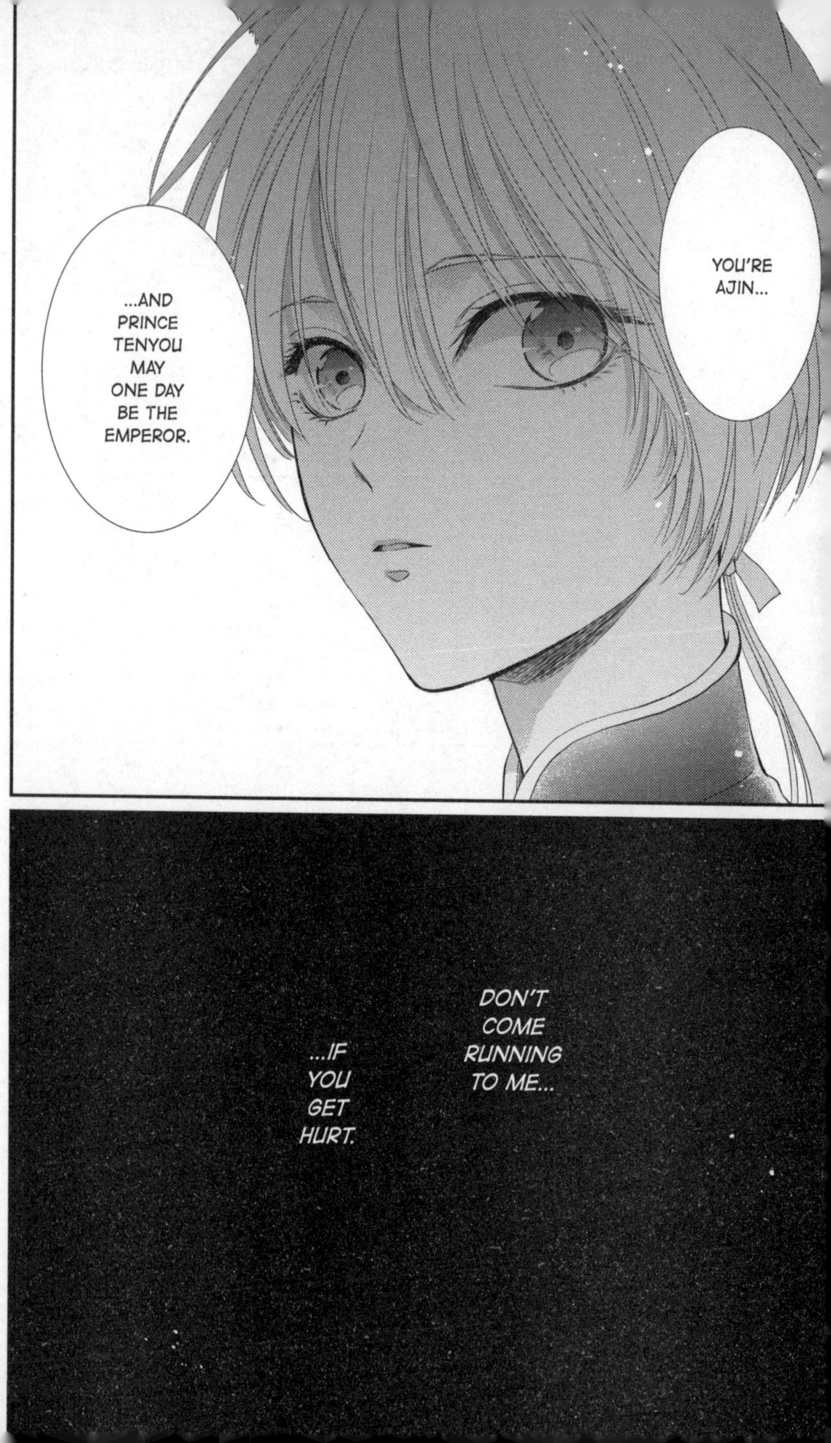
YOU'RE AJIN...
...AND PRINCE TENYOU MAY ONE DAY BE THE EMPEROR.
DON'T COME RUNNING TO ME...
...IF YOU GET HURT.

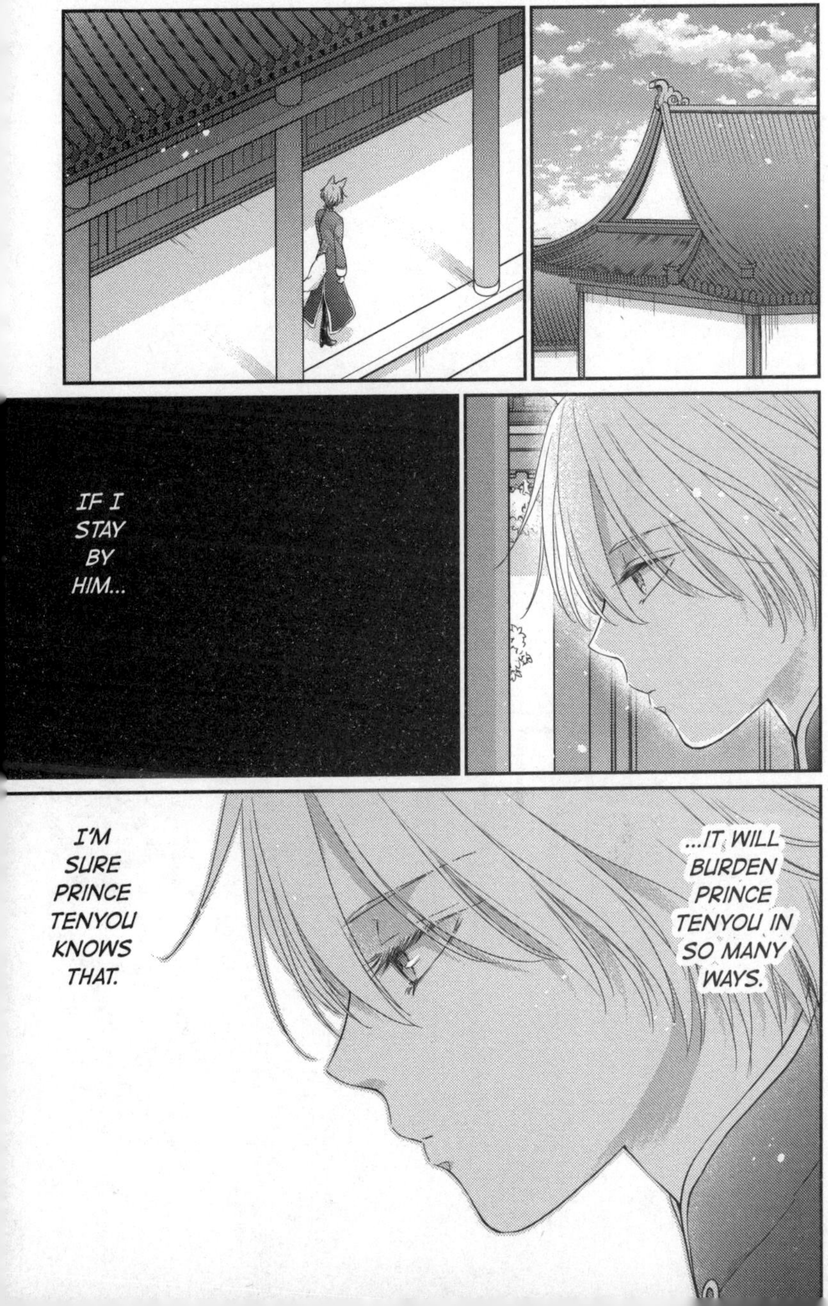
IF I STAY BY HIM...
...IT WILL BURDEN PRINCE TENYOU IN SO MANY WAYS.
I'M SURE PRINCE TENYOU KNOWS THAT.

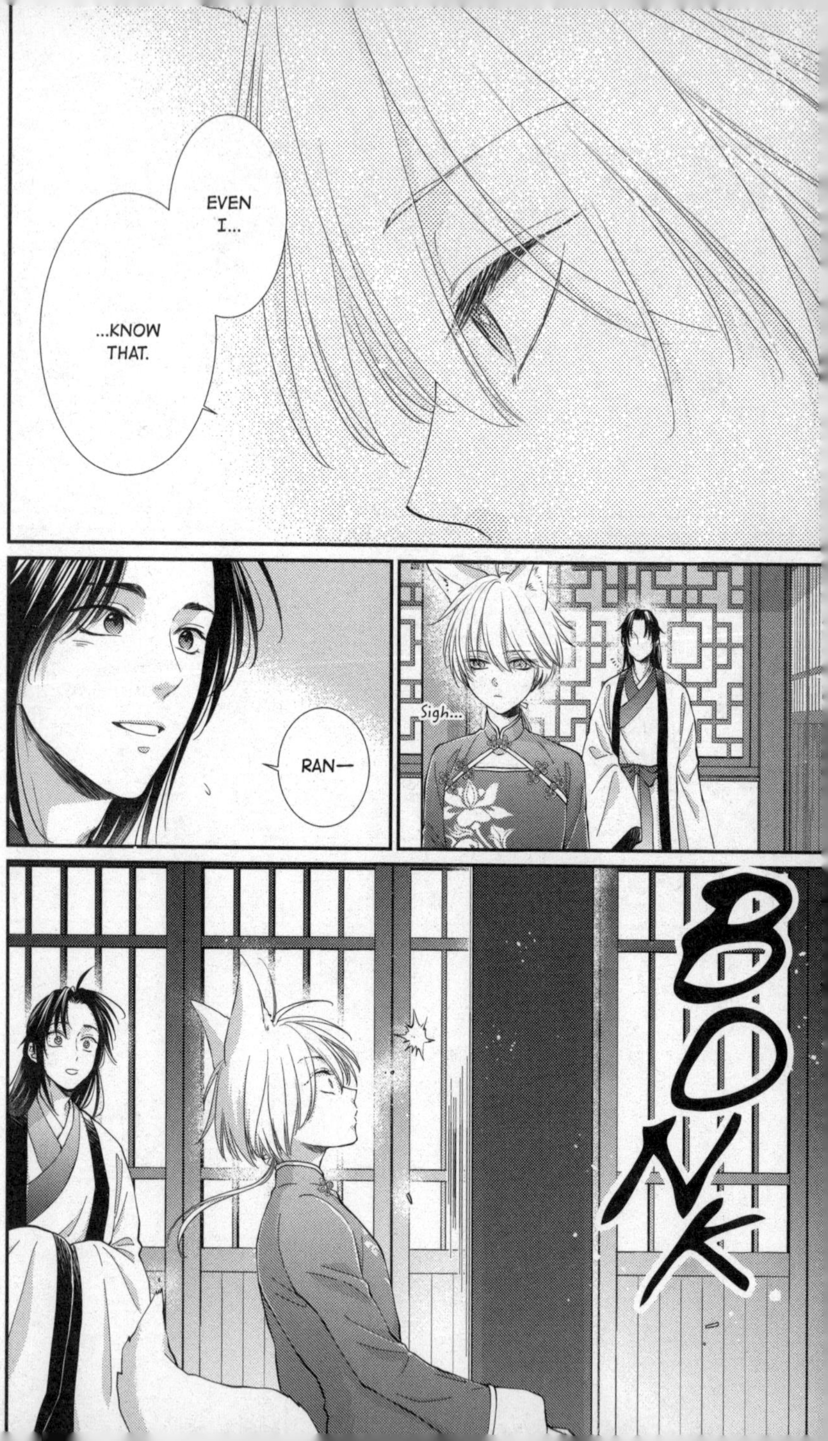
EVEN I...
...KNOW THAT.
Sigh...
RAN—
BONK

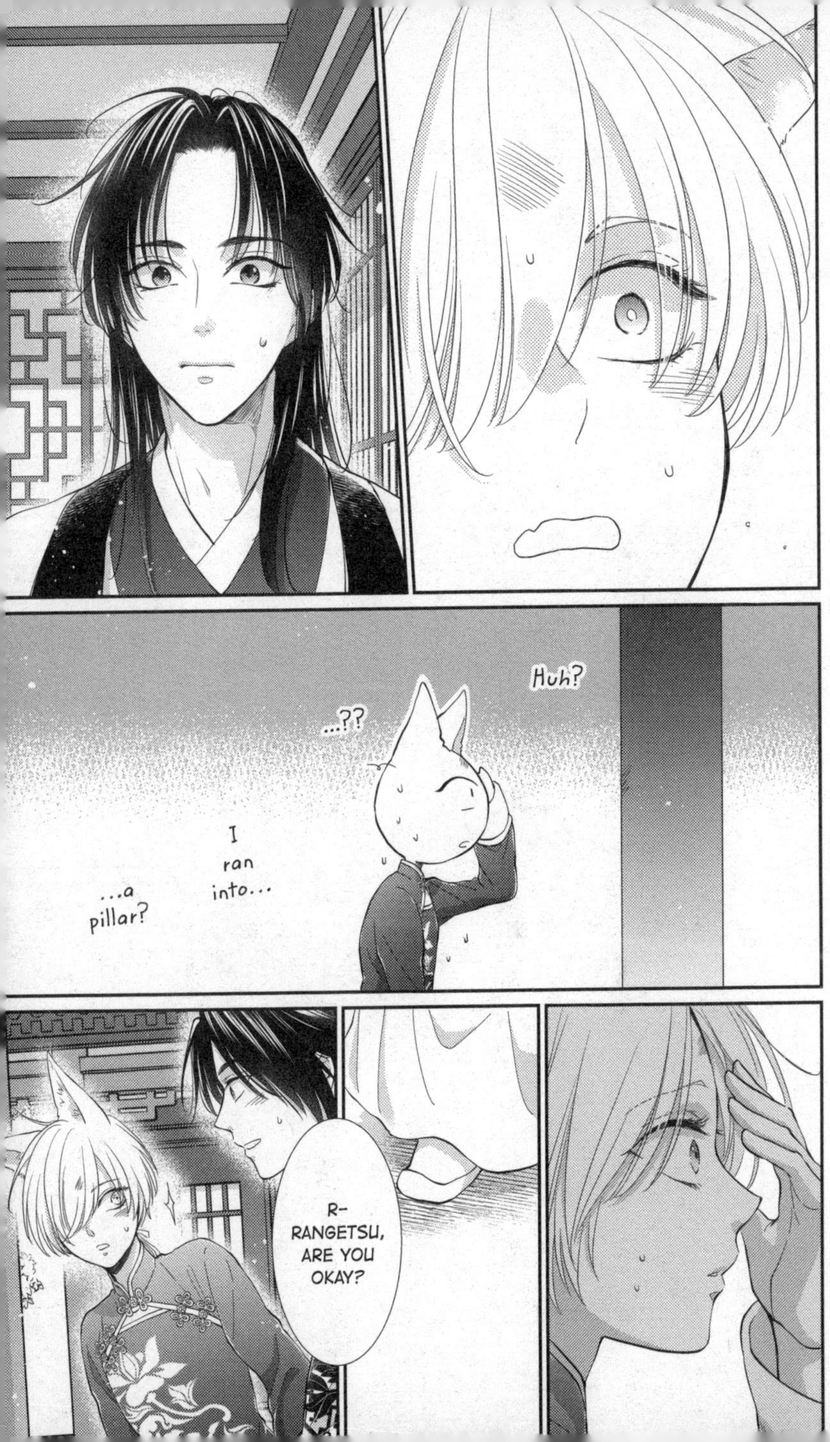
Huh?
...??
I ran into...
...a pillar?
R-RANGETSU, ARE YOU OKAY?

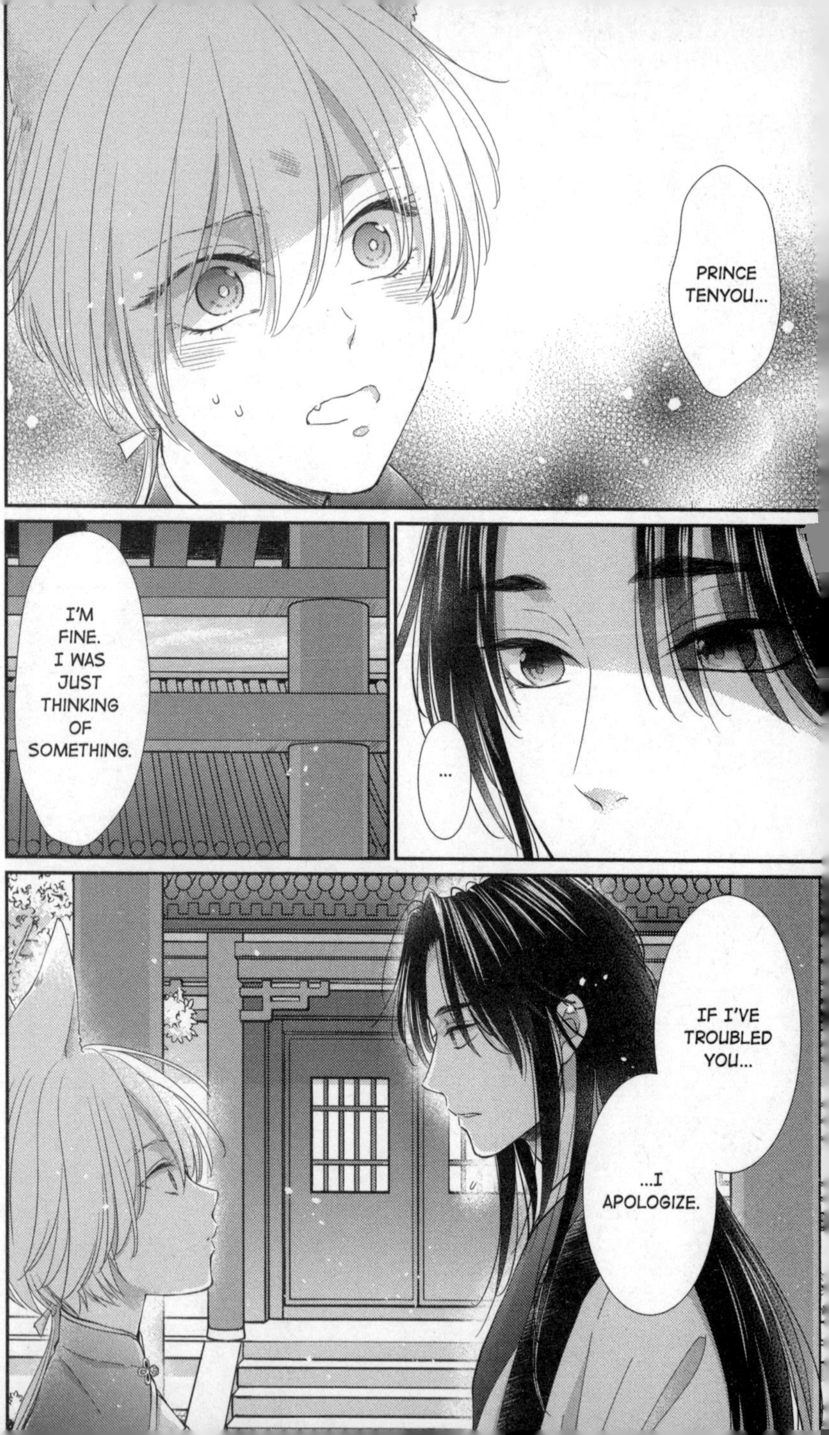
PRINCE TENYOU...
...
I'M FINE. I WAS JUST THINKING OF SOMETHING.
IF I'VE TROUBLED YOU...
...I APOLOGIZE.

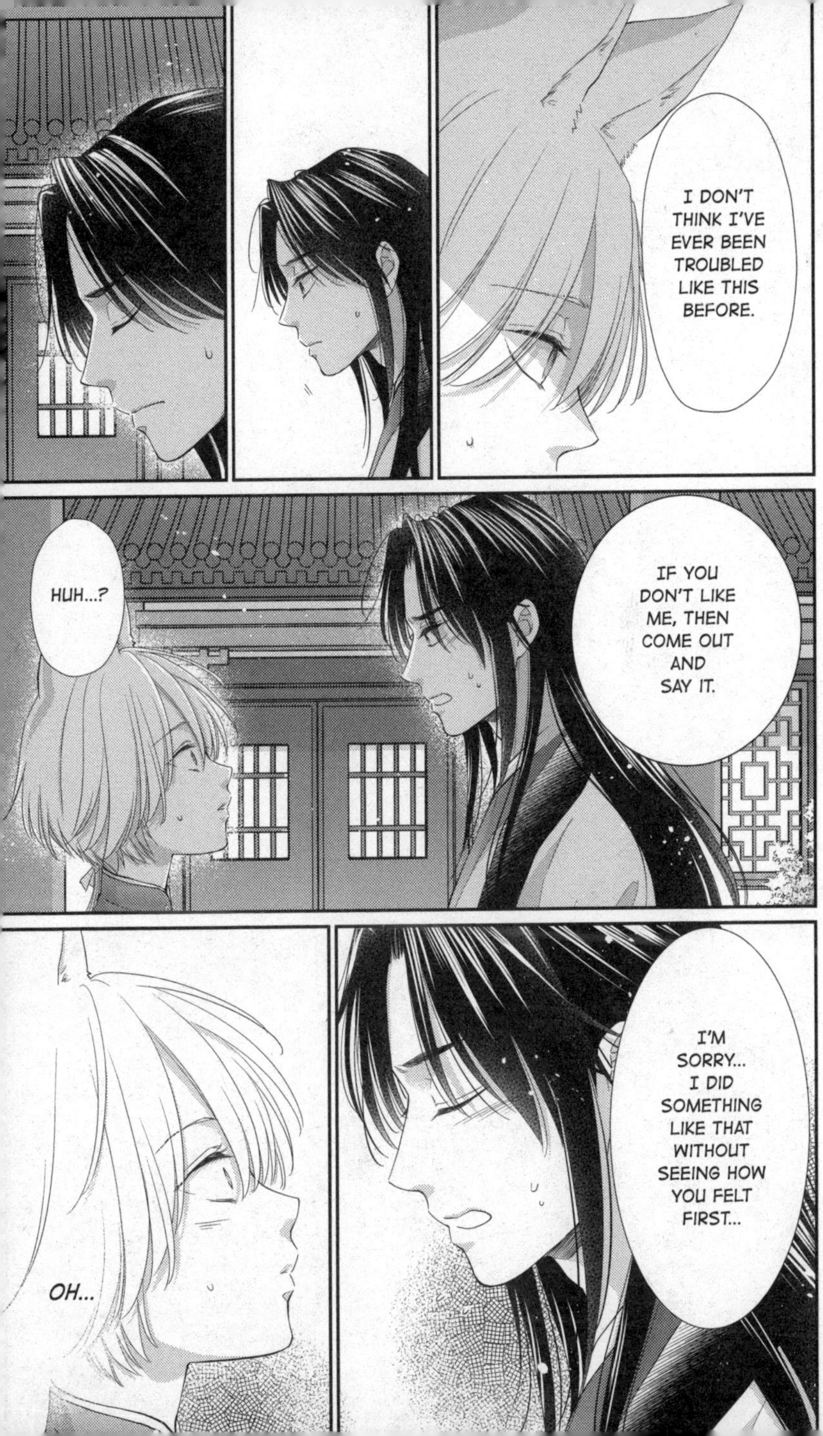
I DON'T THINK I'VE EVER BEEN TROUBLED LIKE THIS BEFORE.
IF YOU DON'T LIKE ME, THEN COME OUT AND SAY IT.
HUH...?
I'M SORRY... I DID SOMETHING LIKE THAT WITHOUT SEEING HOW YOU FELT FIRST...
OH...

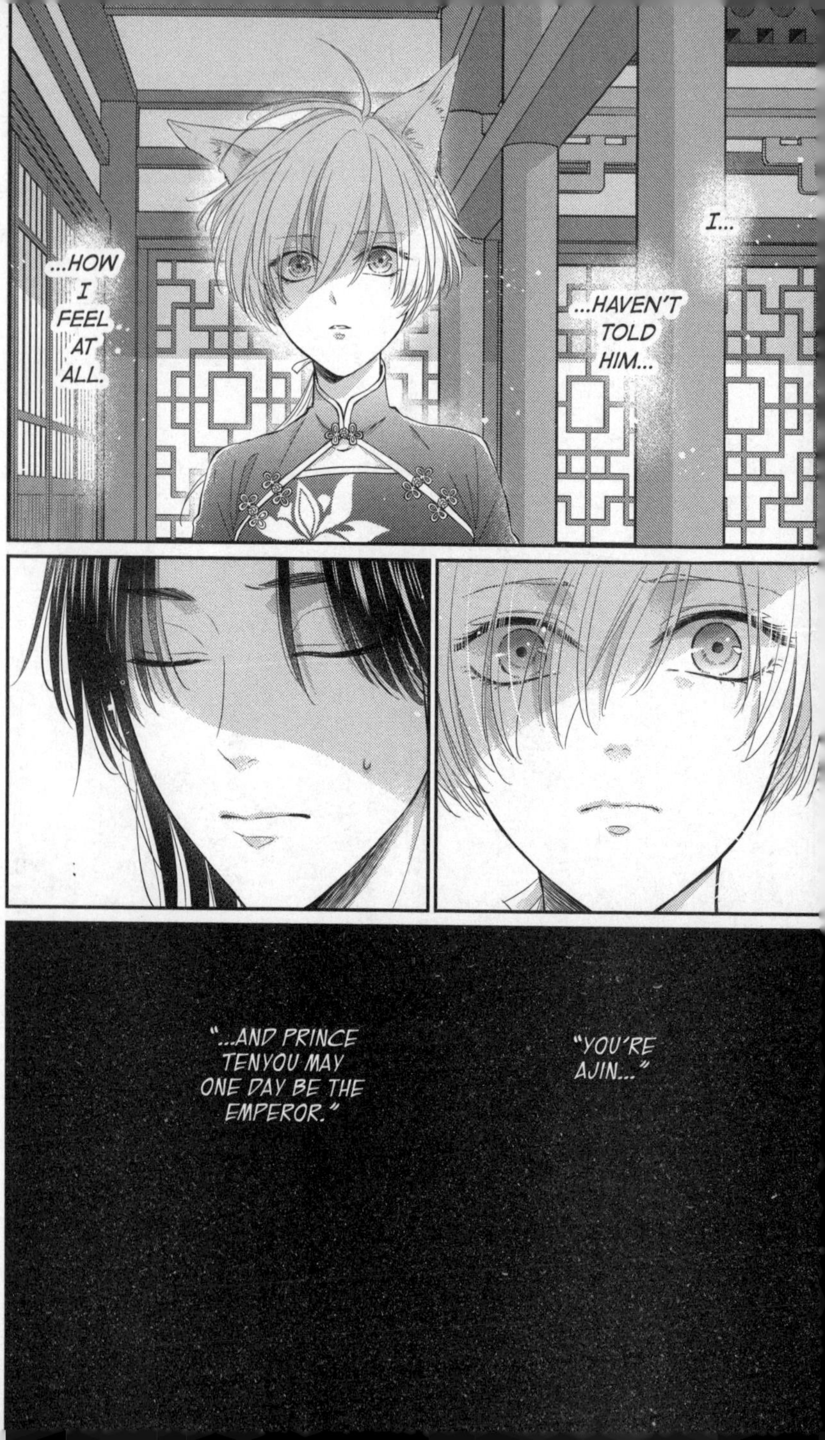
I...
...HAVEN'T TOLD HIM...
...HOW I FEEL AT ALL.
"YOU'RE AJIN..."
"...AND PRINCE TENYOU MAY ONE DAY BE THE EMPEROR."

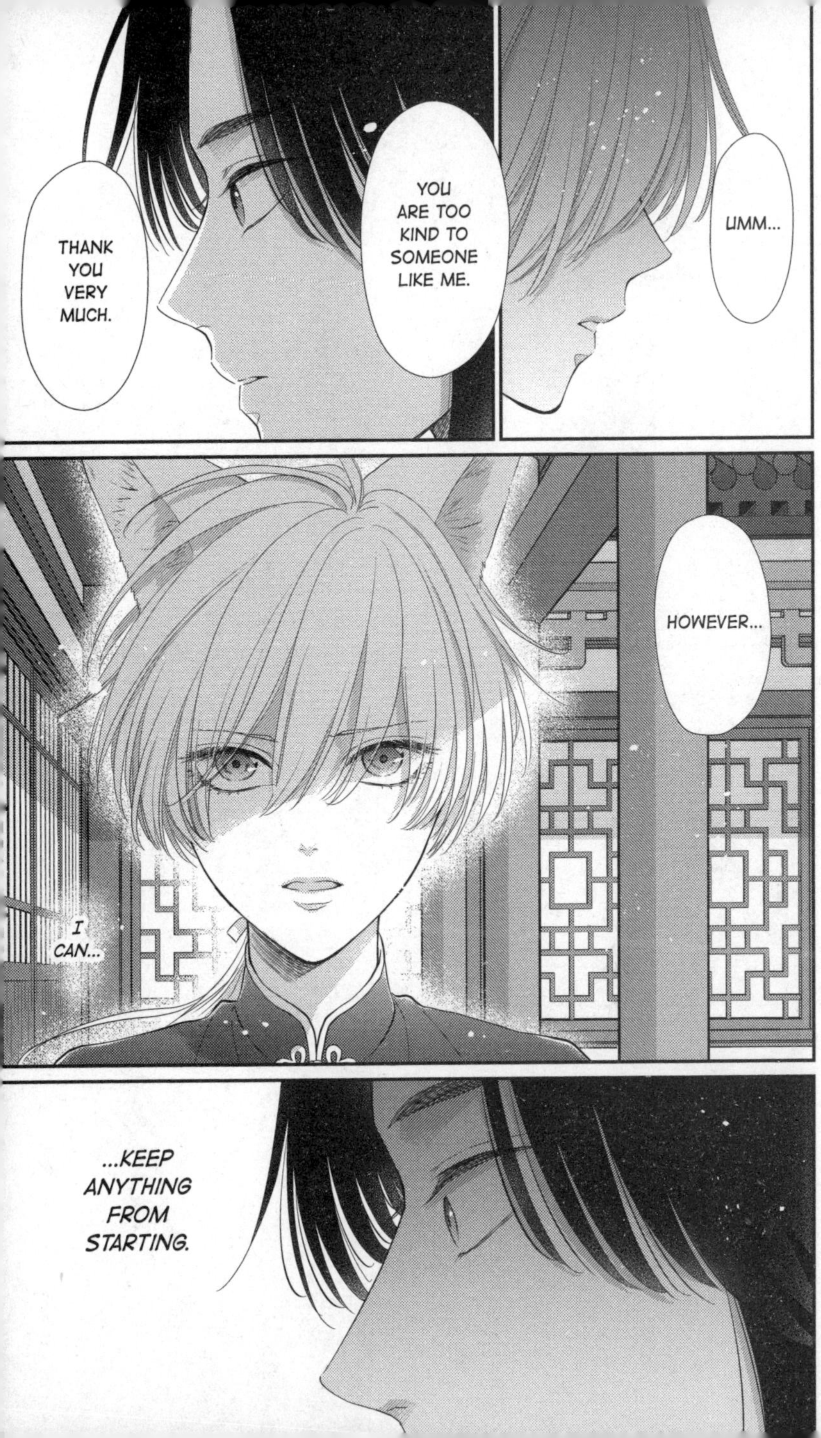
UMM...
YOU ARE TOO KIND TO SOMEONE LIKE ME.
THANK YOU VERY MUCH.
HOWEVER...
I CAN...
...KEEP ANYTHING FROM STARTING.

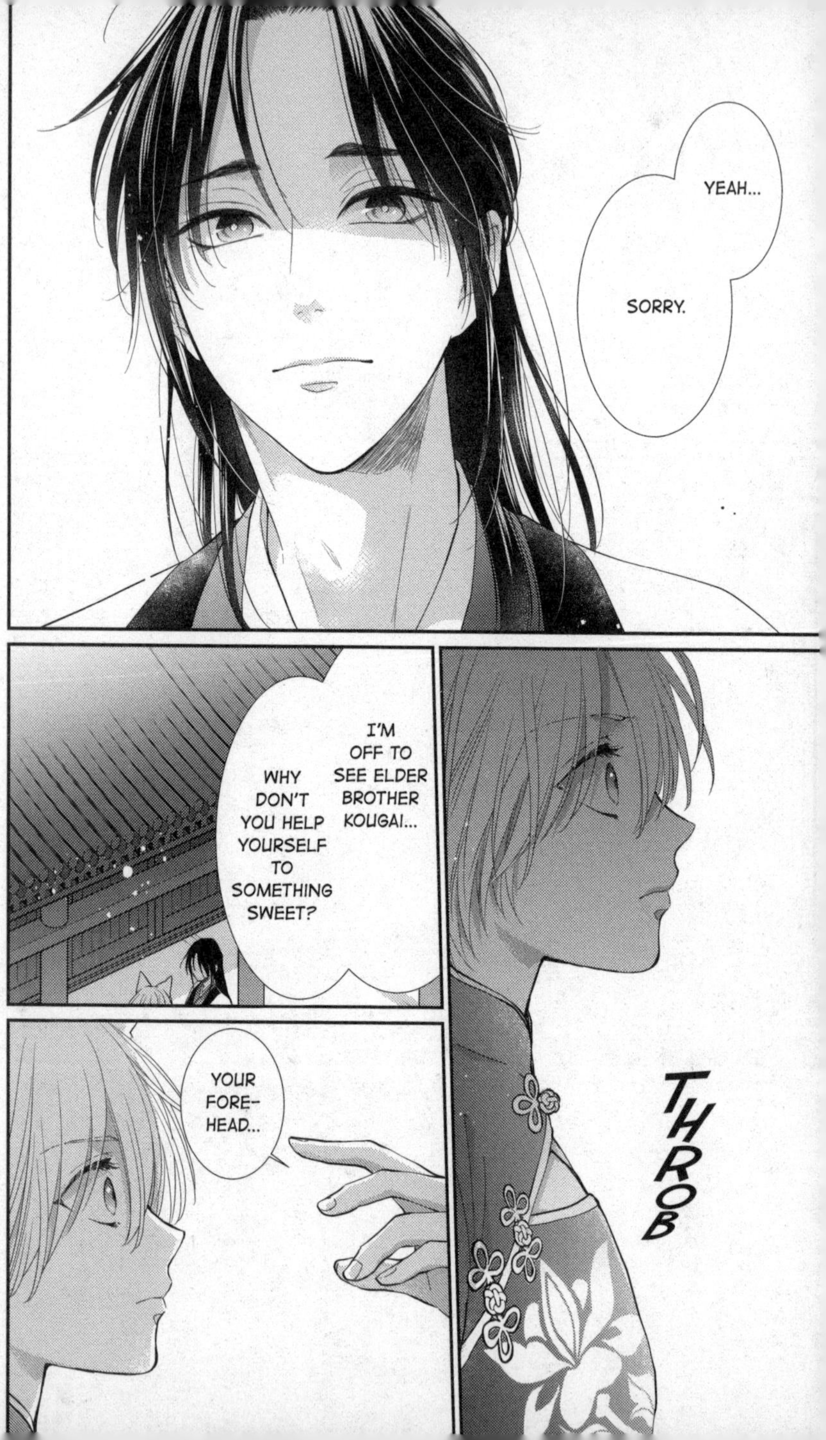
YEAH...
SORRY.
I'M OFF TO SEE ELDER BROTHER KOUGAI...
WHY DON'T YOU HELP YOURSELF TO SOMETHING SWEET?
THROB
YOUR FORE-HEAD...

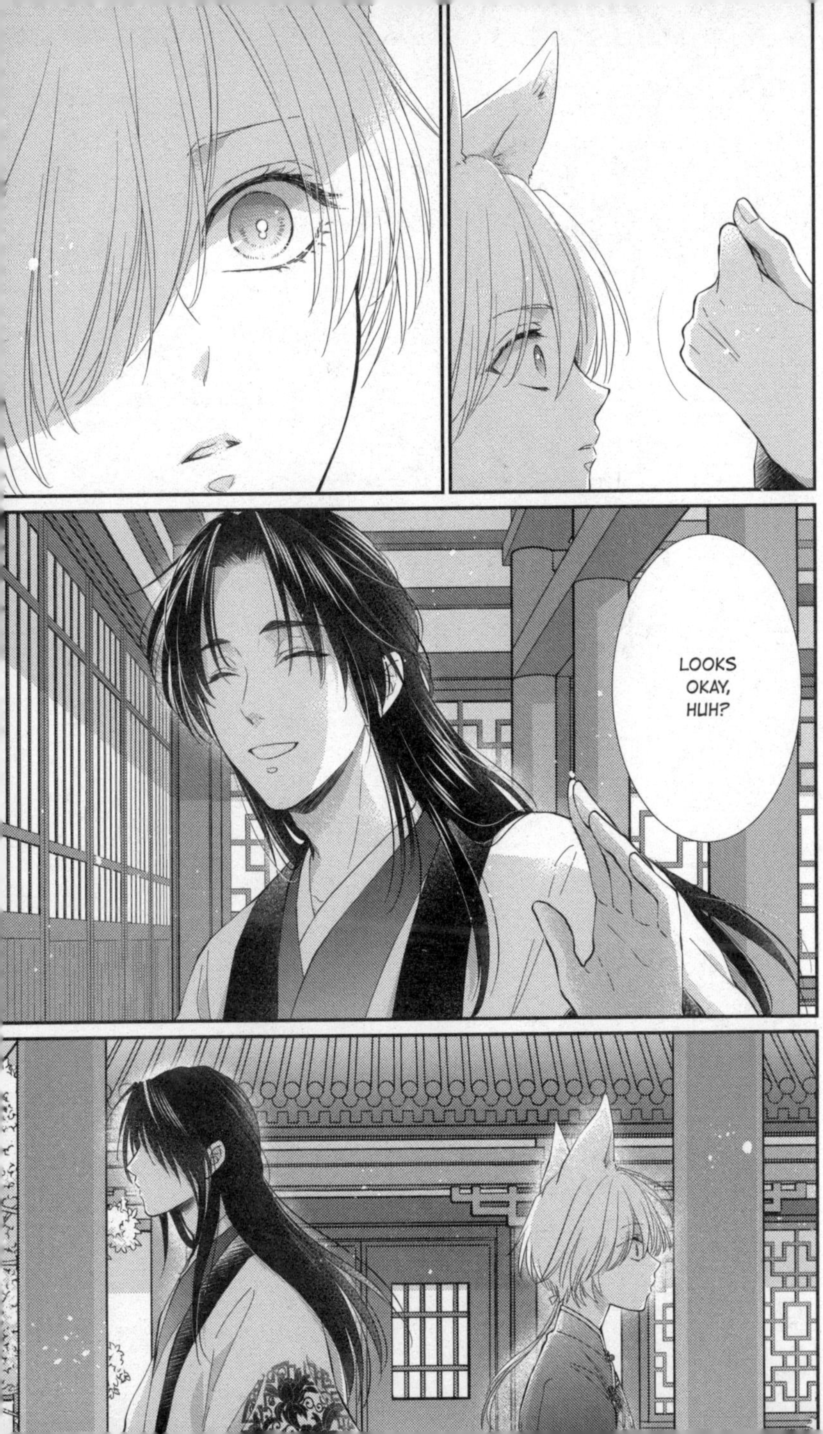
LOOKS
OKAY,
HUH?

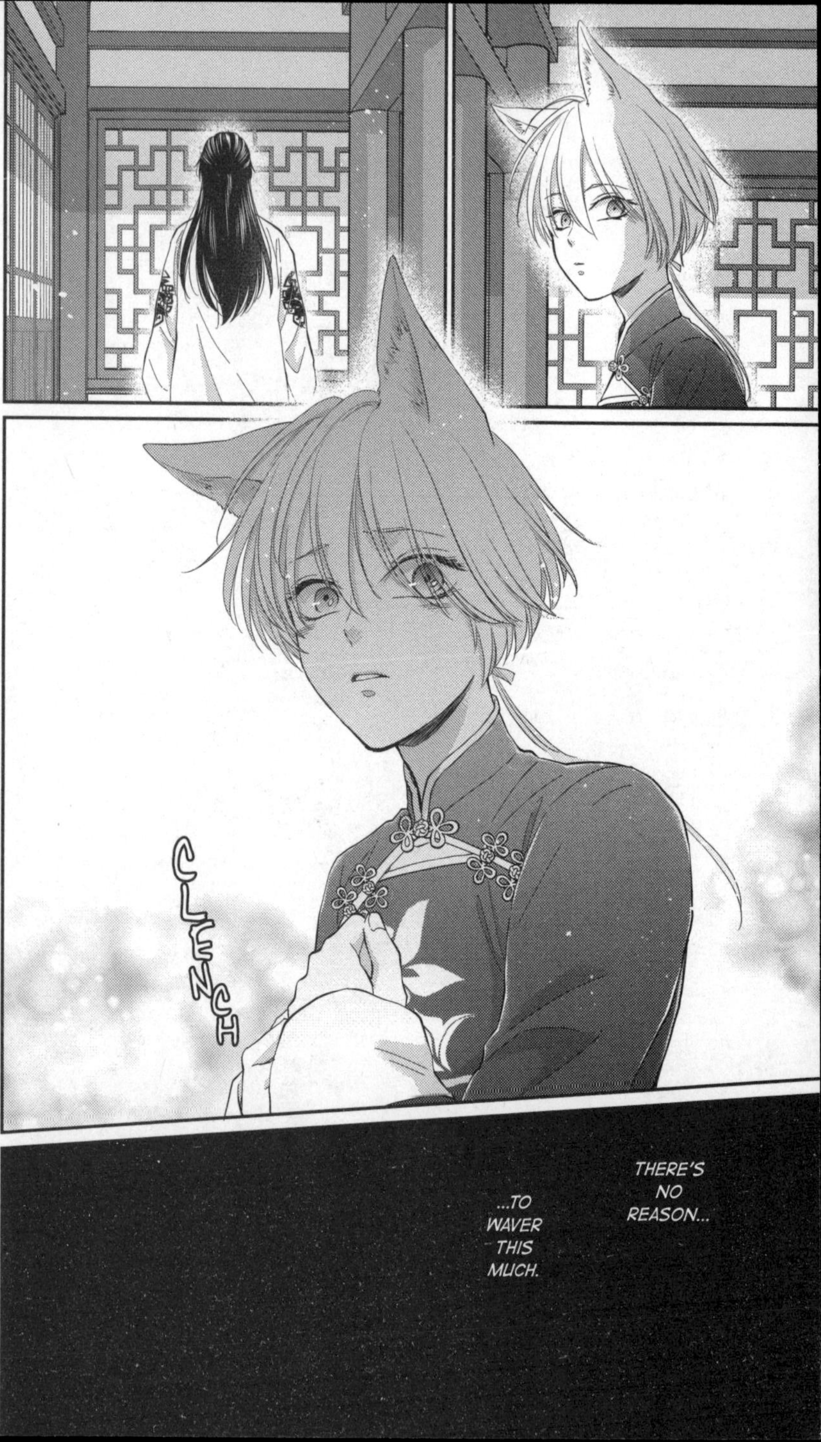
CLENCH
THERE'S NO REASON...
...TO WAVER THIS MUCH.

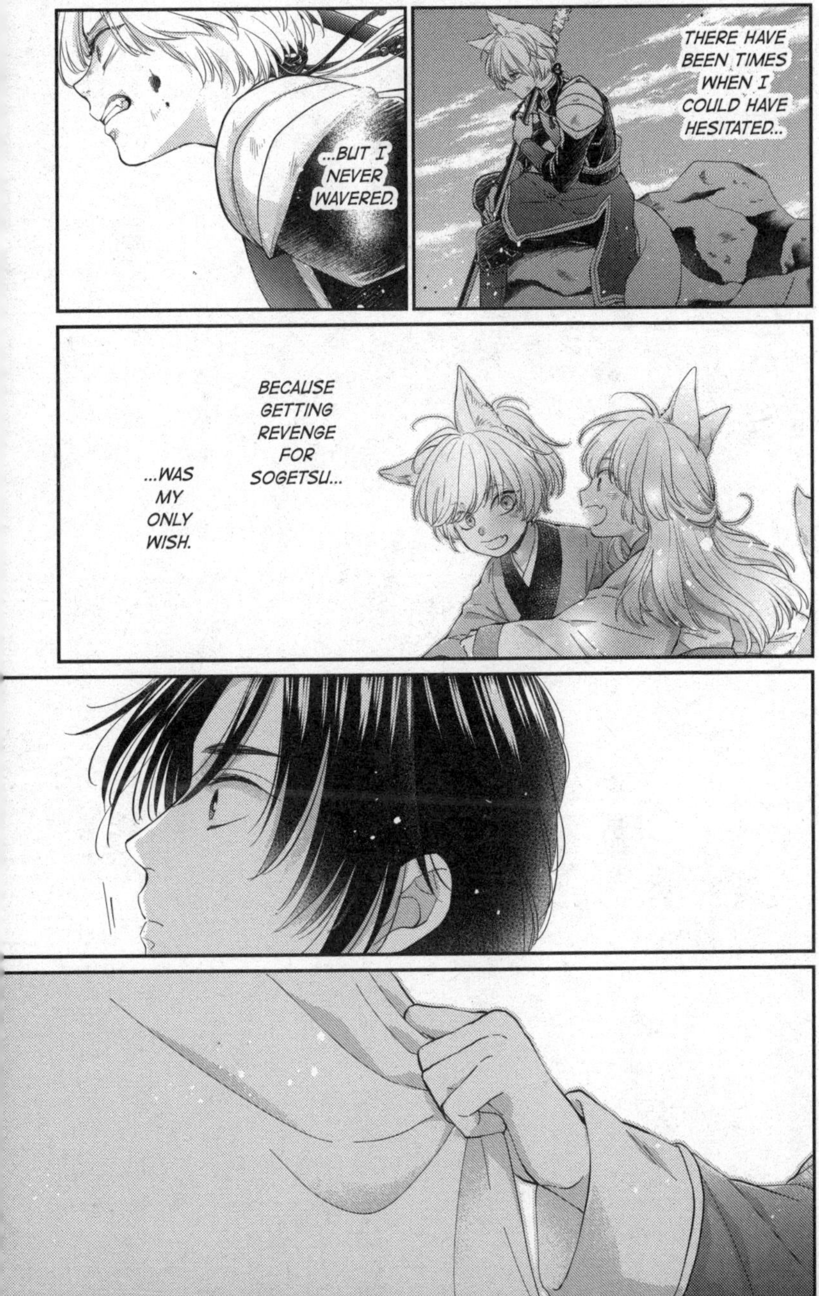
THERE HAVE BEEN TIMES WHEN I COULD HAVE HESITATED...
...BUT I NEVER WAVERED.
BECAUSE GETTING REVENGE FOR SOGETSU...
...WAS MY ONLY WISH.

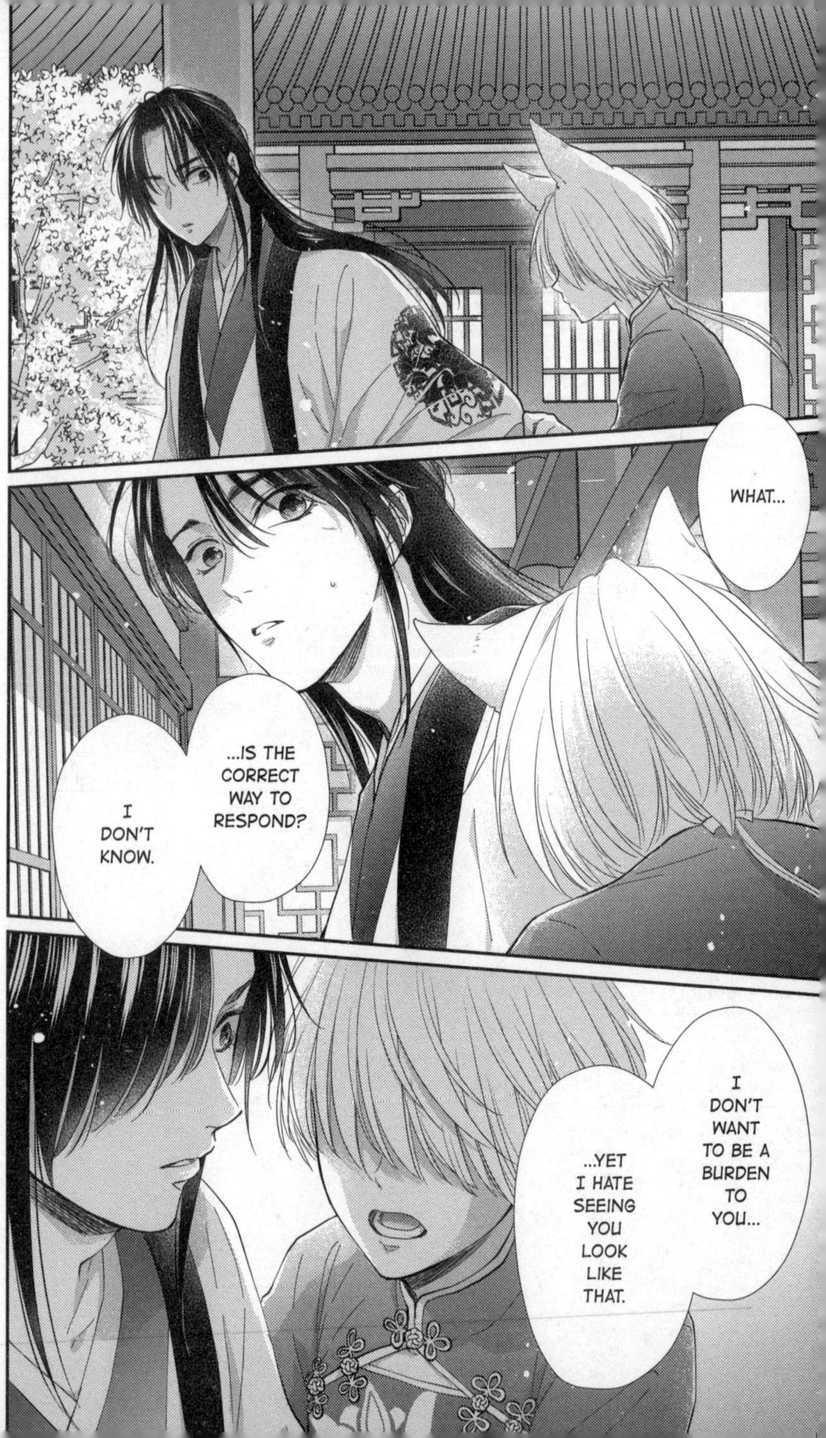
WHAT...
...IS THE CORRECT WAY TO RESPOND?
I DON'T KNOW.
I DON'T WANT TO BE A BURDEN TO YOU...
...YET I HATE SEEING YOU LOOK LIKE THAT.

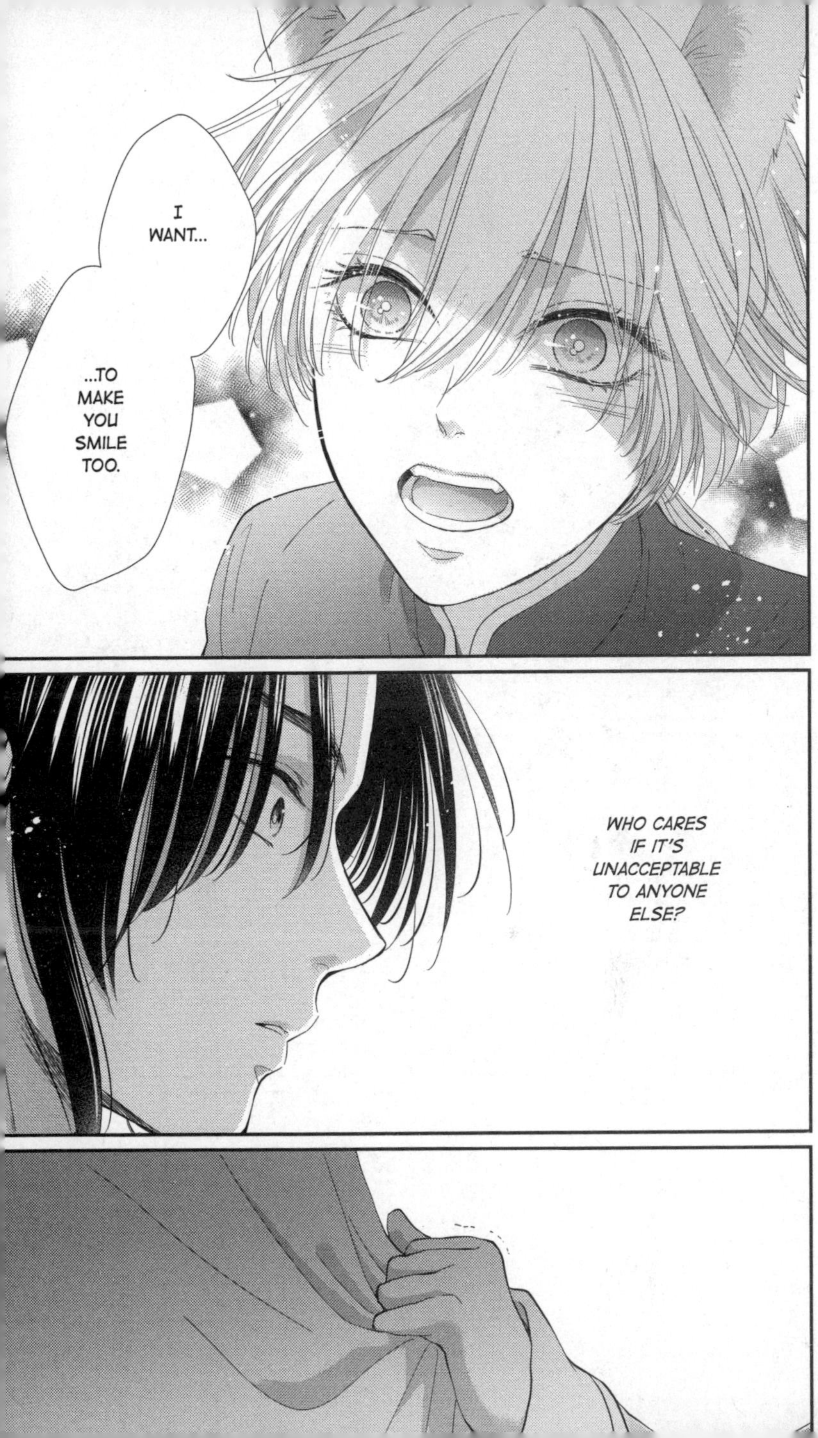
I WANT...
...TO MAKE YOU SMILE TOO.
WHO CARES IF IT'S UNACCEPTABLE TO ANYONE ELSE?

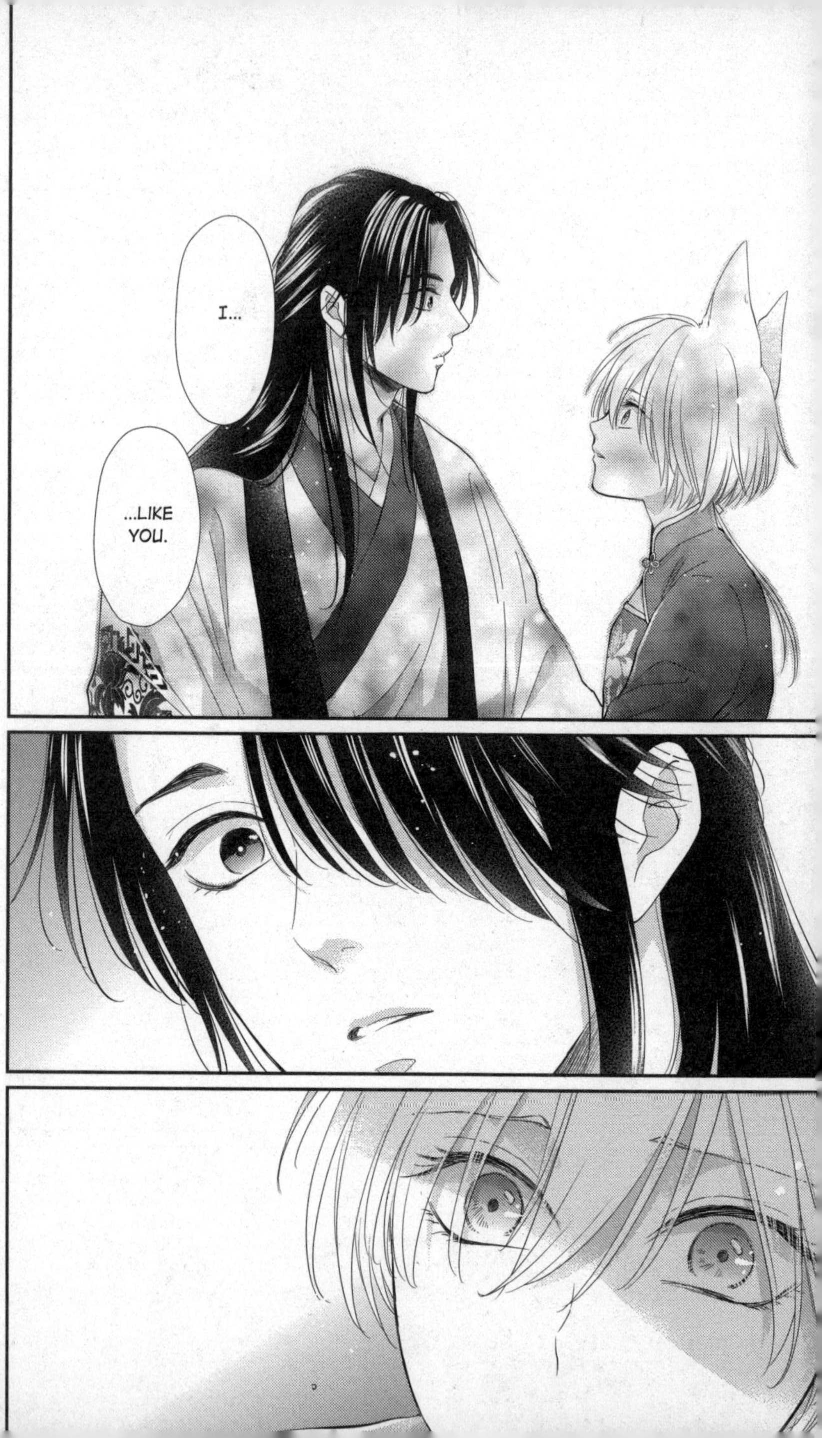
I...
...LIKE YOU.

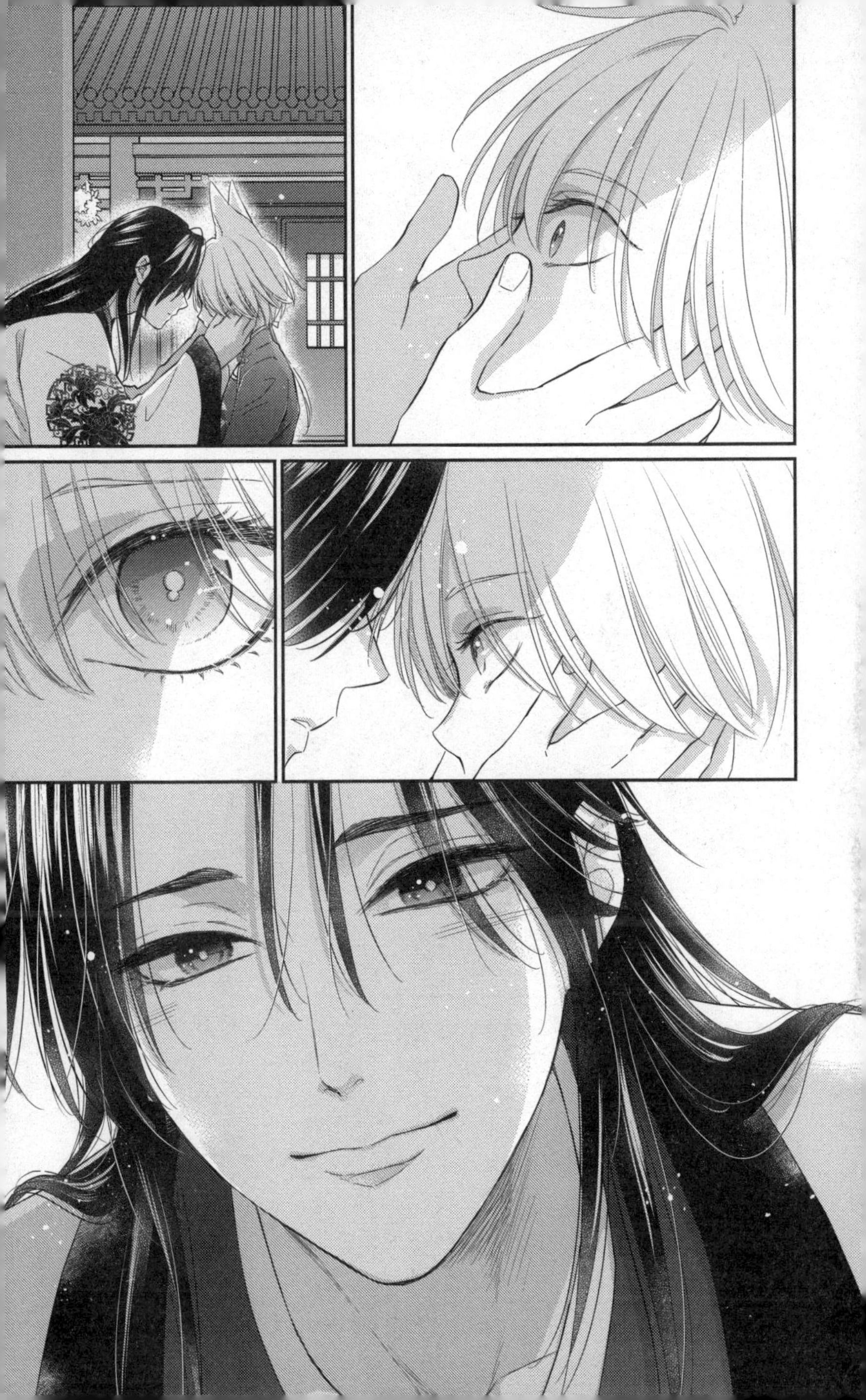

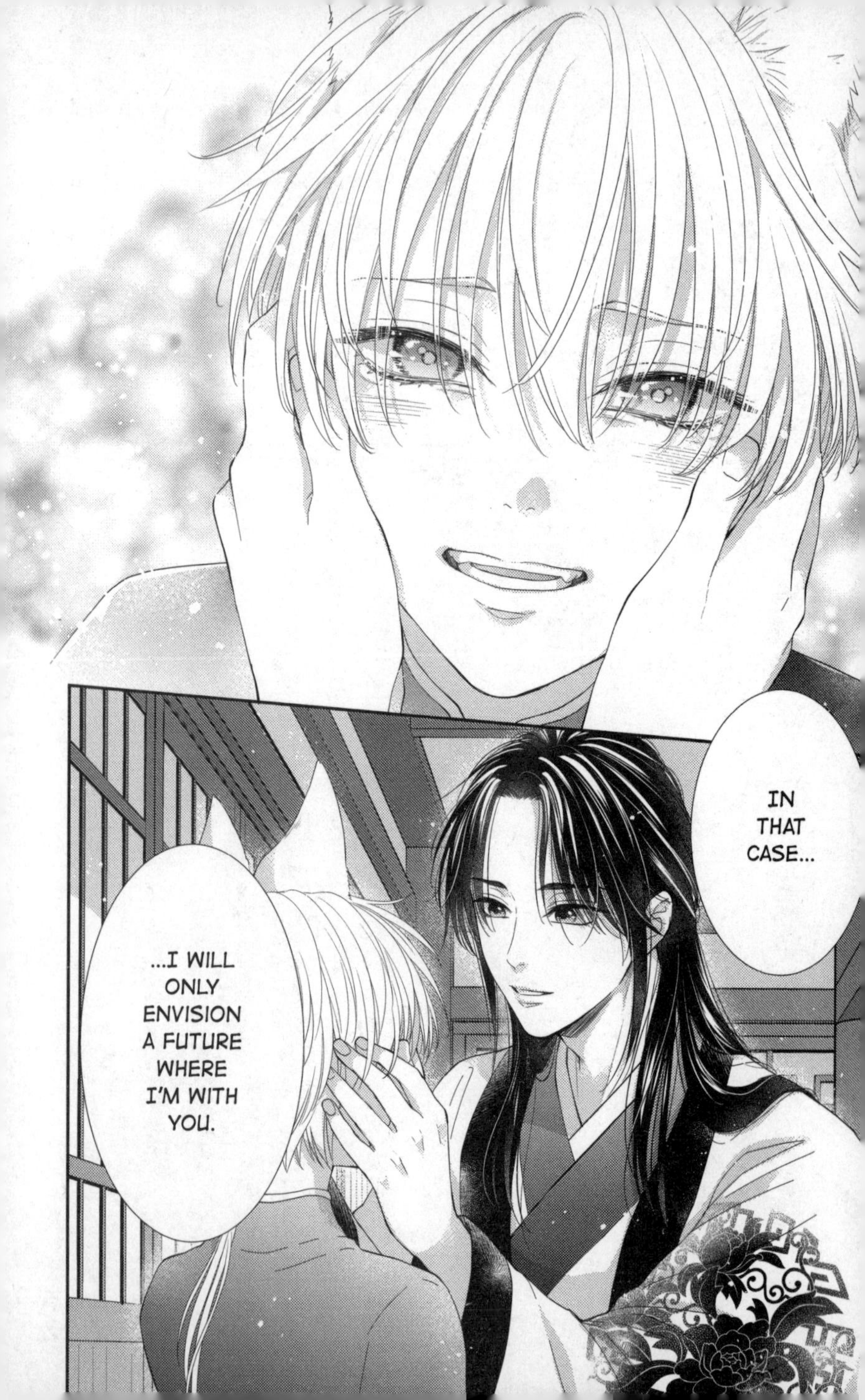
IN THAT CASE...
...I WILL ONLY ENVISION A FUTURE WHERE I'M WITH YOU.

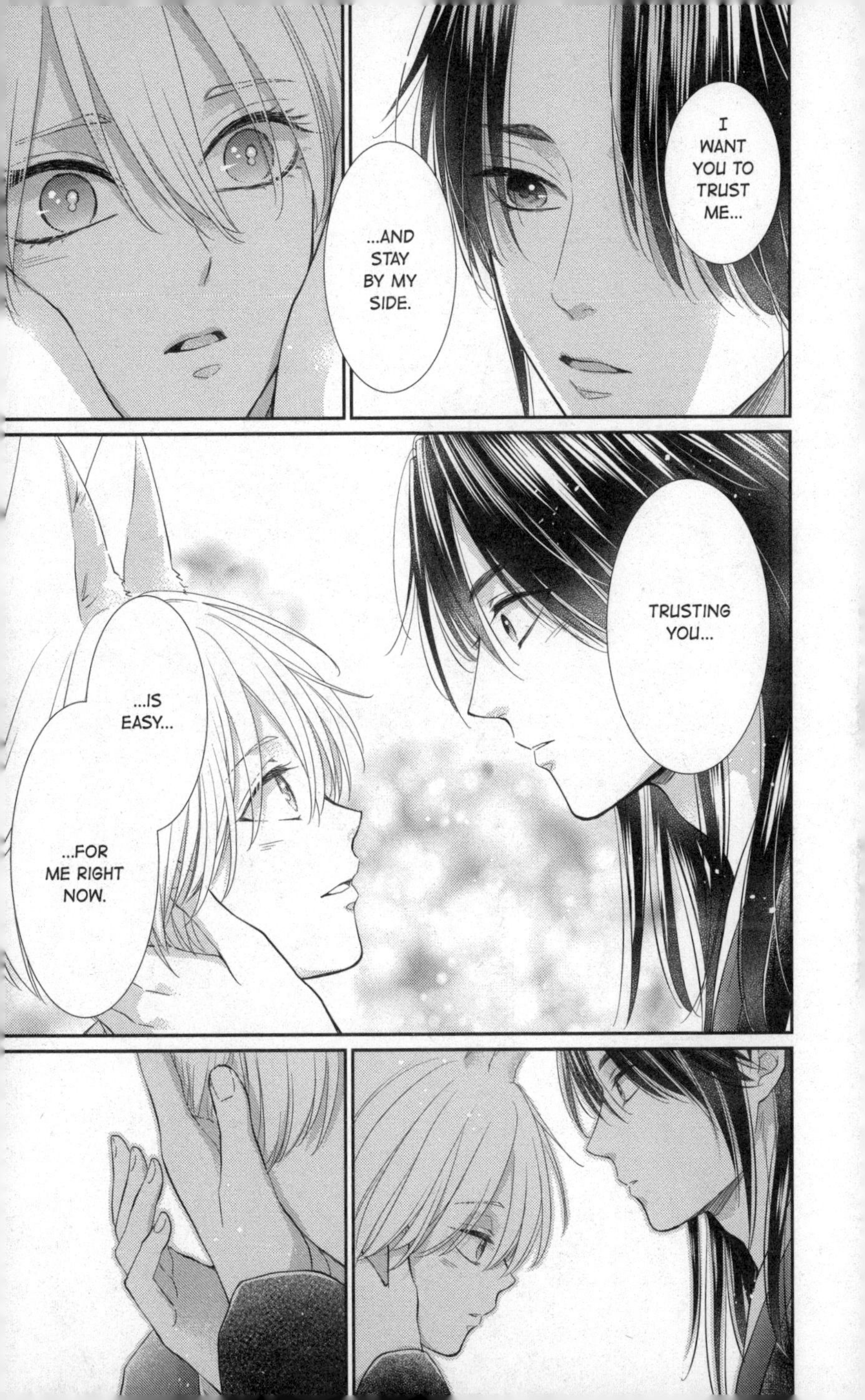
I WANT YOU TO TRUST ME...
...AND STAY BY MY SIDE.
TRUSTING YOU...
...IS EASY...
...FOR ME RIGHT NOW.

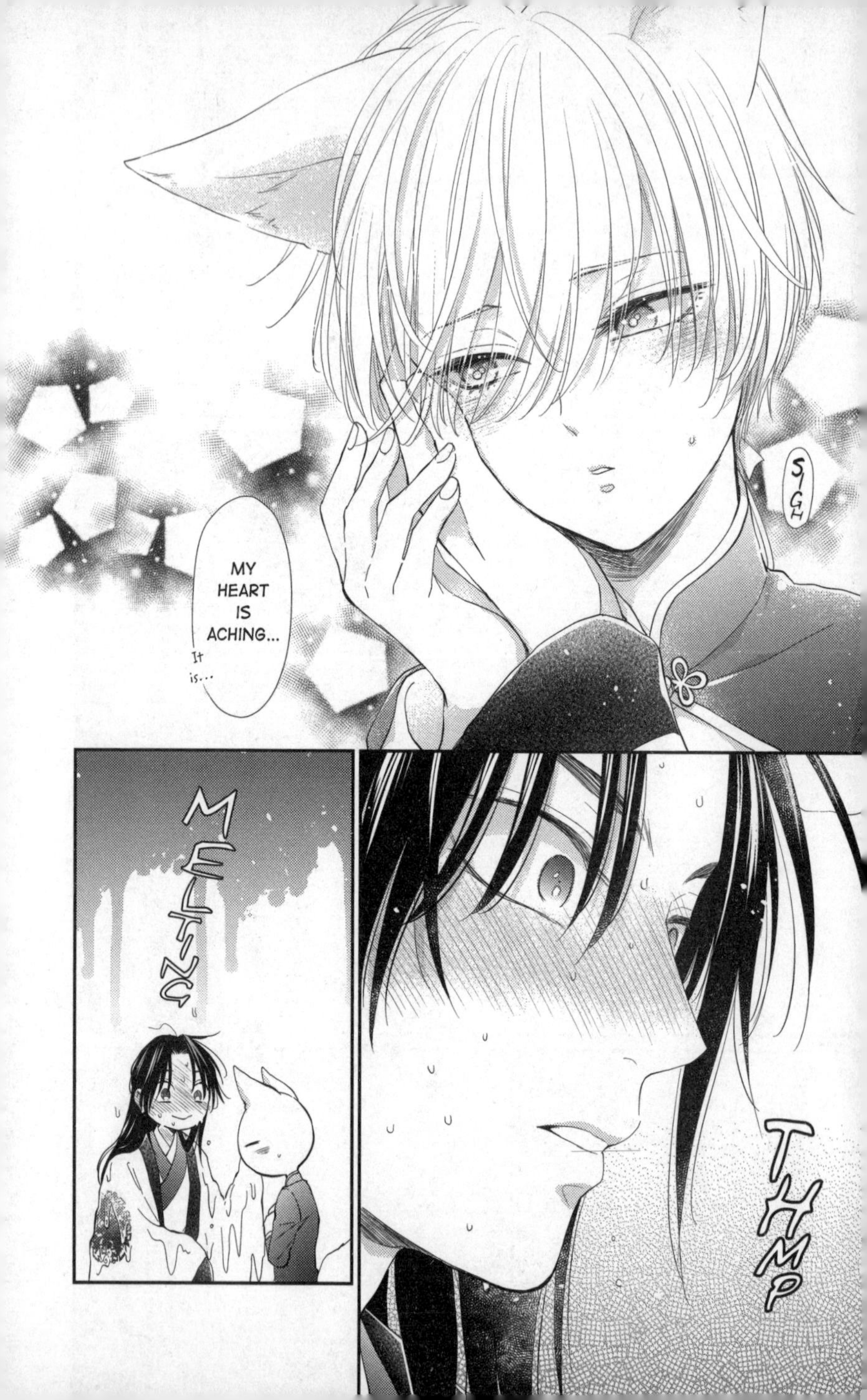
SIGH
MY HEART IS ACHING...
It is...
THMP
MELTING

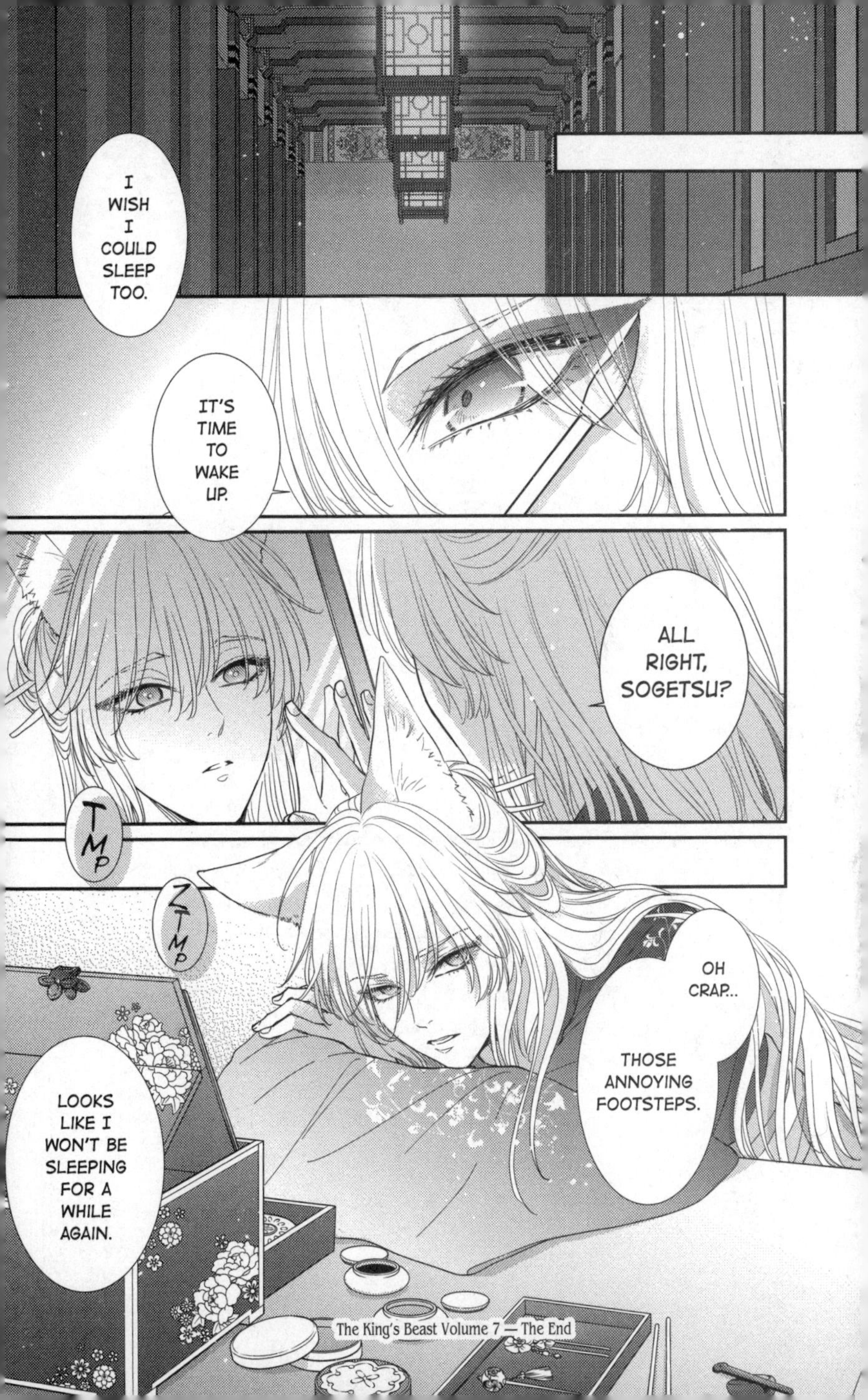
I WISH I COULD SLEEP TOO.
IT'S TIME TO WAKE UP.
ALL RIGHT, SOGETSU?
TMP
TMP
OH CRAP...
THOSE ANNOYING FOOTSTEPS.
LOOKS LIKE I WON'T BE SLEEPING FOR A WHILE AGAIN.
The King's Beast Volume 7 — The End

I love voice comics! They're so fun.
Hope you get a chance to listen to everyone's voices!*

*Refers to the Japanese voice comic release.

—*Rei Toma*
麗

Rei Toma has been drawing since childhood, and she created her first complete manga for a graduation project in design school. When she drew the short story manga "Help Me, Dentist," it attracted a publisher's attention and she made her debut right away. After she found success as a manga artist, acclaim in other art fields started to follow as she did illustrations for novels and video game character designs. She is also the creator of *Dawn of the Arcana* and *The Water Dragon's Bride*, both available in English from VIZ Media.

THE KING'S Beast 7

SHOJO BEAT EDITION

STORY AND ART BY **Rei Toma**

ENGLISH TRANSLATION & ADAPTATION **JN Productions**
TOUCH-UP ART & LETTERING **Monaliza De Asis**
DESIGN **Joy Zhang**
EDITOR **Pancha Diaz**

OU NO KEMONO Vol. 7
by Rei TOMA
© 2019 Rei TOMA
All rights reserved.
Original Japanese edition published by SHOGAKUKAN.
English translation rights in the United States of America,
Canada, the United Kingdom, Ireland, Australia and New
Zealand arranged with SHOGAKUKAN.

Original Cover Design: Hibiki CHIKADA (fireworks. vc)

Fox Mask Design Inspired by W. Mushoku (WALTZ)
Kitsune Kuchi Men Ajisai Komendou
https://www.komendou.com/SHOP/Kom-Kt-03.html

Printed in the U.S.A.

Published by VIZ Media, LLC
P.O. Box 77010
San Francisco, CA 94107

10 9 8 7 6 5 4 3 2 1
First printing, August 2022

viz.com

shojobeat.com

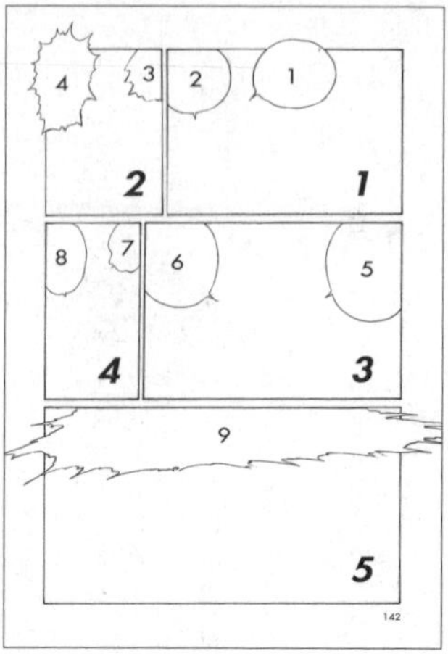

THIS IS THE LAST PAGE.

THE KING'S BEAST has been printed in the original Japanese format to preserve the orientation of the artwork.

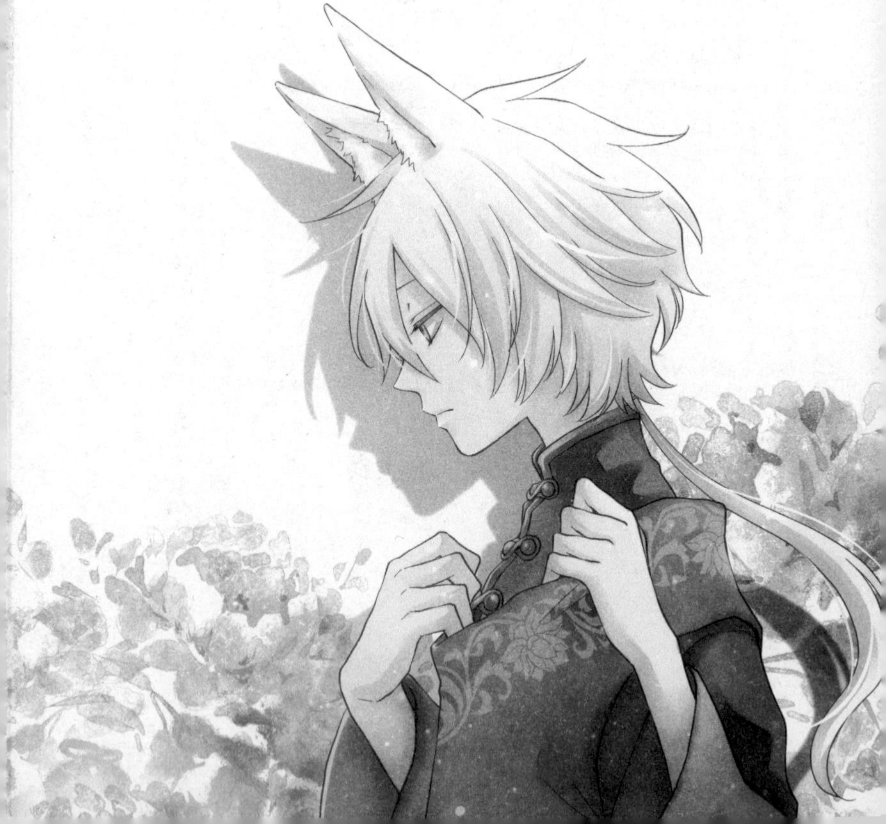